Also by Roy Blount Jr.

Alphabetter
Juice

Alphabetter
Juice

{ or, The Joy of Text }

Roy Blount Jr.

Sarah Crichton Books
Farrar, Straus and Giroux
New York

Sarah Crichton Books
Farrar, Straus and Giroux
18 West 18th Street, New York 10011

Copyright © 2011 by Roy Blount Jr.
All rights reserved
Distributed in Canada by D&M Publishers, Inc.
Printed in the United States of America
First edition, 2011

Grateful acknowledgment is made for permission to reprint an excerpt from "An Old Joke" from *Twigs & Knucklebones* by Sarah Lindsay, copyright © 2008 by Sarah Lindsay. Reprinted with the permission of Copper Canyon Press, www.coppercanyonpress.org.

Library of Congress Cataloging-in-Publication Data
Blount, Roy.
    Alphabetter juice : or, the joy of text / Roy Blount.— 1st ed.
      p.   cm.
    "Sarah Crichton books."
    ISBN 978-0-374-10370-5 (alk. paper)
    1. Vocabulary—Humor.   2. English language—Dictionaries—Humor.   I. Title.

  PN6231.W64 B49 2011
  818'.5407—dc22

                        2010039937

Designed by Ralph Fowler / rlfdesign

www.fsgbooks.com

10 9 8 7 6 5 4 3 2 1

2JGw/OX

ELSIE: *What's that, Daddy?*
FATHER: *A cow.*
ELSIE: *Why?*

—from a 1906 issue of *Punch*, quoted by Ernest Weekley as an
epigraph to his book *An Etymology of Modern English*

When we reflect that "sentence" *means, literally,* "a way of thinking" *(Latin:* sententia*) and that it comes from the Latin* sentire, *to feel, we realize that the concepts of sentence and sentence structure are not merely grammatical or merely academic—not negligible in any sense. A sentence is both the opportunity and the limit of thought—what we have to think with, and what we have to think in. It is, moreover, a* feelable *thought, a thought that impresses its sense not just on our understanding, but on our hearing, our sense of rhythm and proportion. It is a pattern of felt sense.*

—Wendell Berry, "Standing by Words"

Captain Smith . . . , *happening to be taken Prisoner among the* Indians, *had leave granted him to send a Message to the Governor of the* English Fort *in* James Town, *about his Ransome; the Messenger being an* Indian, *was surpriz'd, when he came to the Governor, . . . for that the Governor could tell him all his Errand before he spoke one Word of it to him, and that he only had given him a piece of Paper: After which, when they let him know that the Paper which he had given the Governor had told him all the Business, then . . . Capt. Smith was a Deity and to be Worshipp'd, for that he had Power to make the* Paper Speak.

—Daniel Defoe, *An Essay on the Original of Literature*, 1726

Alphabetter Juice

Introduction

This book includes two disastrous wedding nights, several touches of romance (aside from the long-deferred union of *scratch* and *itch*), and lots of animal life (*eels*, crabs, *elephants*, *flies*), but it all springs from things going on among letters on a printed page.

Where almost anything can happen. I'm reading a fascinating piece by Oliver Sacks in *The New Yorker* about a novelist who woke up one morning and couldn't read, couldn't recognize letters (see *O*), which makes my blood run cold to begin with, and I'm reading that people with certain ocular disorders "may be prone to visual hallucinations, and Dominic ffytche et al. estimate . . ."

Oh my God, I'm having one. *What the hell kind of phantasm is "ffytche et al."?*

Then I go back, reread, and settle down. Some medical researcher's name is Dominic ffytche. I've heard of such names. But I want to say to this man, "Dom. Please. I have name issues myself—Blount pronunced [*sic*] Blunt. That is no doubt one reason I'm so hipped on phonetics, that my own name is blatantly not spelled the way it's pronounced, so I have to spend a great deal of my time arguing with people about how to pronounce my *own damn name*, which is a centuries-old English pronunciation and I am not about to change it. And I wouldn't try to tell you, sir, that you should turn your *y* into an *i* and lose your *e*. All I ask of you is this: find it in your heart to capitalize one, at least, of your *f*'s. You don't know what a start you gave me."

What do we have, if we don't have letters? The police chief on *The Simpsons* advised people to "follow the Four A's: Always Act According to the ABC's." There is more to life than that, but it's a good start. This book, like its only slightly worse predecessor, *Alphabet Juice*, is not, except in irritable moments, a book of advice. It does **urge** you to **dwell** upon the literality and the physicality of language.

Wait! Hold on a minute!

Almost lost you, didn't I? I had the TV reference nailed down. (Quick, here's another one: remember in *The Simpsons* when the local library had a big neon sign outside that said, "We Have Books by People on TV"?)

But then I drifted off into *-ity* words. Not **nitty-gritty** *-ity* words, like *pity* or *Fitty* (there, you young folks, there's a hip-hop reference, and see **blob**), but longish . . . Excuse me, this damn phone . . .

Ah, well. Where were we? These days, with so many demands on our— what?—our *attention*, it may seem hard to bring words into close focus. Hard and also retro. **But**, to paraphrase Gerard Manley Hopkins (see **foil**), there is a freshness deep down in words, and you never know when it's going to flash out. Here's a little teaser from this book's entry on **garden path phenomenon**:

> . . . a review, by Janet Maslin in *The New York Times*, of a memoir by Barbara Walters:
>
>> Ms. Walters . . . will acknowledge this much: She's old enough to have had the daughter of one of the Three Stooges . . .
>
> *WHAT? WHAT?* Which one? Surely not Curly! . . .

Yet another TV reference. And for you sports fans, how about the pleasures of the narrow-box-score phenomenon: *Zmmn. DvMrp.* (See **vowel**.)

It's a shame, isn't it?, that people who use words in public don't pay more **granular** attention to the words they use. On public radio I hear a concerned interviewee: "We—including the president—are not doing nearly enough to ensure that our children eat healthy food."

Hmm. We, including the president. Why not throw in Young Jeezy, the World Trade Organization, Stephen Hawking, the Phoenix Suns, Calista Flockhart, and the supermodel Gisele Bundchen? Don't tell me any of them *are* doing enough. When something is not being done enough—and when isn't something not?—it brings so many people together, conceptually. I'm thinking maybe this book could use an entry on the interviewee *we.* But then the interviewer says: "Do you think it's because the president doesn't want to open up that whole can of worms?"

Here we go! Talking about children, right? And eating, right? Can of worms? Huh? My guess is, the interviewee will respond to that figure of speech in one of three perfectly natural ways:

1. "Funny you should mention that. Studies show that a can of earthworms contains more nutrients, without the trans fat, than three cans of SpaghettiOs."

2. "Hmm. You may have hit on something. If someone would market high-fiber, sugar-free, organic school-lunch snacks convincingly resembling earthworms, it might go a long way toward solving this problem—anyway for **boys**."

3. "**Ew**." (See **succinct**.)

In fact the interviewee responds in none of those ways. She plows on ahead with her message. She doesn't even chuckle, nor does the interviewer.

People! We're using *figures of speech* here! Figures of speech have specific words in them, and words have specific sounds in them, and attention must be paid. I don't mean pissy, constrictive attention, I mean lip-smacking attention. But not sloppy lip smacking. That spoils it for others. (See **Dionysian, Apollonian, blended, briefly**.)

There is a widespread tendency today, even on the part of people who write about English usage, to eschew finickiness. I'm sorry, but when it comes to wording, I intend to finick till the day I die. Because there's **kicks** in it, as Louis Armstrong used to say. You can even enjoy slovenly syntax (see **first sentence**) if it conjures up an image. When the sign at a temporary warning light says, "Be Prepared to Stop When Flashing," you can picture someone throwing open his or her raincoat while poised to desist. When you read in an obituary, "At the age of seven, his grandfather died," you can imagine three extraordinarily compressed generations.

In a Whole Foods store, I am waiting as my eat-it-there pizza slice is warmed. The pizza will disappoint (there is no more excuse for floppy, doughy pizza than there is for floppy, doughy sentences), but I don't know that yet. My heart has been warmed, and lifted, by the sign next to where my slice is warming:

HAVE IT WARMED IN OUR HEARTHOVEN

Heart-hoven! A Gerard Manley Hopkins word (*hoven* as an archaic past participle of *heave*), surely:

Soul-flung, rump-sprung, heart-hoven I rise . . .

Then I come back to earth. I lack the chops to fake even one line of Hopkins (see *foil*). And what that Whole Foods sign means is *hearth oven*. But thanks to close reading, I have had a moment there, one that "saved some part of a day I had rued," as Robert Frost wrote of snow shaken down on him by a crow.

Recently I read a book that stated flatly, "Language is intrinsically neutral." That is doctrine, I think, passed down to linguistics majors (I am a proud English major) so that they can look beyond words, which resist abstraction, toward notions of universal grammar, which thrive on abstraction. To me, calling language neutral is like (no, worse than) saying "Pizza's pizza. Depends on who's eating it and where and when, what it's eaten with, how it's marketed . . ." Okay, pizza does depend, to some extent, on such considerations. I'm not an absolutist. But there is such a thing as pizza that hits the spot. Such a thing as pizza that's unusually interesting, on purpose. Such a thing as pizza that makes you say, "Now *that's* pizza." There is also such a thing as sorry-ass pizza. And to an undismissible extent, those such-a-things depend upon the pizza's ingredients and how they've been assembled, baked, and slid from the oven. Pizza essences. Alphabet juice.

Anatoly Liberman is a leading scholar of English etymology. "The more expressive human speech is," he writes in *Word Origins, and How We Know Them: Etymology for Everyone*, "the more 'echoic' words it contains." He adds:

> The criteria for calling a word echoic are not clearly defined. *Grunt* is an onomatopoeia. A grumpy person may be prone to growling and grousing, though even without *gr-* in his or her name such an individual would be equally obnoxious. Consider *hump*, which rhymes with *grump* and means "a fit of ill temper," its soft sound texture notwithstanding. *The Oxford Dictionary of English Etymology*

suggests that this sense of *hump* is rooted in the idea of humping the back in sulkiness. Whether such a conjecture deserves credence is a matter of opinion. Kipling had a similar explanation of the origin of the camel's humps; his camel was irascible and spiteful.

Fine. That's all I ask from linguisticians: the *hump* (and the *gr-*) under the tent. Once *hump*, the noun, is in play, so is *hump*, the verb, in various meanings—and how about **jump** and *slump*. And *humph*. I rode a camel for four days in Kenya, and I can tell you that a camel has its *humph*'s, to put it mildly. Have you ever heard a camel being awakened at dawn, cinched up, and introduced, as if for the first time, to the notion that camels are beasts of burden? The camel's response begins way up high like a teakettle at just-boil and works its way down through the expostulation of an arch-bishop being contradicted, the gurgle of ancient plumbing, the cry of an emeritus member of the Explorers Club (see **device, narrative, what would you call this one**) being violated in his leather chair, and on down down down into some deep body cavity unknown to man.

"The consonants and vowels of human speech," writes Liberman, "cannot do justice to animal cries." Agreed. Those letters can, however (see intro to *Alphabet Juice*), try. An attempt I have made to spell the plaint of the camel is this: *Eeeeurghgr'gl'gl'gblglglglghg'blegh*. Another is *eeeurngh'gla blalala'bleagh'l'leh*. Neither is exact. The protest of the camel is richer; it's more crowded in there, more *b*'s, maybe—*b*'s and *g*'s and *l*'s on top of one another.

I know of no single English word that violates neutrality quite that expressively. But we all know many words that significantly engage the senses. Consider the political writer Paul Berman's grounds for preferring *fascist* over *totalitarian*: "*totalitarian*, being abstract, is odorless. *Fascist* is pungent. To hear that emphatic *f*-sound and those double different *s*'s is to flare your nostrils." (See **ouistiti**.)

Sonicky, the term I devised for *Alphabet Juice*, works better for me than *echoic*, or *imitative*, because it seeks to *combine sonic* (evocative of sound) and *kinesthetic* (evocative of body movement). The most expressive English words, *hump* among them, engage the ear, the vocal apparatus, and by implication other parts of the body: call me suggestible, but I can feel *hump*, which first appeared in English as part of *humpback*, in my upper back and shoulders. In the current dark economy of virtual, ephemeral assets—in which people receive enormous compensation for borrowing thirtyfold against other people's money, causing it all to go away—shall we not honor intrinsic value where we can? I speak of the juice inherent in letters and their combinations. See, for instance, **blurt**, and **bubble**, and **hunch**. And how about this one: *draw* means to pull along, *drag* to pull along against resistance. Resistance resides in that hard *g*.

"Most etymologists are very reluctant to admit echoism," writes Otto Jespersen in his 1922 book, *Language*. Under *sound symbolism*, the *Oxford English Dictionary* quotes Jespersen, from that same book, as follows: "The idea that there is a natural correspondence between sound and sense, and that words acquire their contents and value through a certain sound symbolism, has at all times been a favourite one with linguistic dilettanti."

But that is only the first sentence of the sixteen-page chapter that Jespersen devotes to that idea. "Of course it would be absurd," he says,

> to maintain that all words at all times in all languages had signification corresponding exactly to their sounds, each sound having a definite meaning once for all. But is there really much more logic in the opposite extreme, which denies any kind of sound symbolism (apart from the small class of evident . . . "onomatopoeia") and sees in our words only a collection of wholly accidental and irrational associations of sound and meaning?

For a century or so, that opposite extreme has been a linguistic tenet, even though Jespersen demolished it in 1922 by pointing out various forms of what I would call the sonicky element in language. Everyone, Jespersen notes, "must feel that the word *roll, rouler, rulle, rollen* is more adequate than the corresponding Russian word *katat', katit'*." He speaks of the fluidity of so many words with *l*'s in them. He sees "a natural connexion between action and sound in the word *tickle*" and its German (*kitzeln*), Old Norse (*kitla*), Danish (*kilde*), Nubian (*killi-killi*), and Latin (*titillare*) equivalents. He observes that "expressions for an uncertain walk," like *totter, dodder,* and *teeter,* "may come to be felt as symbolic of the movement as such." Not imagined, felt.

My impression, in fact, is that contemporary etymology is rewarming to the connection of sensory perceptions and sense. OED used to say *pebble* came from Latin *papula* and pretty much leave it at that. Now a March 2010 online revision concedes that "the first element of *pebble stone* may be imitative in origin (compare later *popple*), arising either from the sound pebbles make when walked upon or from the association of pebbles with flowing water. Perhaps compare **Frisian** *babbel-stientsjes* to little round stones washed up at the beach."

Thank you. But I want to go farther. I am quick to agree with Otto Jespersen that if any word is echoic (but see discussion in *Alphabet Juice*) it is *piss*, but I want you to notice, as well, that *piss* is *sip* backward. OED defines *fluff* as "Light, feathery, flocculent stuff." Fine. But OED's etymology says *fluff* is "app[arently] connected with *flue*; perh[aps] an onomatopoeic modification of that word, imitating the action of puffing away some light substance." Oh, please, with the *app* and the *perh*. Can't we give *fluff* fully unhedged credit for sounding precisely like fluff? *Fluff* is head and shoulders better than *flocculent stuff*, because it eliminates everything (the *-occulent st-*) in *flocculent stuff* that doesn't sound fluffy.

And let's branch out from there. Does OED recognize the porn-industry word *fluffer*? (Yes, as of June 2010.) With "head and shoulders," I have unintentionally evoked dandruff—how did the *uff* get in there? According to all rigorous sources, *dandruff* (or *dandriff*) is an etymological mystery. My hat is off to rigor, but I love to speculate. Can't we start with *dander* and then, just to see what happens, fit it out with *drift*, *fluff*, even *ruff*?

Let me quote (courtesy of Jeffrey Kacirk's *Forgotten English*) Francis Bacon. Though he was rightly skeptical about alchemy (and would be equally skeptical today about the notion that he wrote Shakespeare), Bacon found a "silver lining" in it:

> Alchemy may be compared to the man who told his sons of gold
> buried somewhere in his vineyard, where they by digging found no
> gold, but by turning up the mould about the roots of their vines
> procured a plentiful vintage. So the search and endeavors to make
> gold have brought many useful inventions and instructive
> experiments to light.

To be clear, I don't believe in pseudoscience. I don't aspire to turn base metals into gold. I want to rummage around in base metals and see what I can put together. I'm a writer. I like to handle words and pass them on by hand. The letters of the alphabet are my stuff.

In response to an article titled "It's Not Dry Yet," about a resurgence of actual *painting* in contemporary art, Shane Neufeld of Brooklyn wrote this to *The New York Times*: "Paint has awakened from a coma in which the medium's intrinsic, exuberant and uniquely liquid qualities were held at bay for the sake of purely intellectual and ideological concerns. It's lovely to think that painting has the chance to regain its cultural power in a visually virtuosic medium." My wife, Joan Griswold, is a painter, an expressively brushy one, who represents (lets there be) the play of light. I doubt I could love an artist of any other stripe. Abstract could work, if sensuous enough. The acrylic-layering abstractionist Robert Natkin said, "You need to look at a painting with the tongue of your eye." Once, when guards at the Frick Collection weren't looking, Natkin licked a Vermeer.

Literally licking written letters is not called for. Letters *come* from the tongue. But give me writing that reeks of sound and motion. Which is not to say sloppy writing. Sneer (and what a sonicky word that is) if you will, but I even believe in making every diligent effort to spell words correctly. Or incorrectly on purpose, as in, "I like it when a whole lot of butter is melting down in my hot baked sweeptater." To my way of thinking, the following passage from a customer review (headed "Interesting, but not practical") on amazon.com would be more telling if the last two words were spelled right: "I will not use most of the words discussed [in *Alphabet Juice*] in day-to-day proffesional writting."

"Various media labs are now testing algorithms that assemble facts into narratives that deliver information," writes David Carr in *The New York Times*, "no writers required. The results would not be mistaken for literary journalism, but on the Web, pretty good—or even not terrible—is often good enough."

Not for my purposes. There's something to be said for *terrible* writing, or for little bits of bad writing by someone you don't approve of (did I mention **first sentence** before?), but not-terrible writing? I don't even have any patience for not-terrible guacamole. (The chunkier the better. See Winona LaDuke at *fox*.)

The Web is a wondrous thing, Google wot (see **Godwottery**), but so many people who publish things on it seem not to be aware of that heretofore traditional stage of composition that involves reading over what you have written before you present it to the world. That's one of the key advantages of writing as opposed to chatting: you can look at what you wrote and see whether it makes sense to, for starters, yourself, in which case it *might* make sense to *somebody* else.

It's hard for me to believe that any algorithm can *feel* the wondrousness entailed in carefully, **hopefully**, fitting bits of alphabet together. And the feeling is crucial. Calvin Tomkins writes in *The New Yorker*, "I have a theory that the beauty of tennis, like the beauty of dance, is kinesthetic, in that we respond to certain shots as though we had made them ourselves." Yes, and that's how we may feel when we read something well written by hand.

I don't believe in magic. (I do in prestidigitation, I've seen it done—has to be precise, I believe.) Nonetheless I am moved to make a connection between **spelling**, as in *c-a-t*, and a magic spell. The former *spell* seems to have come to us from the Latin and the latter from Germanic tongues, but both *spell*'s surely derive from the PIE root **spel-*, "to say aloud, recite." And *c-a-t* is as marvelous an incantation, if you think about it, as *abracadabra* (see *Alphabet Juice*)—more marvelous, because it works. Daniel Defoe, 1726:

> The writing Words, in all Languages, agreeable to the Idiom of every respective Tongue, joining them in Monosyllables, joining the Monosyllables again into compounded Words, and giving every Letter its right Place, with its Accent or Emphasis, is a surprising Thing in the Nature of it, and if fully and seriously considered, carries us beyond Nature it self, ending only in Astonishment and an unresolv'd Wonder.

Note: As in *Alphabet Juice*, when a word or phrase appears in **boldface**, it is the subject of a separate alphabetical entry. In **boldface italic**, it is under consideration qua word or phrase as opposed to topic.

Abbreviations of reference books frequently cited:

AHD: *American Heritage Dictionary of the English Language*
Chambers: *Chambers Dictionary of Etymology* (I realize this was originally Barnhardt, but the current, in-print edition is Chambers.)
OAD: *New Oxford American Dictionary*

OED: *Oxford English Dictionary* (online)
RHU: *Random House Webster's Unabridged Dictionary*
WIII: *Webster's Third New International Dictionary, Unabridged*

PIE stands for Proto-Indo-European. See *Alphabet Juice.* Sometimes, because I don't want to have to explain what Proto-Germanic or Proto-Teutonic means (because I'm not sure myself), I use PIE somewhat loosely. So let's just say PIE stands for Pre-historic, Id Est (That Is).

a · A · a

Can you tell whether a newborn is male or female from his or her first cry? Certainly, according to Richard Rolle of Hampole, in his poem "The Pricke of Conscience," circa 1340. A boy baby first cries "*a. a.*"

Why? Because *a* is the first letter of *Adam*, "our forme-fader," or fore-father.

And, according to Rolle, a girl baby first cries "*e. e.*"

Why? Because *e* is the first letter of *Eve*, who "bygan our dede," that is, who began our death, by allowing the serpent to inveigle her into biting the apple, so that humankind no longer dwells eternally in paradise.

Pricke! I know. In any contemporary context, "**prick** of conscience" would seem oxymoronic, and that is something, believe me, I am not even raising an eyebrow in protest of. But Rolle, at least consciously, meant *prick* in the sense of **pang**.

Here's why I bring Rolle up: six hundred and seventy-one years after "The Pricke of Conscience," we are more enlightened about sex-linked charac-teristics. But we still don't know how to spell the sounds of the letter **A**.

You think capturing sound in letters is simple? Take a look at WIII's take on *eh*:

> **eh** \ '(h) $\bar{a}$ $(^n)$, '(h) ai $(^n)$, '(h) e (e) $(^n)$ (?), '(h) a (a) $(^n)$ (?), '(h) $\dot{a}$ ($\dot{a}$) $(^n)$ (?), *all with interrogatory intonation* \ *interj* [ME *ey*]—used to invite confirmation or to express inquiry or slight surprise.

All those letters and marks, and those parenthetical *h*'s (whose rele-vance eludes me) and tiny *n*'s (for whiffs of nasality) are attempts to render various pronunciations of what Ernest **Weekley** calls a "natural exclamation." Canadians, at least stereotypically, say "eh?" a lot to mean something in the range of "right?," "*n'est ce pas?*," and **yo**. But English speakers in general say "eh?" often enough that you'd think we would have figured out a better way to spell it. The sound is *ay*! After all, *eh* without the question mark spells a dismissive sound rhyming with *feh*, *meh*, *yeh*, and *heh-heh*.

Eh? can't be spelled *a*, because *a* is a word, usually pronounced *uh*. Way long ago, a commonly used word was *ay* (or *aye*) pronounced *ay* (in Middle English, though, *oo*) and meaning "ever." At that time, then, *ay?* might have looked like it meant "ever?"

Might we spell *eh?* by borrowing *eigh* from *weigh* and *sleigh*? Too heavy. Perhaps when the Normans took over Britain they experimented with the *et* from *beret* or the *é* from *touché*, but they must have shrugged, *enh*, and moved on to more pressing issues such as trying to replace *will* with *testament* and *lawyer* with *attorney*.

I say we should have stuck with the Middle English spelling of *eh?*, i.e., *ey*. As in *obey* and *they*. Too late now, though, eh?

See **aid, marital** and *I*.

> *abacus*

This most basic of calculating machines started out—at least as far back as the fourteenth century—as a board or tray sprinkled with fine sand in which lines could be drawn: figures and geometrical diagrams. Maybe *abacus* only happens to begin with the first letters of the alphabet—from a Greek root spelled alpha beta alpha (not gamma, though—the English hard *c* derives from either a xi or a kappa). The Greek word may have come, says Chambers (OED declines to speculate), from Hebrew *'ābhāq*, dust.

See *granular*.

> *accentuation*

Merritt Moseley, professor and scholar of literature and language at the the University of North Carolina at Asheville, writes me: "When people try to write Southern dialogue, they routinely have people saying *anythin'*. Or *everythin'*. Now I'm a Southerner and know a lot of them and I don't think people say that. We say *nothin'* and *somethin'* (or *sumpthin'*), but *anything* and *everything*. So . . . is it the trisyllabic thing that makes us give the full *ng* on some words but not on others? Another funny place to get the *any-thin'* or *everythin'* pronunciation is with British rockers trying to sing like Mississippi bluesmen, but I don't think anybody says it naturally."

I agree, and I guess the number of syllables is a factor. We can't say Southern speech abhors a dactyl (*dum*-da-da), because we turn *umbrella* into one: *um*-brel-la instead of um-*brel*-la. (*Insurance*, though a comparable case, comes out more like two syllables: *in*-shunce, or even *in*-shawnce.) I must say, I am always startled when people pronounce *alphabet* as *alph*-a-bit. That's how OED pronounces it, but I want some stress on that -*bet*, and American dictionaries bear me out.

OED puts all the stress on the first syllable of *anything*, too. At its thickest, a Southern accent may reduce *something* to *sum'm*, but it tends to relish an emphatic -*ng*, as in *thang*, *dang*, *whang*, *chicken wang*, and *weddin' rang*. In *nothin'* there's something to chew on, but *anythin'* is just a string of little mincy-ninny noises, hardly consonant with folk music, much less the blues.

See **you-all**.

➤ *accompaniment*

Louis Armstrong: "I work with two bands, the one on stage and the one in my head. If they sound good on stage, okay, I'll play with them. If not, I just turn up the volume of the band in my head."

When one is writing, does one have an ear tuned to some kind of readerly play-along? I don't want to think about it. At any rate, one has got to trust the backup within.

➤ *acnestis*

Given a cat's suppleness and scratchy tongue, there is no such place as this on a cat, which is why a cat can be so smug. As for humans, there would be far more hermits if it weren't for this, the only part of the body that gets larger, more active, and more conducive to maintenance of an intimate relationship as we get older. It is the spot, back between your shoulder blades, that you can't reach, yourself, to scratch.

Which is so often—and don't tell me it just *seems* that way—the place that itches. There must, for that place, be a more **sonicky** word, which I can't quite put my finger on.

WIII doesn't extend itself to *acnestis*, but it's a venerable term—OED traces it back to 1743—and not without currency, perhaps because it appears in Ammon Shea's 2008 book about reading the entire OED in one year. Wordsmith.org cites, from a Malaysian newspaper in 2008, "the last five months have felt like an acnestis upon our collective soul," and various online book purveyors offer a British-published paperback titled *Acnestis in Elysium.* (Even in paradise, there's always something.)

Acnestis derives from ancient Greek, either from the word for spine or cheese grater, or from *a-* meaning un- (more or less) and *knestos*, meaning scratched.

➤ ad hominy

The fallacy of asserting or assuming that a statement is invalid—or, okay, that it is valid—because it was made by someone from the South.

➤ *adulation*

Why is this pronounced with a *j* sound where the *d* is? Same in *education*, *gradual*, *modular*, *schedule*. And in *idgit* for *idiot*, *Injun* for *Indian*, *didja* and *wouldja* for *did ya* and *would ya*. Instead of tripping from the hard-palate *d* to the soft-palate *yoo*, the tongue wants to compromise on *j*. Somehow we manage to say *adyoo* for *adieu*, though, maybe because it's French.

The key syllable in *adulation*, pronunciation aside, is *ul*, from the Latin word for tail. To adulate is to fawn, to flatter, to approach someone with tail wagging.

➤ adverb

Adverbs get a bad rap. To be sure they can be (intentionally or unintentionally) flaccid. In 2006, a group appointed by Congress presented President Bush with a report outlining new approaches to the invasionary quagmire in Iraq. The president's response to the report was that it had "some really very interesting ideas."

But consider the adverb in this passage from a poem by Sarah Lindsay, "An Old Joke," in which she imagines an ancient girl's succumbing to a horrible gut-spilling disease:

> They buried the husk of her
> in the front room,
> tiredly crying.

Not a common word, *tiredly*, and not euphonious—*wearily* would be more conventionally poetic. But *tiredly* is inspired, somehow. I wonder if Lindsay remembered it from the short story "The Best of Everything" by Richard Yates. At the story's beginning, a woman named Grace recalls that after her first date with a man named Ralph, her roommate, Martha, was scornful of him: "Isn't he funny? He says 'terlet.' I didn't know people really said 'terlet.' " Martha prefers men who use "words like 'amusing' all the time."

Well, Martha is a college graduate, lah-di-dah. Now it's the night before Grace will marry Ralph. To give the two of them some privacy for a change, so they can consummate their love a night ahead of time, Martha is graciously spending the night elsewhere. When Grace *hopefully* presents herself to Ralph in her new negligee, however, Ralph says he has to rejoin the boys, who are throwing him a party. But first, "I'm fulla beer. Mind if I use ya terlet?"

Let's turn our eyes from jerky Ralph and poor Grace for just a moment to ask, what *is* a sufficiently polite yet straightforward term for the john? *Toilet*, euphemistic as its derivation may be (originally, from *toile*, a cloth), has itself a coarse ring in English. I guess *bathroom* will have to serve, but inasmuch as a *half bath* has no bathing facilities—oh, never mind.

It's not *terlet* in itself that brings home to Grace and us how dismal her marriage is likely to be, but the word *door* does resonate, as they say.

And Ralph is on his way out on the town, after showing his thoughtfulness by reminding Grace to show up for the wedding.

"She smiled tiredly and opened the door for him. 'Don't worry, Ralph,' she said. 'I'll be there.' "

➤ aid, marital

The rock my marriage is founded on is one simple four-letter word:

Hunh?

I (the party of the first part, let us say, only for the sake of convenience not priority) may sometimes speak in what I *might* stipulate to be a perceived mumble. And the Mrs. has suffered a spot or two of OMOY (Overloud Music of Yore)—related hearing loss. And vice versa. And at least one of us—who, arguably, could on occasion be me, though not necessarily usually, from my point of view—has a *tendency*, yes, okay, a *perceived* tendency, to address the other in a normal (not to say murmuring) tone of voice from a room or two or three away. AS IF I HAVE NOTHING MORE TO DO WITH MY LIFE THAN HOVER CONSTANTLY IN CONVERSATIONAL-TONE RANGE!

So we frequently do not hear each other distinctly the first time. And there's always the possibility that a given statement is something that she or I, as the case may be, will *want* to hear—or at least something the not-hearing of which will leave himself or, indeed, herself open to the charge of:

Not listening.

Here is what I have learned: that a person is more likely to listen to something that he or she has *asked to hear repeated*. Well, not *fully* repeated. It is acknowledged, I believe, on the part of both parties, that the addressed party should, ideally, say *Hunh?* before the other party finishes making the statement in question, so that he or she—the original speaking person—will not have to say the whole thing over again, FOR GOD'S SAKE.

Often, it is even a good idea to ask a spouse to repeat a statement that one thinks one *has* heard distinctly. Once I told the Mrs. that she looked "perfect." As indeed she did.

"*Hunh?*" she said, which was fortunate because she thought I had said she looked "puffy."

I realize now that *eh?* would be *nice*r.

See *A*.

➤ *airplane*

It was *aeroplane* before such a thing existed, and still was *aeroplane* to the Wright brothers in 1905 and as late as 1934, and still is *aeroplane* in British

English, though according to John Ayto's *Dictionary of Word Origins*, that spelling is acknowledged even in the UK to have "a distinctly old-fashioned air." Let's not get off into that other meaning of *air*. Let us ask, why *-plane*?

From Latin *planus*, flat, we get plane geometry, a higher plane, the Great Plains, and the verb *plane* as in when your motorboat gets down onto an even keel. When people dreamed of an aeroplane, it was because they had given up on mechanical wings that flapped. Eventually aeronautic research established that fixed wings had to be rounded and pitched.

So planes take us up, now, but the miracle of human flight has become, if I may speak for humanity, a downer. In my occupation as a loosely based wordsmith, I have flown many, many times. Most recently from Chicago to New York. The day before, I had flown vice versa. During that night's taping of the radio show *Wait, Wait . . . Don't Tell Me!*, I had somehow not managed to come up with many—with *any*—scintillating remarks in time to get them in edgewise, and on the following morn I had awakened earlier than necessary and had lain there heavy-headed with worse than usual sinus congestion. Is there anything more boring than the symptoms of chronic sinusitis? I arose and dragged myself to O'Hare airport, where I have spent far too many involuntary hours to ever feel in any way pleased to be there yet again. And I had been booked into *a window seat*.

I don't care what the Wright brothers, if they have some way of reading down upon this, think. I have looked out of all the airplane windows I ever need to look out of. To be sure, a middle seat is worse; I don't even want to talk about being in a middle seat. But in a window seat you are crammed up against a wall—the wall between you and cloudland, I know, but a wall. A plastic wall. A wall that makes me want to be some*where*, with some*body*, not here in jam-packed limbo cheek by jowl with people I only hope will not try to engage me in conversation.

I tried to change to an aisle seat, but no dice. By virtue of the many miles I have flown, I possess credits exchangeable for upgrades to first class, which I define as a part of the airplane where there are *padded, uncontested* places to put your elbows. I wait-listed myself. I was fourth in line. The three ahead of me got the only slots. As so often happens.

So there I sat by the window. Praying that the other two seats would not be filled by extra-large, hairy, leg-jiggling people dressed for the gym. Then here those seat fillers came. **Nice**-looking people. But large. Not fat, but long limbed, expansive, and the worse of it: ebullient. From the Latin for boiling, that is to say, bubbling over.

He bubbled into the middle seat, she into the aisle. An African-American woman in her late thirties, I would say, with her adolescent son—they looked alike in a fresh-faced way, and he called her Mom. Both of them were beaming.

"It's his first flight!" she said.

Ah.

"And his sixteenth birthday!" she said.

Ah.

"Could I look out the window?" he asked, craning around me.

"I'm sorry," I said, "but I can't take the *middle*—" And then it hit me. First, that he was asking only that I pull up the window shade. Second . . .

"Would both of you like to move down, and I'll take the aisle seat?"

"*Would* you?" she said. "So *nice* of you."

I took the aisle. Which was better. But I was still on an airplane, and my head all clogged up with snot.

As we took off, the youth's face was pressed against the window, and the rest of him was bouncing in his seat. "*We're going to hit a bus!*" he cried, delighted. "*Highways!* We're flying over cars!"

She was trying to peer out over his shoulder. She turned to me and said, "It's just *my* second flight," she said.

Ah. I was trying to read about Afghanistan.

They rejoiced between themselves for a while, and then for an hour or so, they slept. Both of them. Strangely chummy, this teenager and mom. Did I ever fly with my poor mother? If I did, it wasn't like this.

They awoke, smiled, stretched. He had his face in the window again. She smiled at me and confided: "I arranged something special for him."

"*Mom,*" he said kiddingly (I can remember saying that to mine, only desperately), "don't talk to strangers."

"Oh, I'm not a stranger," I said, not being a terrible person, "I'm your row mate." But I was still *down*.

She looked expectant. And then, the announcement:

"We have a special passenger on board. This is his sixteenth birthday. And this is his first flight, ever. Let's have a big hand for . . . Roy!"

General applause. Air passengers are easily led. But "No!" Mom said—
"LaRon!" Then she looked at where LaRon was sitting, and back over at me.

"Are you Roy?" she said.

I said I was.

"Yo, Roy!" said LaRon. "Now we're both Roy!" We shook hands across
Mom's lap, and he turned, bouncing again, to watch us land. "*Ohhhh* me.
Ohhhh-*oh*. We're coming down over a *bridge! Ohhhh! Oh!*"

On the ground I took their picture on their phone. Then I took it again
on mine. I show it to people. LaRon is holding up the certificate the flight
attendant had given him, fortunately (though I don't think he would have
minded) without filling in his name.

➤ *and*

Perhaps by way of twitting the sort of English teacher who insists that one
must never, ever, begin a sentence with *and*, Garrison Keillor begins each
installment of his daily literary-history spot on public radio as follows:
"And here's the Writer's Almanac for July 10, 2010," or whatever. It's as if
the listener were arriving in the midst of an extended conversation, which
after all is what public radio is. We may think of Wally Ballou, the nasal-
toned roving reporter played by Bob Elliott and created by him and Ray
Goulding, the great Bob and Ray. Wally would always come bouncing in on
the second beat of his self-introduction: "-ly Ballou here!"

And leans forward, provides action for a spring ahead. **But**, on the other
hand, brings the reader/listener to a halt, a pre-turnaround snag. Consider the following statement:

"You gotta do what you gotta do and sometimes you do it with tears in
your eyes."

That is what reputed Genovese capo Thomas Ricciardi testified that
mob hit man Michael "Mikey Cigars" Coppola told him, and other pals,
with regard to his, Coppola's, whacking of their associate John "Johnny
Coca-Cola" Lardiere.

To recap: according to Ricciardi, Coppola admitted to Ricciardi and others that he, Coppola, had whacked Lardiere. And this, Ricciardi alleged, was
Coppola's philosophical gloss on the thing:

"You gotta do what you gotta do and sometimes you do it with tears in your eyes."

This new dimension to an old cliché befits a time when wiseguys are reduced to being named after soft drinks. But who would have expected the sentiment to be so *nice*ly metrical? It flows as if inevitable, as if it comes from an age-old ballad:

> Let's say some day I gotta shoot you,
> Or you, or you, or all of you guys.
> You gotta do what you gotta do
> And sometimes you do it with tears in your eyes.
>
> On occasion—you know this is true—
> You off your old lady. Everyone dies.
> You gotta do what you gotta do
> And sometimes you do it with tears in your eyes.

What I find most striking about Coppola's homily, however, is that he didn't say *but* sometimes you do it—shoot a friend and colleague to death in cold blood—with tears in your eyes. That would have suggested a qualm, a touch of regret.

He said *and*. As in, "I did what I had to, and I did it even though it made me feel a little blue." Or, "I did it, and I did it in the right spirit, too." With *but*, there's an element of grimness. With *and*, the whacker's tears make his response to duty's call even finer. Who says hit men don't need to feel good about themselves?

But not everyone has a hit man's moral agility. The other day in the grocery store I heard a small child mutter to an adult, "I'm sorry."

"And . . . ?" said the adult.

"An' won't do it again," the child said quickly.

"But . . ."

"But . . . I 'said that last time'? And . . . but—okay okay what *what*?" said the child.

➤ arbitrary

The notion that the connection between words and their meaning is arbitrary, for crying out loud, is generally credited to Ferdinand de Saussure. What made Saussure so sure? Well, he had special insights into letters and their connections. He said he experienced the French letter-sound *a*, for instance, as

> off-white, approaching yellow; in its consistency, it is something
> solid, but thin, that cracks easily if struck, for example a sheet of
> paper (yellowed with age) drawn tight in a frame, a flimsy door
> (in unvarnished wood left white) that you feel would shatter at
> the slightest blow, an already broken eggshell that you can keep
> cracking by pressing on it with your fingers. Better still: the shell of
> a raw egg is *a* (whether in colour or in the consistency of the object),
> but the shell of a hard-boiled egg is not *a*, because of the feeling you
> have that the object is compact and resistant. A yellowed pane of
> glass is *a*; a pane of ordinary colour, offering blueish reflections,
> is the very opposite of *a*, because of its colour, and despite its
> consistency being just right.

The phenomenon of *synesthesia*—one aspect of which is associating letters with colors—is discussed in *Alphabet Juice*. I'm always interested in connections between letters and the senses. But in my opinion, the concept of **sonicky** helps us appreciate the nature of, say, **blob** a lot more than all that eggshell shit helps us appreciate the nature of French *a*.

Okay, now, this just in. Here's a more serious rejoinder to the notion that words are arbitrary: not even letters are. In his *New Yorker* piece about a writer who was deprived, by a stroke, of the ability to read, Oliver Sacks quotes the French neurologist Jules Dejerine, who had studied the brain of a man who suffered the same loss. Dejerine concluded that "letter shape is not an arbitrary cultural choice. The brain constrains the design of an efficient writing system so severely that there is little room for cultural relativism. Our primate brain only accepts a limited set of written shapes."

See *O*.

➤ *architect* (the verb)

On *Wait Wait . . . Don't Tell Me!* a caller said his work was "architecting software." Peter Sagal, our host, asked him whether that was the same as "designing software."

    Caller: Designing is a more user-friendly term.

    Peter: And *architecting* is what you say when you want to sound **snazzy**.

    Caller: Exactly.

➤ *awesome*

Sadly diminished by overuse. *Time* magazine should not be reduced to describing an Olympic boxer's victories as "jaw-droppingly awesome."

b · B · b

Bee, the insect, perhaps goes back to PIE root *bhi-*, to fear, or more specifically to quiver, and by extension to buzz. (The word *bees* sounds like a buzz.) *Be*, the verb, in its many forms (*am*, *are*, *is*, *was*, *were*) is, to quote Etymonline .com, "the most irregular verb . . . and the most common" verb in Modern English. Ernest **Weekley** called it "an accidental conglomeration" of Old English dialects. The *b* parts go back to PIE base *bheu-*, grow or become.

A *bee*, we may assume, never brings up to itself the question, "to bee, or not to bee." It's too busy. It just be's that way.

➤ *back in the day*

No one under fifty (and that's being generous) should be allowed to get away with saying "back in the day."

➤ *bean*

Nobody knows the source of this ancient English word. Baked and canned in England, beans are close to the staff of life, but—you know critics are forever trying to work out what manner of person Shakespeare was? I'll tell you one thing: he didn't like beans. In his whole corpus, beans come up only twice, in both cases they're food for horses, and in one of those they are "as dank . . . as a dog" and will make a horse sick.

Bean meaning head we may associate with P. G. Wodehouse's utterly unaggressive Bertie Wooster: "I'm a bit short on brain myself; the old bean would appear to have been constructed more for ornament than for use, don't you know." (Remarkable that the same actor, Hugh Laurie, has portrayed both the blithe British *nincompoop* Bertie and the acerbic American wizard Dr. House so well on TV.)

But *bean* meaning head is primarily an American word, and a violent one. It first crops up in baseball slang, in connection with attempts to hit people in the head with a pitch. In 1905 a sportswriter wrote that the distinguished Native American pitcher Charles Albert "Chief" Bender "places much reliance on the bean ball."

This was back before batters wore any sort of head protection. Not until 1971 did the major leagues make hard plastic batting helmets mandatory, and even when you're wearing one of those, having a hardball thrown at your head is a lot like being shot at. One major leaguer and several minor leaguers have been killed by beanballs, and quite a few prominent players have suffered brain damage. Part of the game. Christy Mathewson was not only one of the greatest pitchers but also an esteemed Christian gentleman (never played on Sunday) and high-minded straight arrow. In 1912 there was published under his name a book, which conceivably—he was class president at Bucknell—he wrote. According to that book, *Pitching in a Pinch: or, Baseball from the Inside*, when a rookie came to bat, the catcher would warn him against the pitcher's "mean 'bean' ball. . . . There's a poor 'boob' in the hospital now that stopped one with his head." Then the catcher would call for the beanball, and if it drove the rookie away from the plate, "Bing! Up comes another 'beaner.'" If the rookie showed fear again, the catcher would conclude, "He won't do. He's yellow."

I'll bet it's that *Bing*, more than the shape of a bean, that gave rise to heads being called beans. *Bam. Bong. Boink.* OED cites six examples of *bean* meaning head, 1905–1924, and every one entails violent cranial contact—even one from Wodehouse: "Have I got to clump you one on the side of the bean?"

Christy Mathewson describes a battle of wits between Bender and the Giants' Freddie Snodgrass. Snodgrass had managed to reach base twice by getting hit harmlessly. When he came to bat next, "the Indian showed his even teeth in the chronic grin" and told Snodgrass to look out.

"Then Bender wound up and with all his speed drove the ball straight at Snodgrass's head."

Didn't hit him that time. Got him out on the next couple of pitches, though.

Ty Cobb, who was vicious but shrewd, called Bender the most intelligent pitcher he ever faced, and Mathewson praises Chief Bender as "brainy." (Wouldn't you think we'd know where the word *brain* came from? OED tells us *brawn* was "originally a part suitable for roasting," and therefore from an old Germanic word meaning to roast; but *brain* we are able only tentatively to associate, maybe, with a Greek word for forehead.)

According to Bender's biographer, Tom Swift, he was paid less than half what other star pitchers on his own team made, and he endured a lot of bigoted razzing—derisive war whoops, that sort of thing. I checked his record for hitting batters. In the 1903 season, as a rookie, he hit one (not necessarily in the head, of course) roughly every 10 2/3 innings. I'd say he was establishing a reputation, like in prison. If he had kept up that pace, he would have set the all-time record for hit batsmen, and maybe killed one of them. But over the other fifteen years of his career, he hit only one batter every 35 2/3 innings. The great paleface pitcher Walter Johnson, who was said to be at pains to avoid hitting batters for fear he would kill them, hit one every twenty-nine innings, which is slightly more often than Bender's lifetime average even including his formidable rookie year.

Getting back to the comestible bean, you might like to know that an old cowboy term for beans is "prairie strawberries."

➤ *bearless*

Doesn't mean without bears. Doesn't mean anything now, but before becoming obsolete it meant, according to OED, barren, not bearing anything.

Compare **toadless**.

➤ beauty, depth of

What a poor tragic sap was Sir Thomas Overbury, the first person known to have written that beauty is only skin deep. It's in his poem, first published in 1614, "The Wife":

> And all the carnall *beauty* of my wife
> Is but skin-deep, but to *two senses* known;
> Short even of pictures, shorter liv'd then life,

And yet the *love* survives, that's build thereon:
>   For our *imagination* is too high,
>   For *bodies* when they meet, to satisfie.

Pretty much as a result of that poem, Overbury was murdered—poisoned bit by bit, like Ingrid Bergman in *Notorious*, only terminally. In Overbury's notorious story, the closest equivalent to the Cary Grant character was in on the poisoning. To top it all off, Overbury seldom gets credit for his skin-deep line. Anne Somerset never mentions it in her absorbing 524-page book about the case, *Unnatural Murder: Poison at the Court of James I.* What is worse, *Bartlett's Familiar Quotations* credits the image not to Overbury but to John Davies of Hereford, who borrowed it for a heavy-handed spoof of Overbury's poem, "A Select Second Husband for Sir Thomas Overburie's Wife":

> *Beauty's but skin-deepe*; nay it is not so:
> It floates but on the *skin* beneath the *skin*,
> That (like pure *Aire*) scarse hides her fullest flow:
> It is so *subtill, vading, fragile*, and *thin*:
>   Were she *skin-deepe*, she could not be so *shallow*
>   To win but *fooles* her *puritie* to hallow.

That came out in 1616, by which time Overbury was dead. He had attained great influence in King James's profoundly corrupt court and had shared that influence with a flaxen-haired young man named Robert Carr, who, if you don't mind a weak chin, was quite pretty. Then Carr fell for a woman, Lady Frances Howard, countess of Somerset. Her portrait sustains her reputation as one of the most beautiful women in the court.

When Carr met her she was already married, but to a man who—there were two sides to the story. According to Frances's friends, her husband on their first night together "laboured a quarter of an hour to know her," then said, "Frankie, it will not be," and bade her good night. According to his friends, as soon as the couple were alone, Frances "reviled him . . . terming him cow, coward and beast . . . which things so cooled his courage that he was far from knowing, or endeavoring to know her."

That marriage annulled, she was dead set on capturing Carr. Overbury hadn't minded Carr's dalliance with Frances—in fact he had ghostwritten

Carr's love letters to her—but he didn't want Carr to *marry* this "base woman," and so he wrote "The Wife" and presented Carr with a copy. Overbury had never had a wife himself, nor been linked to any woman, but his poem undertakes to describe the subcutaneous virtues a *proper* wife would have. In the course of forty-six stanzas it takes some unexpected turns. The skin-deep image is all very well; more striking is the dismissal of a woman's shapely body as nothing "but well-digested food." There is gender-bending:

> At first, both *sexes* were in *man* combinde,
> Man a *she-man* did in his body breed;
> *Adam* was *Eve's*, *Eve* mother of mankinde,
> *Eve* from *live-flesh*, man did from *dust* proceed.
> > *One*, thus made *two*, *mariage* doth re-unite,
> > And makes them both but one *hermaphrodite*.

> Or rather let me *love*, then *be in love*,
> So let me chuse, as *wife* and *friend* to find,
> Let me forget her *sex*, when I *approve*:
> *Beasts* likenesse lies in *shape*, but *ours* in *mind*:
> > Our *soules* no *sexes* have, their love is cleane,
> > No *sex*, both in the *better part* are *men*.

Carr and Frances were creeped out by "The Wife," and so was the king. James liked the cut of Carr's jib himself, but he had found a new young man, George Villiers, who, judging from his portrait, was more beautiful, if you don't mind really skinny legs and a blank expression, than Frances and Carr put together. Frances and Carr had the king's blessing. Overbury lost favor and found himself in the Tower.

He appealed to his friend Carr, who he assumed would be able to bring James back around. The response, through nefarious intermediaries, was judiciously poisoned jellies and tarts. Overbury grew sicker and sicker, thanks not only to the steady flow of tainted treats but also to the attentions of fashionable physicians. One of these, Dr. Theodore Turquet de Mayerne, was the author of a book recommending, for internal application, "a syrup made with the flesh of tortoises, snails, the lungs of animals, frogs and **crawfish**, all boiled in scabrous and coltsfoot water, adding at the last sugar candy" and, for external application, a dressing called "balsam of bats," which contained "three of the greater sort of serpents or snakes cut into pieces, their skins being first stripped off; twelve bats; two very fat sucking puppies; one pound of earthworms washed in white wine; common oil; malago sack; sage, marjoram and bay leaves," to be boiled and then supplemented with two pounds of hog's lard, "the marrow of a stag, an ox's legs, liquid amber, butter and nutmegs."

Overbury hung on for months. Finally he lost faith in Carr and succumbed. In his day he had been described, by James's wife, the long-suffering Queen Anne, as "a pretty young fellow," but in death his skin was covered with pustules and grievous ulcers. Frances and Carr had a gala wedding. John Donne, hoping for an income from Carr (who never delivered, so Donne had to take holy vows for a living), wrote a poem for the occasion, including these lines:

> For every part to dance and revel goes,
> They tread the air, and fall not where they rose

which may have come back to disturb Frances and Carr a couple of years later when they were sentenced to hang.

Rumors had gone around. Public sentiment had been aroused. And Carr had developed an ill-advisedly outspoken case of jealousy toward Villiers, whom James never ceased to dote on, even after a friend of Carr's who had an epicene son "took great pains in tricking and pranking him up," improving the youth's complexion by "washing his face every day with posset curd," and parading him before the king.

Frances and Carr were imprisoned, tried, and convicted. Eventually the king pardoned them—too pretty for the rope—but the trial and incarceration had been an ordeal, and sources close to the couple said that although they lived under the same castle roof, their love had not survived. There they were, stuck with each beautiful other, each proof to the other that beauty can in fact run deep-trouble deep.

➤ belch

OED traces this robust word back to Old English *bealcian*, which meant the same thing; compares it to Dutch *balken*, to bray, shout; and leaves its etymology at that. Chambers breaks down and admits that *belch* is "almost certainly imitative in origin," which is surely so. But an audible eructation of gas from the stomach doesn't make the sound *belch*. *Eructation* is closer, or *urp*, or *burp* if one prefers, but even though I have known some highly creative eructators, I have never heard anyone put a *b* sound into a belch. Nor, for that matter, a *ch*. Not onomatopoeic, then, but **sonicky**. *Belch* looks like it *ought* to sound like a belch. Maybe because we so often labor to **squelch** a belch.

See **blurt**.

➤ *bigth*

Neither WIII nor OED recognizes *bigth*, even as an obsolete word, but it used to be used. According to Alice Morse Earle in *Customs and Fashions in Old New England*, early apothecaries "did not measure the drugs with precision. . . . The asbestos stomachs and colossal minds of our forefathers were much above such petty minuteness; nor did they administer the doses with exactness. 'The bigth of a walnut,' . . . 'as bigg as a haslenut,' . . . 'the bigth of a Turkeys Egg.'"

Why did *bigth* die out? *Breadth*, *depth*, *length*, *width*, and even *strength* have the advantage of being more specific and measurable; but *bigness* is in OED and still has some currency. The problem with *bigth* is that it's ugly to look at, confusable with *bight*, and a pain to pronounce. Shifting from a hard *g* to *th* is a jolt. *Big thing*, or *big thighs*, gives the tongue time to make the transition. *Length* ends in *gth*, but the *n* softens the *g* so it flows into the *th*.

➤ *blab, blabber*

OED:

> Words of similar form appear in other Teut. langs.: cf. ON. *blabbra* . . . Da. *blabbre* to babble, gabble, Sw. dial. *blaffra* to prattle, G. *blappern*, . . . *plappern* to blab, babble, prate. But the evidence is not sufficient to show whether any of these were actually connected with the English word, or whether they agree only in being natural

expressions of the action involved, which seems to be essentially that of producing a confused repetition or combination of labial (*b*) and lingual (*l, r*) sounds.

That is to say, words about loose lips and a flapping tongue, formed by loose lips and a flapping tongue.

➤ bless

This word is peculiarly English, with no kin in other languages. OED traces *bless* back to Old English *blóedsian*, whose "etymological meaning was . . . 'to mark (or affect in some way) with blood (or sacrifice); to consecrate.'" For instance, to splash sacrificial blood on doorways to keep out the Destroying Angel.

When the Bible was translated from Hebrew into Latin, scholars needed a word for the Hebrew *brk*, which meant, according to OED, "primarily 'to bend,' hence 'to bend the **knee**, worship, praise, bless God.'" They came up with *benedicere*, literally to speak well of. By the time the Bible was translated from Latin into English, *blóedsian* had softened, in form, to *bless*, which was chosen as the equivalent of *benedicere*. That selection, OED suggests, is how *bless* gained unbloody connotations—sort of like the way people hoped your aunt Peaches would be influenced by being chosen to play Mary in the Christmas pageant.

But wait a minute. Where did that soft *ss* ending come from? If *blóedsian* had held on to more of itself, Elvis in "All Shook Up" would have sung something like "Blodze my soul, what's wrong with me?" The *s* sound in *bless* didn't come from *benedicere*, because the Latin *c* had a *k* sound. (Cicero, the great Roman orator, to whom we owe "While there's life, there's hope," would turn over in his sarcophagus if he heard us praise an eloquent speaker as ciceronian, pronounced *sissy-ronian*. In Cicero's place and time he was *kicker-o*.)

In OED we find *bloedsade* circa 950, *bletsode* circa 1000, *bletcaed* in 1154, and *Blettcedd* circa 1200. A softer-sounding verb was needed for gentler rituals. When *blessed* turns up at last in 1377, it is with regard to the breaking and blessing of bread.

"At a very early date," says OED, "the popular etymological conscious-ness . . ."

Love that notion, "the popular etymological consciousness." I didn't even know we had such a thing going on, but I like to think about us all floating in a rootsy ken, without quite realizing it. Maybe popular etymo-logical subconscious would be more accurate, but who am I to quibble with OED?

". . . the popular etymological consciousness began to associate" the verb *bless* with the originally unrelated noun *bliss*, whose roots, neither bloody nor sacramental, are akin to those of *blithe*. In haphazard Middle English, *bliss* was often spelled *bless* and vice versa (or either of them, *blyss*). "Hence," says OED, "the gradual tendency to withdraw *bliss* from earthly 'blitheness' to the beatitude of the blessed in heaven, or that which is likened to it."

In Old English, *bliss* was already lispingly close to itself: *bliths*. As early as the year 971, it was already *blisse*. OED suggests that *bliss* and *bless* influ-enced each other as to meaning. I'm thinking form, too. I'm thinking *bliss* got sanctified by sharing its *s*'s with *bless*.

See **-ed**.

➤ *blob*

Appears first in the fifteenth century as a verb meaning to make a bubble and in the sixteenth as a noun meaning bubble, in either case, by common acknowledgment, **sonicky**: "expressing the action of the lips in producing a bubble," according to OED, which says the same about *bleb*, a small blister or bubble. "In relation to *blob*, *bleb* expresses a smaller swelling; cf. *top*, *tip*, etc.," adds OED—*eh* and *ih* are shorter sounds than *ah*. That's why we say *tip-top* and *hip-hop*: *top-tip* would be top-heavy, *hop-hip* a stumble. Com-pare *topspin*, which orally enacts its meaning twice: pushing forward to *p* then cutting back to sizzle a bit at *s*, then forward again to *p* and back again to nail it with an *n*. That *psp* juncture, in particular, packs lots of represen-tative action. The only words I can think of where that sequence appears are made-up inversions, *lipspread*, *upsprung*—no, wait, there's **rumpsprung**, in which the neighboring *m* and *r* spread the pressure out.

See **bubble**.

➤ *bloggerheads, at*

The situation of people calling each other names, anonymously, on the Internet.

➤ *blurt*

OED's first definition of this word is not current except in dialect, but you have to like the smack of it: "To emit the breath eruptively from the mouth; to snort in sleep." Presumably OED lists that definition first—although its first citation in print dates from 1611—because it is more closely linked to the body than the current, more abstract definition, "To utter abruptly . . . , to burst out with," which is supported by an earlier (1573) citation in print. If a word has ever had a bodily meaning, that is presumably the one that it started with.

So what's the etymology? OED says "app[arently] a modern onomato-poeia, expressive of a discharge of breath or fluid from the mouth after an effort to retain it; with the *bl*- element, cf. *blow*, *blast*, *blash*, etc.; with the rest cf. *spurt*, *spirt*, *squirt*, etc.: see also BLIRT."

When we do see *blirt*, which means to burst into tears, the OED gives us more on the nature of *-urt* and *-irt* words: "expressing the forcible emission of liquid." I would say the *ur* or *ir* part is what does that (as also in *burst*, *gurgle*, *burble*, *splurge*, *purge*, *hurl*—the *uh* sound without the *r* gives us *gush*, *flush*, *upchuck*), and the *t* evokes termination. I know that when I blurt something out, I often bring it to an abrupt halt and hope I can pass it off as a snort.

I love it when the highest lexicographical authority acknowledges that many words are intrinsically, nonarbitrarily expressive of their meaning. But was even the original snort-in-the-night *blurt* onomatopoeic in the usual sense? OED defines onomatopoeia two ways. First: "The formation of a word from a sound associated with the thing or action being named; the formation of words imitative of sounds." Second: "The use of echoic or suggestive language, esp[ecially] onomatopes, for rhetorical effect." In the second definition, it's hard to see why *onomatopes* adds anything, since OED defines *onomatope* as "a word formed by onomatopoeia." The definitive example of *onomatope* that OED cites is Noah Webster's in 1828: "a figure in which words are formed to resemble the sound made by the thing signified; as, to buzz, as bees . . . A word whose sound corresponds to the sound of the thing signified."

Because *onomatopoeia* is narrowly associated with imitative sound, it can't do justice to *blurt*, or *spurt*, much less, say, *finagle*. Perhaps my grandchildren will see the day when OED acknowledges the kinephonic concept of **sonicky**.

➤ *body*

No other language has a word like this one. Old High German *botah* and *potah* had the same meaning, but etymology cannot link that word to our *body*, and it died out of German many centuries ago. In English, as OED puts it, "*body* remains as a great and important word."

It would be interesting to make a study of all the English words, like *body*, that go back to earliest print and seem to come from nowhere. Others include *curse*, *guilt*, and *dog*. The groundbreaking nineteenth-century etymologist Walter W. Skeat compared *body* to a Sanskrit word and said the original, Old English sense related to bondage—the body "considered as confining the soul." Etymologists don't believe that anymore.

Is it just me, or does *body* sound more emotive, and fleshier, than any of the various forms of the Latin *corpus* in Romance languages and German? More emotive, fleshier, and also more embracing: "the whole material organism viewed as an organic entity" (OED). The physical self rolled into a ball.

See **bubble** and **beauty, depth of**.

➤ *boo*

In the sixties it was a term for marijuana. Maybe from *taboo*, suggested an article in *High Times*. Now it means boyfriend or girlfriend. Perhaps an alteration of *beau*, suggests OED. Old Slavic for loved one was *l'ubu*, if that's any help.

To scare someone, people used to go *bo*. A "combination of consonant and vowel especially fitted to produce a loud and startling sound," says OED.

Now people go *boo*. (Ghosts put more *o*'s into it, more syllables, even.)

People used to go *boo* to sound like cows. Which is why audiences started going *boo* to express disapproval of a performance. Boo birds—people who get off on expressing disapproval—may also hoot like owls or hiss like geese or snakes, or they may utter catcalls (OED: "From the nocturnal cry, or 'waul' of the cat"), which were originally produced in English theaters by means of a special squeaking instrument.

Or they may jeer. Nobody knows where *jeer* comes from. **Weekley** hazards a perhaps: corruption of the Dutch *den gek scheeren*, to make a fool of someone, *gek* meaning fool.

OED says *bah!* was probably picked up from modern French. Not from sheep, then.

To sound like cows these days, people generally go *moo* (or in German, *muh*; French, *meuh*; Spanish, *mu*; Russian, *mu*; Lithuanian, *mū*; Latvian, *mau*).

Back to *hiss*. Charles Lamb, the illustrious nineteenth-century British essayist, wrote a play, a farce, which he titled *Mr. H.* "How simple! how taking!" he wrote to a friend before opening night: "A great *H* sprawling over the play-bill, and attracting eyes at every corner." *Mr. H.* was hissed off the stage. Lamb wrote to another friend:

> Mercy on us, that God should give his favorite children . . . mouths to speak with, to discourse rationally, to promise smoothly, to flatter agreeably, to encourage warmly, to counsel wisely, to sing with, to drink with, and to kiss with, and that they should turn them into mouths of adders, bears, wolves, hyaenas, and whistle like tempests, and emit breath through them like distillations of aspic poison, to asperse and vilify the innocent labors of their fellow-creatures who are desirous to please them! Heaven be pleased to make the teeth rot out of them all, therefore!

Lamb had thought it would go over so cool, how subtly he had set up the disclosure (the *reveal*, a screenwriter would say) that the *H* of Mr. H. stood for *Hogsflesh*.

➤ books, randomly readable

"I won't begin in any particular spot," said Mark Sanford, governor of South Carolina, to kick off a press conference about having got himself into a spot by going to Argentina to see "the woman who I've been un-faithful to my wife with."

Would **whom** have been too punctilious there? Perhaps. I just thought Sanford's opening would be a good way to start an appreciation of the sort of book that you can open up at any page and plunge into. One of these is *Lo!* by the collector (and perhaps example) of unexplained phenomena Charles Fort. Here is what I have just turned to in *Lo!*:

> Louth, Lincolnshire, England, May 29, 1920—the River Lud, which is only a brook, and is known as "Tennyson's Brook," was babbling, or maybe it was purling—
>
> Out of its play, this little thing humped itself twenty feet high. A ferocious transformation of a brook sprang upon the houses of Louth, and mangled fifty of them. Later in the day, between banks upon which were piled the remains of houses, in which were lying twenty-two bodies, and from which hundreds of the inhabitants had been driven homeless, the little brook was babbling, or purling.

See **purl**.

➤ *boy*

According to John Ayto's *Dictionary of Word Origins*, the latest etymological theory connects this word to the Old French *embuier*, fetter. In English, *boy* originally meant male servant or churl. Anatoly Liberman in *An Ana-lytic Dictionary of English Etymology*, however, says the Modern English *boy* is a "blend of an onomatopoeic word for an evil spirit . . . and a baby word for 'brother.'" (Sounds about right.) For many years, especially in the segregated South, white people invidiously called black men "boy." But by the fifteenth century, *boy* had come primarily to mean a young male, un-pejoratively, and if there weren't something engaging about the sound of the word, a rapper would never refer to his entourage as "my boys" and people of both genders would never exclaim "Oh boyoboyoboy!"

In his book *Try and Stop Me*, Bennett Cerf told a story about Herbert Bayard Swope, who in the twenties, thirties, and forties was an enor-mously self-important and yet widely enjoyed newspaper editor and man of affairs:

One night a Broadway friend and his blue-eyed babe taxied Herbert Swope home from a theatrical party. Swope, as usual, carried the conversational ball. "The era of the economic royalists and predatory robber barons went out with the Hoover administration," he boomed. "I have told Franklin and I have told Wendell—I'm sure you agree with me—that if they ignore the portents and pussy-foot back to the tenets of the McKinley era, I will not be responsible for anything that happens to them." The little lady sitting next to him gazed at him in wide-eyed wonder and said softly, "Hey, hey, Big Boy."

See **gillie, girl**.

➤ *bubble*

No evidence has been found, we are told, to link *bubble* etymologically to any of the words for *bubble*, similar as they are, in other languages: Latin *bulla*, Swedish *bubble*, Dutch *bobbel*, Danish *boble*, German dialect *bobbel*. "As likely as not," says John Ayto, "the whole family of *bubble* words represents ultimately an attempt to lexicalize the sound of bubbling, by blowing through nearly closed lips."

Hmm. I have been sitting here for twenty minutes trying and failing to make anything like the sound *bubble* by blowing through nearly closed lips, with spit or without.

OED is much closer to the mark, saying of all these versions of *bubble*, "it is not clear how far they are related to each other, or are merely parallel imitative words, suggested either by the sound of bubbles forming and bursting, or by the action of the lips in making a bubble."

But why "merely"? What is so *mere* about a series of letters managing to convey an evanescent material object? It's wonderful. It's damn near too marvelous for words.

And when words across several languages are so similarly **sonicky**, why can't they be called "related"? They may have cropped up unaware of one another, but they all go way back, they all may be seen to evince the lips of the same species, and as soon as they encountered one another, they knew.

And can't we readily imagine that *bulb* and *boil* and *ball* and *bowl* and *bob* and *buoyant* and *belly* and *bulge* (and maybe, just maybe, **body**) are all to some extent rooted in the oral evocation of roundness? I don't know. I'm just asking.

See **blob**; **bum**.

➤ *buckra*

In every source I've found, this old derogatory African-American term for white people is said to be from an African word, *bakra* or *mbakara*, meaning white man, European, or master. From a verb, *kara*, meaning to encompass or master. I wonder whether *buckra* was influenced, at least, by a word that goes back to the thirteenth century in English and appears right after *buckra* in most dictionaries: *buckram*, as in (AHD) "a coarse cotton fabric heavily sized with glue, used for stiffening garments and in bookbinding" and "resembling or suggesting buckram, as in stiffness or formality." (Some say probably from Bukhara, Uzbekistan, whence the fabric was imported, but OED says that won't wash.)

➤ *bum*

Let's concede this one to the UK: *bum* is a better, plumper, more affectionate term for the human posterior than American *butt*, which is too hard sounding, like what a goat does, or *ass*, which sounds inherently crass—a quality which, to be sure, improves the following anecdote that I remember from the autobiography of Lauren Bacall:

At a big reception somewhere, the shah of Iran danced with her. Was smitten by her. Told her, "You dance divinely, Miss Bacall."

She responded, "You bet your ass, Shah."

But there's something grating about *ass*. Even when *bum* has negative connotations, as in expressions like *bum leg* and *bummer*, it has a down-home warmth (can this be related to the **M**'s in *me* and *mom* and *yum* and *hum* and *home*?) that comes through in the old antisalvationist hobo song, "Hallelujah, I'm a Bum."

OED calls *bum* "probably onomatopoeic, to be compared with other words of similar sound and with the general sense of 'protuberance, swelling.'" (Or as some might say, it's **sonicky**. See **blurt** and **bubble**.)

In Chaucer's "The Miller's Tale," a smarty-pants student sticks his bare bottom out the window so that a dumb cluck, mistaking it (again) for the face of the lady with **whom** the student is dallying, will kiss it. But the cluck has got wise. He pokes the student with a hot iron. Here's how the story ends in the original:

> And Nicholas is scalded in the towte.
> This tale is doon, and God save al the rowte!

Towte is a long-obsolete term for the buttocks; *rowte*, for an assemblage of people. (From the latter we get *rout* meaning an army's disorderly flight, and by extension an overwhelming defeat in sports.) The best modern translation I have seen of those two lines is Nevill Coghill's:

> And Nicholas is branded on the bum
> And God bring all of us to Kingdom Come.

How would we do that in American?

> And Nicholas is branded on the ass.
> Such things God knows do sometimes come to pass.

> And Nicholas is blistered on the butt.
> Good Lord! Next time he'll keep the window shut.

Why do Brits say *arse* and Americans *ass*? Well, for one thing, Brits don't say *arse*, they say something more like *ahss*, which strikes me as a bit haughty—a quality that, to be sure, adds something to the expression "disappear up one's own arse," meaning, according to OED, "to become excessively self-involved, pretentious, or conceited." OED provides this **nice** example, from a novel by Peter Marshall (I might mention, though, that when I clicked on P. MARSHALL on OED.com—which incidentally I love—I was transported to a bibliography that did not include Peter Marshall, so I had to do quite a bit of surfing before I ran him to ground): "You see, logic cannot stand the application of logic. Under such an application, logic will disappear up its own arse."

In *ass* for *arse* there must be a parallel in American *cuss* for *curse, bust* for *burst*, and *hoss* for *horse*: if the English don't pronounce *r*'s, why should we spell 'em?

In the late sixties when I was covering baseball for *Sports Illustrated* I heard a story that comes to mind here. When Masanori Murakami joined the San Francisco Giants in 1964, becoming the first Japanese-born player in the American major leagues, his English and his acquaintance with American baseball rituals were limited. Two veteran Giants, Bobby Bonds and Jim Ray Hart, fun-loving African Americans, took him aside and gave him a helpful tip about how to show respect. So the first time Murakami came to bat, he bowed to the plate umpire and said ceremoniously, "You can kiss my big black ass."

Fanny for bottom is American. In British English, *fanny* means, as OED puts it, "the female genitals." Origin unknown, though OED is willing to suggest, tentatively, that the British *fanny* meaning "a tin for holding anything to be drunk" might come from "the female name," and AHD is willing to hazard a speculation that the American *fanny* comes from that same name, a nickname for *Frances*.

Another **nice** word is *rump*, but it also has derogatory applications, as in *rump parliament*. *Tush*, like the Yiddish *tuchus* from which it springs, has a friendly sound.

Fundament isn't bad—a bit formal, but that quality lends something to Mark Twain's observation that "by consent of the whole company, when only males are present, it is still permissible, in good society, to remove the embargo on the fundamental sigh."

Buns, from the shape, I guess, seems apt. *Nates* is, like so many words from the Latin, boring. The German *Arsch* is almost unpronounceably harsh. *Keister*, which originally meant suitcase and whose origin is unknown, is too cold for me, and so is *can*, and so is *prat*, from which we get *pratfall*. The origin of this *prat* is unknown, but it goes back at least to the sixteenth century, and I'm wondering, just on my own cognizance, whether this *prat* can have sprung from a sardonic allusion to the Old English adjective *prat* meaning "cunning, astute," related to *pretty*. *Derrière* is perky French from the Latin *de retro* meaning "from the back." Once on *The Wire*, Herc, the dumb cop, was wearing a T-shirt that said, over an outline map of Wisconsin, "Smell That Dairy Air."

See **tutus, the two.**

➤ *but*

In the forties movie *Blue Skies*, Joan Caulfield prods Bing Crosby into admitting he's in love with her.

"Yes," Bing intones (croons, almost), while holding the lovely Joan close, "I guess I am. But—"

"*But*. What an unpleasant word," says Joan.

"You know me, I'm just not the marrying type," says Bing.

Maybe that exasperating little exchange provides context for all the aunts and English teachers who have adjured young people (or so a number of them, now grown, have informed me) to avoid the word *but* because "it's a defensive word." Poppycock. It's a useful word, a word that sounds like what it means. I see a lot of *but*-avoidance in the press. Why would AP write this, about the usually affectless Phillies pitcher Roy Halladay's having smiled and high-fived after pitching a perfect game: "Ordinary stuff for most people, although for Halladay, such signs of emotion may have as well been considered a wild party"?

Forget the bizarre lameness of "may have as well been." Why *although*? Surely that sentence calls for a simple *but*.

I also see a lot of *yet*'s that ought to be *but*'s. *Yet* shouldn't be brought out until you need something stronger than *but*. It means nevertheless. If you say, "I called you, yet you didn't call back," then what have you got left for, "You told me you had called me three times last night, yet somehow, my phone didn't ring"? *Yet* may be the new *but*, because *yet* slides off the tongue, whereas *but* may strike an idiot as bumptious, or something.

Yet *but* can even be a romantic word, as in "I'll be loving you" (and here I paraphrase lest I wind up owing an arm and a leg to the estate of Irving Berlin), not for just a season, not for just a reason . . .

But always.

The word *but* was formed, we are told, as early as the eighth century, by combination of *be* meaning "by" and *ut* meaning "out." Originally, it was only a preposition, as in "I need nothing in my system but roughage and love," or an adverb, as in "Limbaugh, O'Reilly, Father Coughlin, and Tokyo Rose, to name but a few." Not until 1000 was *but* used as a conjunction, as in

She's got freckles on her
But she's pretty.

By scholarly consensus, *but* is etymologically unrelated to the *butt* that means thick end or human posterior. What's more, that *butt* is unrelated to *butt* as in the butt of a joke (which however may be related to *butte*). And none of these are related to the verb meaning to bump with the head. But however *but* and the several *butt*'s differ in provenance, they take after one another at some level. "Only in rock-solid marriages," writes Richard Ford in *Independence Day*, "can you hope to hear that you're a sweet man without a 'but' following along afterward like a displeasing goat."

See *and* and **though**, **the lazy.**

c · C · c

From *Sesame Street*, we know that a *C* is a cookie from which the Cookie Monster has taken a large bite. A cookie-cutter shark, according to OED, is a small one that "takes distinctive, non-lethal bites from large prey." *Cookie* derives not from *cook* but from Dutch *koekje*, little cake. An attractive woman said "See ya, Cookie" to me once, and it felt like a nibble, but I was in a relationship, as they say, with another, who never called me "Cookie." That's the way it crumbles.

Kooky, meaning eccentric to the point of craziness, is possibly from *cuckoo*, meaning a bird that goes *coo-coo*, just that, over and over and over again, *coo-coo, coo-coo*, which is possibly why *cuckoo* means crazy. *Cootch* is a catchy—if in most contexts too familiar—word for what I would have to say is the most extraordinary, if you think about it, part of a woman. Maybe *extraordinary* is not the word, but you know what I mean. You know what I mean? To babies we say, "Coochy-coo."

See *ch*.

celebrity

Originally, in the fourteenth century, a celebrity was something less common: a solemn ceremony or celebration. More recently I saw a TV commercial in which someone unrecognizable popped up to say, "Hello, I'm Fitness Celebrity . . ." and her name. Can you truly call yourself a celebrity if you have to introduce yourself as one?

➤ *ch*

You can't tell me there is nothing inherently catchy in the *tch* or hard-*ch* sound of English, especially American English, as in *catchy*. Or *clutch*, or *cinch*, or *notch*, or *niche*, or *chink*, or . . .

*Dontcha just know it? You betcha. Gotcha. Natch. Cha-cha, choo-choo, chow-chow, got a **hunch**, comin atcha, ka-ching, chill, thanks much, chop-chop, chin-chin, cheers, ciao, cheerio, check, watch yerself, oo-chi-wa-wa, charmed, buenas noches, right back atchu.*

"The Man Right Chea." "I Wanna Get Wit Chu." "Rock Witchu." Da Brat and Tyrese favoring us with "What 'Chu Like."

Scratch, itch, chafe, coochy-coo, hoochie-coochie, nautch dancer, crotch, hunch, punch.

Pitch. Chuck. John Clare, in the mid-nineteenth century, referred to throwing a ball back and forth as "chuck ball and catch it."

Chuckle. Chatter. Chugalug. Hooch. Crunch. Munch. Lunch. Choppers. Chomp. Champ. Chew. Manolha Dargis in *The New York Times*, on Jack Black's accent in *Nacho Libre*: "You hear the quotation marks in the delivery and the thought that goes into every phrasing. That gives the lines chew."

Chicken. Cheese. Charley. Macho. Honcho. Mensch. Butch. Britches. Bitch. Tchotchke.

Chockablock. Chocolate chip. Woodchuck chuck. Chain chain chain . . .

English has two affricates, *j* and *ch*. (See **adulation**.) An affricate, according to AHD, is "a complex speech sound consisting of a stop consonant followed by a fricative." A fricative (also AHD) is "a consonant . . . produced by the the forcing of breath through a constricted passage." From the Latin "to rub against." The sound of *ch* is that of *j* without vocal-cord vibration.

People—even those who see no charm in driving a car in such a way as to "scratch off"—like to say *ch*. It's a catch. It sets up a release.

Ahhh-*choo*.

See **sneeze**.

➤ *chimera*

When my daughter, Ennis, was a moppet, we had a talk about what words not to use in the hearing of her grandparents. She assured me that, for

example, "I never say *fart* to anybody until I've heard them say it first." I
hope I followed that policy for most of my life with the word *chimera*, because I knew it meant a wild fantasy, but I pronounced it, in my head, shi-
mer-ra, because I associated it with *shimmer*, as in a mirage. Then I heard
somebody pronounce it correctly, kie-*mir*-a. I hastened to the dictionaries, which trace it back to a mythical Greek monster with the head of a
lion, the body of a goat, and the tail of a serpent. Or, sometimes, a lion's
body and head with a second head, that of a goat. A wildly improbable
combination of things, then. The rabbitfish, which has rabbitlike teeth, is
of the family Chimaeridae.

➤ Chinese sense of time

A man I met said he'd been involved in negotiating a big-money agreement
with a Chinese company. The Chinese balked at the term "in perpetuity."
What would they agree to instead? "Fifty thousand years."

➤ Chinese, would-be purification of

According to the *Far Eastern Economic Review*, when the Red Guards were
intent upon forcibly regrooving all of Chinese culture along Maoist lines,
they tried to eradicate English-tainted foodstuff terms by instructing the
state-operated provision store in Shanghai to start referring to cocoa (*ke
ke*) as *hong se fen* (red-colored powder); coffee beans (*ka fei dou*) as *huang
la fen* (yellow bitter powder); chocolate bars (*chia ke li*) as *hsiang tsao kuan*
(fragrant grass—or vanilla—bar); and beer (*bi jiu*) as *mi mai chi jiu* (rice
and wheat gaseous wine). These changes failed to catch on.

➤ *clever*

Middle English was *cliver*, nimble handed, from *clivers*, meaning, as OED
puts it, "claws, talons, clutches," connecting with "the use of the hands, a
notion which [**redundancy** alert] still remains in the general sense of
adroit, *dexterous*, having 'the brain in the hand.'" Chambers tentatively
relates to Old English *clifian*, meaning cleave, as in adhere. Not the other
cleave, as in split. The two *cleaves* find a certain extra-etymological, and

extra-grammatical, unity in the hymnal lyric, "Rock of Ages [or, as Kris Kristofferson sang it, "Rita Coolidge"], cleft for me."

> *clown*

Want to hear a sad clown story? No, of course you don't, but this one relates to the war on terror. In 2006, after a slow day of painting faces and twisting balloons for tips in a Manhattan park, a Russian immigrant named Alexander Alhovsky, forty, stopped at Starbucks for a coffee. When he left, his battery-powered balloon pump was still on the counter.

Police were called. They **x-ray**ed the pump and determined it was not a bomb, but they could not eliminate the possibility that Alhovsky was a terrorist leaving a fake bomb as a test. Surveillance was set up.

When Alhovsky returned, by his account, police officers knocked him off his bike, kicked him in the kidneys, stepped on his face, held a gun to his head, and dragged him so that his pants and underwear came to his **knee**s in front of neighborhood children.

Alhovsky sued, claiming post-traumatic stress disorder. He wore his clown outfit to court, but the judge made him change. One of the arresting officers was quoted by the *New York Post* as saying the pump looked like a bomb to him, adding that the clown "kept saying, 'I'm just a clown!' That didn't mean anything to me."

The jury ruled that the police did not use excessive force.

A term for "morbid fear of clowns" often advanced earnestly on the Web is *coulrophobia*. Neither OED nor WIII recognizes it, and Etymonline.com says it "looks suspiciously like the sort of thing idle pseudo-intellectuals invent on the Internet and which every smarty-pants takes up thereafter; perhaps it is a mangling of Modern Gk. *klooun* 'clown.'"

On YouTube you can find an affecting clip of a woman being treated for her terror of clowns. Elsewhere online you can buy, in several different designs, T-shirts saying CAN'T SLEEP, CLOWNS WILL EAT ME, which is the name of an Alice Cooper song inspired by a line spoken by Bart on *The Simpsons*—Homer had built him a bed that looked like an evil clown.

Here and there online you can find several terms for "fear of police." The dumbest is *policophobia*. The most psychiatric sounding is *astynomia-phobia*, from the Greek for police. The catchiest is *popophobia*. The cleverest is "common sense." Of these terms OED acknowledges only the last, which it defines as "the plain **wisdom** which is everyone's inheritance," or, more affirmatively, "general sagacity."

> *consonant*

A poem by my friend Jon Swan:

THE CREATION OF WORDS

Hay in the loft. Barn doors
Open wide as the vowels of Iowa
through which swallows slip,
in and out, whispering consonants.

> *coot*

There's something down-home engaging about the sound of this word, isn't there? Rhymes with *scoot* ("Scoot over there, Sugar, and make room for me"), *shoot* (as in "Aw, shoot"), *root*, *boot*, *poot*, *toot*, and *hoot*.

According to Bill Cotterell of the *Tallahassee Democrat*, the colorful former Alabama governor Big Jim (or Kissin' Jim) Folsom in his postgubernatorial years "enjoyed being an old coot, I think. He used to call the UPI bureau in Birmingham three or four times a week when I worked there in 1969, to tell us what he thought about George Wallace. Usually after the cocktail hour, I suspect. He was only 60 at the time but I thought he was much older because when I'd say, 'How are you, governor?' he would invariably reply, 'Well, the business takes care of itself, I got most of my vision in my good eye and the wife's not pregnant, so I guess ah'm doin OK.' "

OED defines the noun *coot* as a bird or a simpleton. But in the United States a coot is a male senior citizen (perhaps owing to the phrase "bald as a coot," the bird's white forehead giving it a baldish appearance). Generally he is an eccentric, entertaining old guy who enjoys messing with people, whether or not they enjoy it all that much.

The OED does not consider the noun's possible relation to the obsolete verb *coot*, which means, as the OED puts it forthrightly, "Of tortoises: To copulate." ("The Tortoises . . . coot for fourteen daies together," 1667.)

OED does recognize *cooter*, "a popular name in the Southern United States of two tortoises." A good deal more than two, I would say, if they coot that much. What other animal can claim to derive its name from its stamina in the hay?

And yet the phrase *cooter along* or *cooter around* is defined in the *Dictionary of Smoky Mountain English* as "To idle, loaf, go around aimlessly." If you cooted two weeks straight, you'd rest up too.

AHD defines *cooter* as "an edible freshwater turtle." If animals could look themselves up! How would you like the second word in your definition to be *edible*?

➤ cotton

We get this word from Old French *coton*, from Arabic *(al) qutn*. (Europe first had cotton fabrics from Arab merchants, around A.D. 800.) Spanish renders *al qutn* as *algodón*. German goes its own way, with *Baumwolle* (tree wool), which reflects the widespread early European belief articulated in 1350 by the unreliable travel writer known as John Mandeville: that in India there grew "a wonderful tree which bore tiny lambs on the endes of its branches. These branches were so pliable that they bent down to allow the lambs to feed."

Mandeville also reported seeing, in lands that he perhaps imagined, "white hens without feathers, but they have white wool on them," and cursed folk with no heads (eyes on their shoulders), and "in another isle be folk of foul fashion and shape that have the lip above the mouth so great, that when they sleep in the sun they cover all the face with that lip," and "in another isle be folk that have great ears and long, that hang down to their **knees**."

The scientific name for the cotton plant, generically, is *Gossypium*, from something Pliny called it for some reason. He used the phrase "*gossippii bombyx*," which would be fun to translate literally as "silk of gossip," but *gossip* derives from Anglo-Saxon originally meaning "godparent," later "close friend"—a person with whom one is likely to exchange loose talk. These days, however, the Internet suits rumormongering better. If your godparent is drooling and going *heee . . . heee . . . heee*, it may affect your desire to chew the fat. On the Web, some of the people you are sharing with may have just washed their hands from dismembering their godparents, but you needn't be aware of that.

Now let us consider *coton* in Louisiana French. According to Amanda LaFleur in *Tonnerre mes chiens! A Glossary of Louisiana French Figures of Speech*, this is an unflattering description of two people who are always together: *comme cul et coton de maïs*, whose "literal translation" would be "like ass and corncob." But not so literal at that. In the French of France, *coton* is still cotton, and corncob is *épi de maïs*. More precisely, *épi* means ear (of corn or other grain). The relation to *épine*, thorn or prickle, may be less relevant than the equation with cob as employed in Louisiana out-houses back before toilet paper became a staple would suggest. Still, within the jocular expression LaFleur cites, another one must be nestled: corncob as corn cotton (poor man's Cottonelle, country two-ply).

The verb *cotton* means "to be drawn to, to get along with," as in "Somehow, although my father was a butthead and my husband is a dweeb, I just don't cotton to Hannity *or* Colmes." According to Etymonline.com, this usage is "perhaps from Welsh *cytuno* 'consent, agree.' But perhaps also a metaphor from cloth finishing." I would have thought it was a straightforward refer-ence to how cotton fibers cling to each other and to other fuzzy surfaces.

Sonicky note: *cotton to* (like *lean-to*) stresses the firm tongue-to-palate connection of *n-t* (for the opposite effect, compare *slough off*); *cling to* holds that connection slightly apart, *ng*, before snapping it together, *t*. The *oo* sound of the *o* in *to* allows us to move on.

See **buckra**.

➤ *cough*

The *gh* here is Old English's attempt to capture the Proto-Germanic *kh*, which was like the *ch* in Scottish *loch* or German *ach*. Good cough sound. But there was something catchy about the tikky cough of the old comic-strip character Major Hoople: *kaf, kaf*, or sometimes *hak kaff*. The major was a hot-air-spewing stuffed shirt with a huge bulbous nose who wore a ratty-looking fez, smoked stinky cigars, and also emitted noises like *HRUMPH*, *EGAD*, *DRAT*, *AWPF*, *HMP*, **PSHAW**, and, when insulted, *SPUTT-TT*.

The surely too polite Latin word for a cough was *tussis*. Hence Robitussin.

See **hiccup**.

➤ *crawfish, crayfish*

What is the difference?

OED says *crawfish* is "now used chiefly in U.S."

AHD says "chiefly Southern and Midland U.S."

OAD muddles the issue by defining *crawfish* as "a freshwater crayfish" or "another term for *spiny lobster*" and *crayfish* (or *freshwater crayfish*) as "a nocturnal freshwater crustacean that resembles a small lobster and inhabits streams and rivers."

I believe some people do refer to small lobsters, such as the French call langouste, or spiny lobsters, such as people around Panacea, Florida, call bulldozers, as crawfish/crayfish, but that's just crazy.

We are talking about mudbugs, crawdads. They look like wee lobsters, three or four or five inches long, and if you wade close to them in the daytime (at night they sleep), they will nip slightly.

Crayfish and *crawfish* both go way back to fifteenth-century Anglo-French enunciatory variations that emerged from the Old French form *crevice*, accent on the second syllable. *Crevice*, morphing into *crevise* and other variations, probably derived from Old High German *krebiz*, meaning "edible crustacean" and coming from the PIE root *gerbh-*, to scratch, from which we also get *crab, carve, crawl, scrawl,* **glamour**, **grammar**, *graffito, diagram, epigram,* and *paragraph*.

Neither crawfish nor crayfish is a fish, duh. The *fish* element crept in from people's pronunciations of *-vice* or *-vise*.

Okay. The difference. I have never heard anybody who enjoyed crawfish thoroughly, to the point of sucking the juice out of their heads, pronounce it crayfish. However, I had to admit that you can get even more intimate with a crayfish, in a sense, after I read in *The New York Review of Books* a review by Sue Halpern of *In Search of Memory: The Emergence of a New Science of Mind*, by Eric R. Kandel: "It is the pursuit of pure science that animates him—hearing for the first time the pop-pop as a neuron fires in the brain of a crayfish . . ."

Wow.

Halpern goes on: ". . . finding his 'voice' as a scientist, solving the biggest of puzzles with the smallest pieces (cells, molecules, genes)." (See *granular*.)

But that pop-pop is what got me. It made me wonder whether I have been callous toward crawfish. When I was a boy in middle Georgia, we would get a long metal tube from somewhere, whittle a cork so it fit fairly tightly into the tube, stick the point of a dart into the cork, and then we'd have a blowgun to take to the creek and shoot crawfish with. We didn't eat them, the way I have learned to do from people in the coastal South; we just wanted to shoot them. It never occurred to us that anybody would ever hear one think.

What, besides the juices of a crawfish boil (salt, lemon, onion, garlic, cayenne pepper, other spices) goes through a crawfish's head?

You can find anything on the Web, right? I Googled "crawfish brain."

Four different sites offered "wholesale crawfish brain," "cooked crawfish brain," "fresh crawfish brain Products," and "frozen crawfish brain Products."

Clicking on each of these produced the same result: a photo of a package of whole crawfish laid in close like sardines, with the headline "Crawfish Brain in Dill," but then, in smaller type, "crawfish brine in dill." Available from "Hubei Shenlu Aquatic Product & Foodstuff Co., Ltd."

That wasn't what I was looking for. At mobilebay.com, I found a chatty posting by Thomas Zew that included this:

> One other part of the crawfish you might want to venture is the crawfish brain. It's located in the deepest part of the head right behind the crawfish's eyes. The brain is dark seaweed-green in color with a wet sandy texture. Once you isolate the brain from the rest of the cavities, suck the pouch encasing the brain. The taste of the brain can be described as bitter mustard like. It's a *nice* contrast of flavor. I use it to clean my palette [*sic*] of the salt and spices so that I can eat more of these addictive crustaceans.

That was more to the point, but we still weren't getting anything from the crawfish's perspective. So I broke down and Googled "crayfish brain."

I can now say I have watched video of a crayfish's brain being removed surgically, with tiny magnified snippers. The brain wasn't dark green, but then it hadn't been boiled in condiments. I surfed on along to Answers .com. An anonymous, teacherish question:

What is the function of the brain in a crayfish?

Only one answer, entirely unpunctuated:

cause then it can think think stuff AND CAUSE GOD SAID SO YOU DUMB

This answer was also anonymous. It may have come from a crayfish. After DUMB, the crayfish may have crawfished: backed away from its position.

See **crustaceous**.

➤ *crustaceous*

The first recorded use of this word in English, according to OED, was by my ancestor Thomas Blount in the 1656 edition of his *Glossographia*. I concede, however, that Henry More used it more provocatively three years later in *The Immortality of the Soul*. More maintained that wasps and hornets "will fly about, and use their wings, a good part of an houre after they have lost their Heads: which is to be imputed to the residence of their Soul in them still, and the intireness of the *Animal Spirits*, not easily evaporating through their crustaceous Bodies."

A wasp or a hornet has a soul? Come on. We just went through something like this with crawfish and crayfish, which is still nagging at me.

I wouldn't seek out a wasp or a hornet to kill it, and even as a boy I wasn't cold-blooded enough to decapitate one to see whether it could still fly, but I have set fire to many a wasp or hornet nest, and I don't care where the wasps that perished, or the ones that escaped, went. What's more, *I enjoyed it*.

I'll tell you something else. Once I subjected myself to considerable hazard in order to get up on a roof and spray, at an awkward angle, a requisite chemical at a hornet nest and then with hornets all around me whap at what was left of the nest with my hat till it came loose and then scramble

down a ladder and then spray the damn nest and surrounding area more
and more until the hornets were all dead, dead, dead; and do you know
how my life partner at the time, a wonderful person, reacted? *She felt sorry
for the hornets.*

I didn't. I am sorry that when I was a boy I wantonly killed crawfish,
because they weren't bothering me and I wasn't going to eat them. If I *had*
been planning to eat them, I would feel okay about it. These are my justi-
fications for ingesting crustaceans:

I. DON'T RECOIL FROM BLUE CRABS, BOILED

True,
Crabs do
Have far too many

Tiny mouthparts and antennae
And eyes at the end of movable stalks.
And as to the manner in which a crab walks,

Or skitters or whatever—how a crab goes—
It doesn't make you want to holler, *"I'll have one of those!"*
Crabs do arise from murky places,

And the looks crabs get on what pass for their faces . . .
Few expressions are foreigner.
And to take a crab apart requires the sangfroid of a coroner,

And after eating several, you may smell like one for days,
But *don't* avert your gaze.
All these drawbacks don't amount to

Much against what crabs boil down to:
Flecks and tidbits, dribs and drabs—
The meat that one with effort nabs

From crabs
Is abs-
Olutely dreamy.

That's why, sweet dining partner, you may see me
Pinch myself, or feel me pinching you.
It's no more than the crab would do.

II. LOBSTERS HAVE IT COMING

A school of thought that I've heard tell of
Holds it's not at all irrelev-
Ant that *lobster*

Rhymes with *mobster.*
But, you say, the *way we cook* . . .
I say, Look,

Is that lobster up to any good?
Are most *prima facie* hood-
Lums half as swarthy

As that lobster? Are they?
That no-neck body, heavy, dense:
Preponderance of evidence

He'd just as soon kill *us* as not.
Toss that character into the pot:
Hey, very

Savory.
Way too delicious
To sleep with the fishes.

And as for
The notion he'll scream, he won't. Or,
If he does, it isn't going

To be a poign-
Ant little *"eek! oh!"*
It'll be *"Mother of mercy; is this the end of Rico?"*

III. ENVOI

He's withdrawn, standoffish—
Why sympathize with a crawfish?
He has a brain? Encephalographable

Doesn't equate to affable.
And don't call him crayfish.
It sounds so *treyf*-ish.

d · **D** · d

Will books ever go 3-D? I was talking with a Google visionary about the imminent future's digital books. They could discreetly feature advertising, he mentioned. I must have looked stricken, because he was quick to reassure me: "You won't turn a page and a dancing monkey pops up."

I *was* reassured, for a moment. And then it hit me: I can do a number of things with words, if I do say so, but I can't make a monkey dance. I can't even kill the dancing silhouette-man who insists upon advertising something right there on the online page I'M TRYING TO READ! I HATE THAT MAN! Where will he pop up next? On my dinner plate as I go to take a bite? On my wife's glasses as I bend to kiss her? If that man were a monkey, he would be even less resistible.

Won't readers of the future (which by now is undoubtedly yesterday) *expect* dancing monkeys? Are we hearing the death knell of the art form I love most? Will words on a page, unassisted by animated graphics, go the way of silent movies, splendid oratory, and Congressional responsibility?

Not if this book can help it. This book is dedicated to the proposition that twenty-six letters (forming forty-five phonemes) can make a monkey dance, or an emperor cringe, if enough writers and readers continue to appreciate the possibilities. William Faulkner made a buzzard hop down the hallway of a house and take off, slowly. William Butler Yeats made an unnamed mythical beast slouch toward Bethlehem. William Blake (in a famous passage I recently heard a TV sports announcer attribute to Robert Blake) made a tiger burn. Emily Dickinson did a snake in the grass ("wrinkled, and was gone") and a spanking-new butterfly: "So from Cocoon / Many a Worm / Leap so Highland gay." Mark Twain rendered a coyote so palpably that Chuck Jones was inspired to create an epical series of Roadrunner-v.-Coyote cartoons that nearly do justice to those few strokes of Twain's pen.

Granted, the *meepmeep* call (if "call" is the word) of the roadrunner is the cartoonist's vocal contribution. *Meepmeep* is a meme. It has caught on—in part (and this goes, too, for the *Aflac* duck) because you can spell it, you can write it out. You know where the words "animated graphics" come from don't you? Respectively, from the Latin for "soul" and the Greek for "writing." The soul of writing is in the *bzzt bzzt* of the letters and their arrangement: syntax sizzle, alphabet juice.

➤ *Daddy*

One of the things about growing up Southern is that you tend to refer to your father as your daddy. It sounds right in conversation (partly because the *y* is pronounced *ih* not *ee*), as when a grown man is saying, "My daddy was always one to tell somebody exactly what was what." But it looks funny in print. Andy Warhol and Truman Capote at the zoo, in *Rolling Stone*, 1973:

> *Andy*: Hello, girls. . . . You're going to the gorilla? Oh, we're going to the deer.

> *Truman*: The yak's right along in here—somewhere . . .

> *Andy*: The hippie look is really gone. Everybody's gone back to beautiful clothes. Isn't it great? . . . Did you ever want someone to call you "Daddy"?

> *Truman*: Call me Daddy?

> *Andy*: Yes.

> *Truman*: No. Nor the other way around, either.

> *Andy*: You mean you don't want to call somebody Daddy.

> *Truman*: Oh, no.

> *Andy*: But isn't "Daddy" **nice**? "Daddy" . . . "Dad" . . . It sounds so nice. . . .

> *Truman*: I've always been . . . strictly on my own.

➤ dangling modifier

You'd think that if anyone would take care not to let anything dangle, it would be someone advertising a treatment for erectile dysfunction. But no. A newspaper ad hails "The Boston Method" as "An Option When Viagra and Cialis Fail," and then, in the second line: "Once Seen as Miracle Pills, Many Now Scramble for Other Options."

This says that pills are now scrambling for other options. Hard to picture. Perhaps they will find work as bracelet beads.

➤ *decapitate*

The New York Times reported in late 2009 that a Mexican drug lord "had been carrying out brutal retaliatory attacks against rivals, dumping decapitated heads and tortured bodies . . ." Well, to decapitate is to behead, to deprive of a **head**. (*Head* in Latin is *caput*, whence *capital*.) So you can't rightly decapitate a head, any more than you can defang fangs or defat fat. Surely the *Times* has someone like the mellow-stickler copy editor at *The Wire*'s version of *The Baltimore Sun*, who when a reporter refers to people who have been evacuated, points out that to evacuate is to remove the contents of, so in emergencies you evacuate buildings; a person who evacuates is one who discharges waste. (AHD's definitions of *evacuate* are all in keeping with this distinction, but then AHD turns around and defines *evacuee* as "a person evacuated from a dangerous area." There's call for a usage note there.)

What term should the *Times* have used? *Severed.*

Behead, by the way, is an unusual word, in that *be-* as the prefix of a verb (*bewail, besmear, bedazzle, bejewel, befoul*) is almost always intensive or at least connotes application, not disconnection. A new and lovely word for me along these lines is *befrumple,* which OED says means "to crease into frumples or clumsy folds."

However, says OED, "an ancient application" of *be-* "was to express the sense of 'bereave of.'" The two examples OED cites are *behead* and *belimb*. (The *-reave* in *bereave* is from a PIE root meaning "to snatch." The title of William Faulkner's comic novel *The Reivers* uses a related old Scottish term for robbers.)

➤ device, narrative, what would you call this one

Geezer in the Explorers Club recounting, to a rapt listener, a narrow big-game-hunting escape:

"As the lion came closer, closer, straight on at me, I took careful aim . . . closer, *closer*, about to spring—I pulled the trigger. And my rifle jammed! Pulled it again, wouldn't fire. And the lion sprang, *Raaarrrrghhh.* . . ."

A pause.

"Yes? Yes? What happened then?"

Puzzled, rather sheepish tone: "I soiled my trousers."

"Well, that's understandable. With a lion upon you like that, anyone—"

"No. I mean just now, when I went, *Raaarrrrghhh.*"

➤ device, similar, but not quite the same

Katharine Hepburn in *Stage Door*, playing an aristocratic character who is striving gamely to fit in with the other girls in a residence for aspiring actresses:

"I'm doing my best to pick up their slang, though I'm not so hot—how is that, 'not so hot'?"

➤ Dionysian, Apollonian, blended, briefly

Satchel Paige is said to have advised, "Work like you don't need to get paid. Love like you've never been hurt. Dance like nobody's looking." Point taken. You do need to get paid, though, and if you've never been hurt you don't know what love is, and you can't help noticing if your dancing makes other people cringe and look away. The other morning I woke up composing this:

> You can write too juicily, just
> As you can too choosily. Lust
>
> And fussiness are faults, whereas
> Taste, desire, and all that jazz

Make language swing. So what's preferred's
The *juicidicious* use of words.

A blend of *juicy* and *judicious*, don't you know. (Peter Viereck once expressed the matter negatively: "aesthetic form is equally betrayed by the anarchic formlessness of the barbaric yawpers and the dead formalism of the elegant wincers.") Fully awake, I realized two things: that "what's preferred's" had no more *juice* in it than a pile of rocks, and that I was too judicious to use *juicidicious* (except like this, with apologies) ever again.

See *juice*.

➤ *discalced*

This is my idea of a bad word. Means shoeless, barefoot. From Latin *dis-* and *calcere*, to fit with shoes. Hardly anyone will recognize it, and it fails to evoke feet.

➤ *distance,* the verb

I don't know that this is a bad word. But it's odd. "The candidate has distanced himself from his father, who has blogged of his love for an enormous stuffed bunny." You wouldn't say "The candidate has nearnessed himself to the book of Revelation."

➤ *dubbed*

Some words get my nose out of joint. *Pooch* (except as a verb, "he pooched his lips out"), *critter*, *osculate*, and this one. On February 9, 1997, the *New York Daily News* carried this much, and no more, of an Associated Press dispatch:

> Jackson, Mich.—A rooster that lost its legs to frostbite will be
> strutting again soon with a pair of artificial limbs.
>   Veterinarian Timothy England has adopted the bird, whom he
> dubbed Mr. Chicken, and is footing the bill for the prosthetic feet,
> which he hopes could become a prototype for injured birds.

The staff also has ordered 14 chicks for Mr. Chicken to enjoy the outdoors with this spring.

Questions:

1. The staff of what?

2. Why is it that people in the news are forever "dubbing" chickens something? Whereby is a veterinarian invested with the authority to dub a living being anything? He gives the rooster feet, and now he is the roost-er's father? Would it not be more fitting to say that this Dr. England *called* the rooster Mr. Chicken?

And does the rooster come when so called? His eyes damp with grati-tude? Does he tell the other chickens, "*Mister* Chicken to you. 'Cause that's what ol' Doc England been an' dub me, when he gimme these feet. The man *gimme* these feet. **Y'all** be lucky if anybody, let alone anybody with a doctoral degree, will stoop so low as to *eat* y'all's feet. Step aside for Mister Chicken, with the pros-thetic, not the pa-thetic feet. A-doodle-doo."

Let us be fair. Dr. England may be as put off as we are by that *dubbed*. The word may not have been his; may not have entered into the interview conversation, even; may have been introduced by a whimsical editor. That sort of thing happens.

3. Why is it that news items with *dubbed* in them tend also to feature coy double entendres? Whether, in this case, "14 chicks" means "14 baby chick-ens," "14 hens," or "14 swinging women," an implication of female com-pany hovers. And according to a publication titled *The Body Connection*, put out by a chiropractic establishment and found by me underfoot on West Ninety-third Street in Manhattan, "Women have about four times as many foot problems as men."

If you are a man, and you are involved with a woman, and you have one foot problem (one foot in the grave, one foot several sizes larger than the other, one foot in a bucket), then she, statistically, has four. How can you take any pursuable counsel from the old saying, "Never go to bed with anyone whose foot problems are more numerous than your own"?

Does the four-to-one ratio apply to chickens? If so, how staggering must be the foot problems of those "14 chicks."

4. Did you think I would even deign to notice "footing . . . feet"? See **peeve**.

➤ *dwell*

I hadn't given this word much thought until I set it down in the introduction, above. The more I looked at it, the more I wanted to look it up. Very few *dw-* words in English, and all the others are pejorative: *dwalm* (to fall in a faint), *dwarf* (see **Xit**), *dweeb*, *dwindle*.

In *dwell* as in dwell upon, the *d* adds a bearing-down heaviness to **well**, as in to well up. But there's no etymological connection. It turns out *dwell* has arisen, or rather resettled, from a negative background. Old English *dwellan* meant to confuse, to lead or to be led astray, as *dwola* meant error and Gothic *dwals* meant foolish. Over time *dwell*'s meaning strayed from "go astray" into "hinder or tarry," which in turn, in the thirteenth century, turned into "remain, stay," and then into "make a home somewhere." Somewhat upbeat story, then, but also a bit of a downer. We go astray (that word is related to *street*) and then find ourselves abiding there.

I guess nobody says *dwelt* anymore, maybe no one ever did outside of poetry—"She dwelt among the untrodden ways"—but I like it, it's springier than *dwelled*. (You wouldn't be charmed by anyone who dwelled among trodden ways.) Then too I am fond of the British *smelt*. And not just in "He who smelt it, dealt it."

e · E · e

Would you like a fresh perspective on the long *e*-sound? Go to YouTube, "Video Stroboscopy of the Vocal Cords." Let me caution you that comments made by previous viewers include: "oh god that was discusting," "that is weard but funny!," and "omg now im scared of wates inside me." But what do they know—they have set down remarks that may last on the Web till the end of time, or at least till the end of the Web, and they couldn't find the time to check their **spelling**. Most of the literate commenters find the video as interesting as I hope you will.

A fiber-optic camera inserted through the unprotesting patient's nose travels down to larynxland, and as mood music plays softly in the background she is asked to "perform a glide." She gives us a long, calm *eeeeeeeee*, and some more *eee*'s, and we see how the gap between the delicate membranous cords narrows to make the high-pitched sound.

Bit of a Rorschach. Eventually, after "the stroboscopy light" was turned on and we got really close—and once I stopped thinking how this might almost do to be projected onto a screen during a performance of *The Vagina Monotones*—I was reminded, visually, of Munch's *The Scream*. But not at all an anguished scream. See if you don't see a vertical mouth (this would be the space between the true vocal cords) pressed nearly shut by a pair of hands (these would be the arytenoid cartilages); and then when the patient takes a break from *eeeeee*, the hands pull aside and the mouth widens into a big sloppy grin that says, in expectation of a compliment, "How was that?"

➤ *e*, short, the new

The other day I overheard a college-age woman say on the radio, "People don't know what to say when I tell them I fance."

"Well of course they don't," I shouted, "because there is no such word!"

To be precise, she didn't say *fance* exactly, she said something between *fance* and *fence*, so that it rhymed with neither *France* nor *tense*. When she went on to talk about being on her school's fencing team, she pronounced *fencing* accurately, to rhyme simply with *sensing*, and she also got *fence* right when it was in the middle of a sentence. But something about "I fence"—her self-defining activity, hung out to dry—had drawn from her a fish-nor-fowl vowel sound that I frequently hear from people of her generation or slightly older. When Paris Hilton pronounces *bed* so that it sounds halfway like *bad*, it may seem right for her, but I don't like hearing young people pronounce *dead* so that it sounds so close to *dad*. (Not that my children resort to such a vowel, but I feel for all fathers.) I think that unnatural vowel is a way to **distance** the speaker from the depressing *eh* sound—not the *eh?* sound (see **A**), but the *eh* that rhymes with *feh*—the *eh* that recently appeared as definition 20 of *eh* on Urbandictionary.com:

> *adj.* Used to describe something or someone uninteresting, boring, or unexceptional.
> "We used to be really tight friends . . . now we're just eh."
> "That movie was kinda eh."
> "She used to be cool, but now she's kinda eh."

The verb *fence* comes from *defense*. Perhaps that *a/e* vowel is a defense mechanism. It sounds affa/ected.

➤ each other

Can be tricky. From *The New York Times*: "At one point, the goalie for each team wrestled each other to the turf." That can't be right. Sounds like they took turns.

The teams' goalies wrestled each other . . .

Each team's goalie wrestled the other . . .

The teams' goalies wrestled together to the turf. Maybe.

➤ ear, writing for the

William Butler Yeats: " 'Write for the ear,' I thought 'so that you may be instantly understood as when an actor or folk singer stands before an audience.' " The poet David Waggoner: "Yeats always sounds like what he means."

➤ -ed, -èd

As a Methodist boy I sang "Blessèd Assurance," *bless*-ed, and heard other people, with more assurance, sing "This Is My Belovèd," be-*luv*-ed. But now I hear people saying "blessed event," pronounced *blest*—which all that does is just throw off the rhythm of the Beatitudes—and "a beloved figure," be-*luvd*, which spoils "Believe it, Beloved."

Originally the past-tense -*ed* was always pronounced as a separate syllable, which is why meter-conscious poets resorted to *inflam'd, fram'd*. Newspapers should have used that apostrophe (*media'd*) when they quoted Tiger Woods's caddy as saying Tiger wasn't doing interviews because "he's all media-ed out." (Newspapers should also desist from spelling the past tense of *medevac* as *medevaced*. That makes the *c* soft, as in *defaced*. It should be *medevacked*, by the same logic as *panicked, picnicked*, and *politicked.*)

So far the adjectives *aged* and *learned* have held on to both their syllables, perhaps because trendsetters have no use for them.

➤ eel

The ultimate origin of this word is unknown. But don't we think (that is to say, don't we feel) that it goes back to people's first reaction to the animal? An extra *e* or two would not be overkill. Compare *eeeek*. I would not fault *ee-ew-eel*.

OED recognizes *eelhood*: "The rank or condition of a full-grown eel." (See **robinhood**.) And *eely*: "Resembling an eel in movement; wriggling, writhing." And *eeler*: "The artful eeler . . . lets down a hank some cubits long of the intestines of a sheep." And to go *eeling*, and *eelery*: "We must not suppose there are no valuable eeleries in the British Isles."

An *eelpout* is not a facial expression available to the eel. It is a fish, with

(AHD) "an elongated body and large head." We are told that eelpouts often "lie under stones or buried in mud." Perhaps this is where the *pout* comes from; or maybe the fact that they have fish lips rather than eel lips gives them, relatively speaking, a pouty look.

According to *New York Waters* by Ben Gibberd, "the last two full-time eel fishermen in New York City" are Larry Seaman and his son Larry Jr. They put traps out in Jamaica Bay. Their bait is chunks of horseshoe crab. In winter, when the eels go to mud, they have to rake them out. They sell the smaller ones to charter boats for bait, and larger ones, up to two and a half feet long, to restaurants that serve them smoked.

With great effort the Seamans haul up a five-hundred-pound bin swarming with eels. "They don't say 'slippery as an eel' for nothing," says Seaman Sr. "Go on, stick your hand in." Gibberd's reaction:

> Unlike snakes, eels are covered in slime, though the real
> unpleasantness in holding them lies less in their texture than in
> their primeval otherness—the sense that they don't belong to the
> world of living things we are familiar with.

I've always had the same feeling about horseshoe crabs, but at least they don't continue to squirm for a while after they're dead and skinned. Eels do, due to muscle contractions. Even after they're sliced up, they can be activated. When Seaman Sr.'s late wife's back was turned, he would sprinkle salt on the slices and send them into frantic wriggling. "Oh God! It used to absolutely freak her out!" he recalls fondly.

Post-9/11, the Seamans are frequently stopped by patrol boats for having "breached a security zone," and although the Seamans say eels and horseshoe crabs are plentiful in Jamaica Bay, conservationists have declared both populations to be threatened. Like so many cool, hands-on trades, including mine, professional eeling is itself threatened, at least in the United States, but Seaman Jr. says, "I'll eel till they put me in jail."

➤ *elephant*

"Of the ultimate etymology," *sighs* OED, "nothing is really known." Other sources suggest the word referred first not to the animal but to the ivory taken from it. When an early form of the word made its way into various early-European languages, early Europeans took it to mean "camel." In English, once the language got the animal straight, early spellings were *olifaun*, *olyfont*, *elifan*, and *olifuntz*, or *olifauntz* (plural): "Of the forme warde [from forward] he herd grete cry, for they were assailed of olifauntz."

In the movie *Larger Than Life*, for which I received sole screenplay credit, the actress playing the elephant (which Bill Murray's character, who has inherited her, must transport cross-country by various means) was named Tai. She was a lovely animal (see, if you feel like it, my memoir, *Be Sweet*). In downtown Los Angeles, during a break in filming (actually, the occasional bit of filming is a break in the not-filming), I got to ride on Tai. Sat in front of the hump, over her shoulders. Moving her slow thighs, she imparted the sensation that her great forelegs were mine.

In Kenya, I had ridden a camel, which I liked, but an elephant is better. Grander, anyway. For living large I'll take either camelback or elephant-back over horseback, as long as there is someone on hand to keep the camel or elephant from shaking me off like a fly. "The Elephant hath joynts, but none for curtesie," wrote Shakespeare in *Troilus and Cressida*, but people train them to kneel so that you can get up on them. "Th' unwieldy Elephant To make them Mirth . . . wreath'd His Lithe Proboscis," wrote Milton in *Paradise Lost*. (I lift these examples from OED, which I guess is not entirely unlike exploiting an elephant.)

The expression "white elephant," meaning an undesired and burdensome gift, comes from the story that kings of Siam would bankrupt a disfavored courtier by presenting him with a rare albino elephant, which was regarded with such veneration that its upkeep was ruinous. People assume that regular elephants are grey, like battleships, but Tai, if you looked closely (see **granular**) was pink and mauve, as was Murray's wardrobe accordingly.

The two of them genuinely bonded, I believe. They swam together, at some risk to Murray, in the movie's best scene, and when they walked side by side she would reach over with her trunk and touch his shoulder. She had been trained, and her trainer was nigh. For company she also had a sidekick and stand-in, whose name I have forgotten.

In the nineteenth century, "to see the elephant" was a slang term meaning to get out and see some real rough life. During the Mexican War and the Civil War, it meant to see action. A. B. Longstreet, in 1835, wrote this: "That's sufficient, as Tom Haynes said when he saw the elephant." When I told Pauline Kael they were going to call the movie *Larger Than Life* (I preferred *She Followed Me Home*, or failing that, *Large as Life*), she sighed, as only she (or perhaps OED) could *sigh*. "It's the *Life* that deadens it," she said.

➤ enough

> Mrs. Gradgrind, weakly smiling, and giving no other sign of vitality, looked (as she always did) like an indifferently executed transparency of a small female figure, without enough light behind it.
>
> —Charles Dickens, *Hard Times*

That "without enough light" is sheer authoriality. Not "with only a thirty-watt bulb behind it," as a writing-class instructor might insist upon, but "without enough." Who is to say it is not enough light? The author. It's an intimacy with the reader, an assumption that the reader will accept "not enough" as enough. The reader goes along with the deal, because Dickens is behind it. Writer and reader strain together for a moment to see Mrs. Gradgrind forever.

Incidentally, the treasures included in the Henry W. and Albert A. Berg Collection of English and American Literature include Dickens's letter opener, whose handle is the actual foreleg of a cat. The blade is inscribed, "In Memory of Bob." Bob was Dickens's cat.

➤ errata

In this book, as usual, there are some. Strain our every fiber as we may, we do not achieve stark perfection. The British columnist Beachcomber (J. B. Morton) put it best, I think: "*Erratum*: In my article on the Price of Milk, *Horses* should have read *Cows* throughout."

➤ ew

A man with the almost biblical name (but never mind that) of Christian Rudder, who founded an online dating service called OkCupid, has told

The New York Times that messages with words like *fascinating* and *cool* are more likely to attract positive responses from potential mates than messages with *beautiful* or *cutie*. "As we all know," Mr. Rudder was quoted by the *Times* as saying, "people normally like compliments, but when they're used as pickup lines, before you've even met the person, they inevitably feel . . . ew."

One thing that strikes me is that *beautiful* and *cutie* both include the sound *ew*. And yet *ew* is a universal—anyway, a broadly recognizable—sound of disgust, not only alone but as part of *pee-yeww*.

Another thing that strikes me is—what is *ew* backward? It's *we*. Could *ew* be a rejection of intimacy? When somebody starts pulling you into a *we* you don't want to be in, one response is, "Who you calling *we*? You got a mouse in your pocket?" Another response might be, *ew*.

Then too, when someone has somehow evinced boastfulness or even boastworthiness, don't people who know that person sometimes go, "*eeewww*"? Or more like, "Look at *yewwwww*, aren't you something"?

See *pu-*.

> *expertise*

In January 2008, *The New York Times* reported that "three body-language analysts who watched Roger Clemens over the past two days" said he "was holding something back." However, Joe Navarro, "a retired F.B.I. agent who trains intelligence officers and employees for banks and insurance companies" and "has also written a book about how to tell whether someone is bluffing in poker . . . , warned against concluding that Clemens was lying. Even the most skilled body-language experts are right in only about half of all cases, he said."

When it comes to lying or not, withholding or not, this seems a low success rate. A coin toss. If I were an expert on experts, I would recommend hiring a *less* skilled body-language expert—one who is right only 30 percent of the time, say—and going with the opposite of his conclusions. That way you're right 70 percent of the time.

f · F · f

When you read online, according to Jakob Nielsen, author of books about people's interaction with technology, "You're just surfing the information. It's not a deep learning." I learned this while skimming *Time* magazine, which goes on to report: "By tracking people's eye movements, Nielsen figured out that our focus moves around the screen in an F pattern. We start scanning horizontally, but pretty soon we're dropping down to see what else is there. By the time we're halfway down a Web page, we're tuning out."

So, I'm just curious, how are you reading this? *E* pattern? *Z* pattern? Huh? Are you with me? Aw, you didn't miss **elephant**, did you?

See **aid, marital**.

➤ *fancy*

The British say, "Do you fancy her?" It comes from *fantasy*. A more holistic question would be, "Do you realize her?"

➤ *feted*

I don't know why anyone uses this word. Depending on the pronunciation (rhyming with either [a] *baited* or [b] *vetted* is acceptable), "The emperor was feted at the cheese festival" sounds like (a), he found his destiny there or (b), he smelled bad there.

➤ *fewer/less*

To some people—many people—it evidently does not ring *wrong* to say, "My Chihuahau has less fleas than yours does." Those people may not realize, or even care, how much effort it requires for me to restrain from responding, "*fewer* fleas, *fewer* fleas!" So let those people go ahead and say it. I can't stop them.

It is good practice, however, to use *fewer* with regard to number of items: "Ever since that whole thing with Wallace Tidwell's **thong**, we're having fewer casual Fridays."

And to use *less* with regard to extent: "Ever since that whole thing with Wallace Tidwell's thong, our Fridays have been less casual."

Ignoring this simple distinction may create misunderstanding. If you say "We will do what we must to ensure that there are less ferocious maniacs roaming the streets," your listeners may justifiably understand you to mean not that you intend to reduce the number of ferocious maniacs roaming the streets but that you intend to temper the current maniacs' ferocity or to replace those maniacs with others who are somewhat less ferocious.

Is that what you want?

See **peeve**.

➤ first sentence

Generally an author takes great pains with the first sentence of his or her book. I know I have never been quite satisfied with any of mine. But then I've never had all the ranks of assistance available to Karl Rove, author of *Courage and Consequence: My Life as a Conservative in the Fight.* Rove acknowledges an editor; a "close friend and trusted former colleague" who "also helped craft every chapter and episode"; a line editor; a researcher; seven research assistants under the "expert guidance" of yet another person, his chief of staff; twenty-two people who read important parts of the manuscript; and ten more people who "devoured and improved major swatches of this manuscript."

An interesting process, devouring and improving, maybe something like free-range chickens turning bugs and scraps into high-quality manure. But never mind that. Here is the opening sentence produced by Rove and his team:

"On September 11, 2001, I was the first person to tell President George W. Bush that a plane had slammed into an office tower in New York City and was aboard Air Force One as it crisscrossed the country in the hours that followed."

The second sentence is nothing to write home about, either. But at least it doesn't place an office-tower-hitting plane aboard Air Force One. The president really would have been slow on the uptake if his trusted aide had informed him that such a plane was crisscrossing the country aboard the president's own plane. I hear people saying, "Oh, you know what he *meant*." I'm sorry, but that don't get it in Sentence Writing 101. Much less *First-Sentence* Writing 101. I have to call him out here: Hey, Karl Rove, you're a writer? Ain't you got no pride? (See **humble**.) When you think of the people who have sweated blood to write good English sentences, you can feel all right to write a sorry-ass *first* sentence like that?

➤ *flies*

Is there any way we can relate positively to *Musca domestica*, the common housefly? No doubt it cannot help that a fly has no sense of personal space, that it keeps insisting, and insisting, "Hey, hey, hold still! So I can get into your nose!"

Traditionally it is ants that ruin a picnic, but ants are linear, and are usually on a surface against which they can be squashed. Flies are at one with the atmosphere. The sight of a fly on a beautiful deviled egg encapsulates so much of the human condition: goody cut with dammit.

Not that flies give a rip for the human condition. Everything else being equal, they would no doubt prefer some good stationary manure to us, but manure doesn't grow on trees these days, and manure is low on sugar. That, science tells us, is why flies find us so attractive: even when we don't have watermelon juice on our hands, forearms, face, and neck, we are sweet, willy-nilly, to flies. Like your old aunt Mae bearing down on your underchin when you were a tot, flies are saying, in the only language they know, "Gimme some sugar."

Flies are excellent at reproducing. How they go about it is something not to be gone into. As to how they eat—they taste things with the hairs of their legs, okay? Then it gets worse. And they feel fully entitled to do this to our baked **bean**s, while we are trying to eat them—our baked beans—

ourselves. I bit down on a fly once, at a picnic. I can still taste it. A little like motor oil, or axle grease, only very slightly crunchy.

But what I was going to ask was, can we find a way to keep flies from getting on our nerves? Maybe, just maybe, we need to consider what we and flies have in common:

1. Reproduction

2. Love of potato salad

3.

Okay, let's do this. Let's give flies credit for having just about the most fundamental name in creation. What other animal is called so simply what it does? (Bee doesn't count.) But come to think of it, that is irritating too. Why should flies get such a cool name? Why wouldn't a pretty bird be called a fly, and a fly be called something worse, a pester, or something that might derive from the Latin for "tastes your food with its leg hairs"? That is just like flies, to get away with being called flies.

When I was a boy, people put **cotton** on their screen doors to keep flies away. I could never understand that, until I learned that the original idea, since forgotten, was to soak the cotton in DDT. These days, restaurants with outdoor dining areas often half fill plastic sandwich bags with water and staple them up where flies would bother diners. Supposedly, a fly's multifaceted eyes are disoriented by reflections from the water. I have yet to see flies frantically backpedaling away from any of these water bags, but I haven't seen any flies perched on them, either.

In fact, I don't think there are as many flies around as there were years ago. Back in the sixties, a friend of mine went to a Coca-Cola bottling plant on business. The receptionist met him at the door. "You'll need this," she said and handed him a flyswatter. The manager who showed him around carried one too. I doubt that Cokes are bottled amid so many flies anymore.

Air-conditioning is hard on flies, for flies like heat. When the temperature drops, they drop, like flies. These days people stay closed up inside their houses, instead of letting fly-bearing zephyrs in through open windows. But let's not delude ourselves that flies are an endangered species. The only way, other than swatting, to get the better of flies . . .

Well, going back to my boyhood again, there were some boys, cruel boys, who would pull the wings off flies, and mock them, saying, "What do you call a fly with no wings? A walk." I didn't do that. For one thing, my motor skills weren't that fine. For that reason, I probably would not be able to do what a college friend of my wife's did with a fly and a strand of her hair, which enabled him to tell a fly, in effect, "Okay, Mr. Essence of flying, *fly for me.*"

When my wife was in college, her hair was fine and straight and long enough for her to sit on. This nimble-fingered friend of hers relieved her of a single strand and tied a loop in one end of it. He caught a fly. He attached the hair to the fly. Then he had a fly on a leash. Eventually he set his pet free, but it flew off trailing the long drifty hair, which must have caused this one fly to provide people—*look at the tail on that fly*—with a little wonderment for a change.

➤ *flulike*

We so often read in the sports pages that D'queem Pong-Roscoe, or whoever, "sat out the first three games with flulike symptoms." Why do we need a word like *flulike*? Why not "flu symptoms," or "symptoms of the flu"? Is the newspaper worried that it will get sued if the sickness turns out to be something other than the flu? It could turn out to be something resembling flu, maybe something much worse than flu. But if symptoms indicate possible flu, they are flu symptoms. The symptoms, themselves, aren't *like* the flu. You wouldn't say something has "a chickenlike taste." Oh, I suppose you could. I still don't like *flulike.*

You wouldn't say "a recoverylike sign." "A doomlike omen." "A disasterlike prediction." "A warlike portent." "Thunderlike clouds."

See **peeve**.

➤ *foil*

Are you ready for some serious alphabet juice? You don't have to be religious. Gerard Manley Hopkins, 1877, "God's Grandeur":

> The world is charged with the grandeur of God.
> It will flame out, like shining from shook foil;

It gathers to a greatness, like the ooze of oil
Crushed.

That's what I'm talking about. Go, thou, and look up the whole damn poem, an astonishing *gush* (not the right word, but if it weren't pejorative, it would be)—an astonishing *eruption* (not the right word either) of vision, movement, sound, and, too, sentiment that in any other setting would be too sweet:

There lives the dearest freshness deep down things.

Setting means a lot. In a toilet stall in a men's room of a highly respectable university's student center many years ago, amid all manner of scurvy allegations, gross insults and counterinsults, directions on how to defecate well and truly ("If you would shit with force and ease / Put your elbows on your **knee**s, / With your hands, grasp your chin / And move your asshole out and in"), talk of rim jobs and ruder-than-necessary drawings of cocks, I discovered this, in a small and not too graceful hand, off to one side: "You know that you are in love when another person's needs become more important than your own." Below this, and connected to it by an arrow, someone had written: "True."

Speaking of Hopkins, check out his "The Windhover," for instance its use of the word *gash* (there, in context, is a right word for you); and note, incidentally, that its connecting *plod* to shining almost contradicts the opposition of *trod* to shining in "God's Grandeur."

But I want to focus on one word in that poem. "English," writes John Ayto in his *Dictionary of Word Origins*, "has three separate words *foil*." The oldest, meaning to thwart, as in "Curses, foiled again," originally meant to trample. It probably derives from the same Latin source as the verb *full*, meaning (AHD) "To increase the weight or bulk of (cloth) by shrinking and beating or pressing." (Compare *felt* and its kinship to the second syllable of *anvil*.) Originally a *fuller* (whence the surname of Buckminster Fuller) fulled cloth by treading on it.

Another *foil*, meaning a light sword with a blunted point used in fencing, which OED first locates in 1594, may in fact be akin, by virtue of the puncture-preventing tip, to the first meaning, but there is no etymological evidence for that, nor for Ayto's on-the-contrary suggestion that this *foil* may have evolved from the meaning of *foil* that we are coming to, as a sword's *blade* evolved from a leaf's.

It is from Latin *folium*, leaf, that we get the meaning of *foil* (and of *folio* and *foliage*) that Hopkins had in mind: metal compressed into a paper-thin (page-thin, as long as pages are paper) sheet, or leaf. This foil shines. Once crumpled and smoothed, it glimmers and glints multifariously. The sense of *foil* as someone who by contrast sets off the qualities of another—as the unprepossessing, five-foot-two, excitable, agonizing, gloom-prone Hopkins set off the Rock of Ages—comes from the practice of enhancing a jewel's brilliance by backing it with foil. We don't ordinarily think of shaking foil blazingly out, but a marvelous hand could do it with a big enough sheet, or poetry can in a few words.

For one thing, *shook foil* shakes it in a way that *shaken foil* would not. "Sprung rhythm" is what Hopkins called the way he would jam two stressed syllables together (or three unstressed ones as in "gathers to a greatness") to generate more torque, more explosiveness, than regular meter could muster. Hopkins, himself, was wound tight. He became a Jesuit priest and lifetime celibate after the shock of finding himself infatuated with a young man named Digby. He was so retiring and his poems so strange that none of them were published until after his death. In his journals and letters he wrote about the "inscape" and the "instress" of things. By inscape he meant something like the complex of characteristics that give a being its individual nature. By instress, a kind of inner force field that holds the inscape together and projects it through the poem to the reader.

The image "flame out, like shining from shook foil" is transcendentally visual, but it wouldn't be without alphabet juice. Consider the inscape and instress potential in the word *foil*: the puff of *f* and the flow of *l* surrounding the bouncy *oi* sound shared by *sproing, boing, oil, boil, coil, loin, joint, joy, ahoy*. (No, not so much by *Roy*. I wish.)

Those three meanings, those three word histories, of *foil* are separate. But we know them all, at once. Unless we have looked up the etymologies, we don't connect the treading of cloth into a dense thinness with metal flattened into a reflective sheet—but why did *full* and *folium* both turn into *foil*?

Full came to mean "spoil a scent or trace by trampling over it." I'm not saying *foil* in the sense of thwart is a mash up of *full* and *spoil*, but I am saying that trading *uh* (as in, *uh*) for *oi* (as in, from the foiler's perspective, *oboyoboy* and, from the foilee's, *oy*) makes a more than casual difference.

Latin *folium* became English *foil* (at first meaning simply leaf) by way of French *foille*, leaf (which evolved into modern French *feuille*, from which we get *feuilleton*, a light essay). French has a sound like Latin *o*, but to the French a leaf called for a more bendable sound.

As for the fencing *foil*, it's metal. It's flexible. Its use entails a lot of thwarting. This is not true etymology, any more than *cockroach* is what you get when you cross a rooster and an insect. But the springiness of Hopkins's image partakes of all the associations that *foil* evokes. Not only the metallic paper but also the sword and the thwarting are foils to the inscape of glory divine.

See **upaya**.

➤ *fond*

The verb *fon* originally meant to lose savor, as in salt that was fonned. Later, to *fon*—also, to *fun*—meant to cheat, to fool, to make fun of someone. So someone who was *fonned* or *fond* was fooled, or infatuated (from the Latin *fatuus*, foolish).

Later *fond* softened, somewhat, into foolishly affectionate. ("Why so pale and wan, fond lover?"—Sir John Suckling, seventeenth century.)

Now, to be fond of someone is a good thing. And fun is, too, but a wisp of caution hovers—"no more fun and games." And to fondle is still to fool around.

➤ fool, e.g., Will Somers (or Sommers)

After I gave a speech somewhere outside the South and mentioned some of the glories of Southern humor, someone in the audience asked:

"How much of Southern humor is intentional?"

"More than you realize," is what I might well have said. But my instinct, perhaps in part Southern, is that to return a fool's unconscious insult with a conscious one is less telling than to return it in a way that pretends it warrants graciousness. So I said, "Some of it. A good deal of it. But no doubt, not all. To be a good fool you have to know first that you are one." Something to that effect.

The word *fool* comes from Latin *follem*, meaning bellows (surely the *f* is not arbitrary) or, by extension, windbag or empty-head. In the old days a great household would enjoy the antics of a "harmless lunatic," as OED puts it, but the best fools were in on the joke. Those jokes have generally not aged very well, as such, even when told by Shakespeare. But here, according to *A Nest of Ninnies* by Robert Armin (1608), is a bit of jesting from Will Somers (or Sommers), royal fool to Henry VIII. The king needs cheering up. Will comes through:

> "Now tell me," says Will, "if you can, what it is, that being born without life, head, lip or eye, yet doth run roaring through the world till it dies?"
>
> "This is a wonder," quod the king, "and no question. I know it not."
>
> "Why," quod Will, "it is a fart."
>
> At this the king laughed heartily and was exceeding merry; and bids Will ask any reasonable thing, and he would grant it.
>
> "Thanks, Harry," says he. "Now . . . I need nothing, but one day I shall. For every man sees his latter end, but knows not his beginning." The king understood his meaning, and so pleasantly departed for that season. And Will laid him down amongst the spaniels to sleep.

Will remained royal jester to Henry's successors well on into the reign of Elizabeth I. It's a wise fool, I'll warrant, who'll call the king Harry and then, for warmth, will sleep with the dogs. Humility, and not just tactical.

See **Xit**.

➤ *form*

When you say the word *form*, slowly and reflectively, don't you feel your vocal apparatus—bear with me—*forming* something? Something sort of ovoid? Starting with a breath-of-life lip puff, *f-*, then making a tour, *-or-*, of the whole oral chamber (wrapping an orb of void), and then coming back around to the lips, together, satisfied, *-m*? You don't get those particular sensations from saying, say, *scratch*, or *gobble*, or *deflate*, do you? I'm just asking. I don't want to weird you out.

So let's get scientific, etymological. Where do we get *form* from? We don't know, for sure. But *form* may have been formed from a morphing (more precisely a metathesis, switching of consonant sounds) of the Greek *morphe*, which means form or shape.

No authority seems to want to entertain, even, the notion that *form* comes from *from*. Soundwise, *morph* is *from* backward. And John Ayto says *frame* comes from *from*, and furthermore that *furnish*, *first*, *for*, *fore*, *foremost*, *former*, and *before* all come from *pr-*, the same PIE root (Chambers calls it *promo-*) from which *from* sprang forth.

Ayto says *former* means, etymologically, "more most before." Chambers makes this clearer: *former* was formerly the comparative of *forme*, meaning first, so that at first it meant, in effect, "more first"—but it was "patterned on *formest*, 'foremost,'" which came before, and that the residual element of *most* comes from "the *m* . . . , a superlative element as old as Indo-European."

Weee-oooo.

> ## *fox*

"The unspeakable in pursuit of the inedible," was Oscar Wilde's definition of foxhunting. Who says you can't eat fox? In the *Dictionary of Smoky Mountain English* entry on *tasted of*, we find: "He said he tasted of everything he ever killed, every varmint, even a buzzard." I talked to a man once who said he ate bear bacon. You know what the old boy said when asked how crow tasted: "About like owl." I used to think "You can kill us but you can't eat us" would be a good slogan for the Florida Marlins baseball team, but I came to find out you can eat marlin.

Fox after a foxhunt is *treyf*. "You shall not eat any flesh that is torn by beasts," it says in Exodus 22:31. This in fact was the original meaning—eventually extended to all nonkosher food—of *treyf*. "The biblical equivalent of 'roadkill,'" as Michael Wex puts it in *Born to Kvetch*. But if you're gentile, or secular, and careful (Oscar Wilde was two out of three), you can eat roadkill.

Foxes may have a gland that causes their meat to become foul, but so do deer and raccoons, you just have to avoid piercing it.

Fox too smart to eat? Foxes are regarded as not just clever but cunning, which suggests uncanny shiftiness. Foxfire is an eery luminescence that emanates from decaying wood, but the *fox* part may derive from *faux*. On the other hand the *fox* in foxglove, the flower, may derive from *folk's*.

Too pretty to eat? A deer is pretty, people eat deer.

People eat snails (though my friend Jan Constantine says she never ate another escargot after seeing one "walking down the street" in Paris), turtle, snake, armadillo, shark, possum, squirrel. I have eaten all those, and ants and fried worms. Never ate fox, never had the opportunity. Not sure how I would react if I did have it.

Too much like dog? People in many cultures eat dog and other animals that Westerners think of as pets. Every year Peruvians consume an estimated sixty-five million guinea pigs—an animal so entrenched in the culture that one famous painting of the Last Supper in the main cathedral in Cuzco, Peru, shows Christ and the twelve disciples dining on guinea pig. Today guinea pig meat is exported to the United States and Japan.

Foxy wine is musky smelling. Maybe foxes stink. It's not what they're known for. And musky isn't necessarily off-putting. In 1640 an Englishman wrote that "the Foxe Grape . . . smelleth and tasteth like unto a Foxe." Sounds bad, but descendants of the fox grape include the Concord grape and the scuppernong, both of which are richly tasty.

Fox's root may be *puk-*, bushy haired. Sanskrit for tail was *puccha-s*, "possibly involving some taboo," says Chambers. *Foxy* means sexy. As far back as 1877 it was American slang for amorous.

Maybe just English people don't eat fox. I'll bet Chinese people have eaten fox, if there have ever been any foxes in China. In a market in Beijing I saw a man making snake tartare by gradually lowering a whole live snake, tail first, into a meat grinder.

Isaiah Berlin quoted the Greek poet Archilochus: "The fox knows many things, but the hedgehog knows one big thing." Berlin sided with the fox, who stands for pluralism, the notion that there are many different, not necessarily compatible but equally valid ways of living. The hedgehog knows to roll up into a spiny ball, and that's about it. The fact that both strategies work, at least for the animals in question, is itself a point for pluralism.

There are foxes, and foxes. In African-American folktales, Br'er Fox's elaborate predatory schemes are always outsmarted by the superior, heartier, freedom-loving trickster, Br'er Rabbit. However he strains, Br'er Fox is a conventional thinker. Br'er Rabbit is spontaneous, inspired, and at home in the maze of the briar patch. He always outfoxes the fox.

In cartoons, it's Coyote vis-à-vis Roadrunner. In the American Revolution, it was regimented redcoats versus wily, light-traveling, indigenous bluecoats. In Vietnam, it was Agent Orange versus black pajamas.

And downhill since then.

It used to be a truism that Americans root for the underdog. Assuming the underdog is no fool. In foxhunting, that would be the fox. If I see a little red free-range canine running for dear life from a pack of baying hounds followed by horsey swells in uniform fancy dress, I am thinking "Go, fox"— not Br'er Fox but, say, the Swamp Fox, Colonel Francis Marion, who outslicked superior British forces in South Carolina with guerrilla tactics and intimate local knowledge of swamps through which to retreat. The world's superpower, on other people's territory, can't very well embody that spirit.

Might eating fox help? Diligent Googling turns up this recipe, from one Ed in Australia:

> First lock away the dogs, those sensitive creatures. Skin the body (of the fox) and soak the carcass in running water for three days. Gut the beast, clean it and cut into joints. Heat olive oil in a large enamel pan. Brown.
>
> Fox meat can be bitter and acrid and the secret to overcoming this is to wait for the juices to be released and reabsorbed. Then add some mashed garlic cloves. Add thyme, tarragon and fennel fronds plus salt—my current fave being the eco-sound Murray River Salt.
>
> When browned add a glug or two of decent full-bodied red wine, tinned tomatoes (this is really a winter recipe), two bay leaves and some home made beef stock.
>
> Cook in the oven with the lid on at 150C until the flesh melts.
>
> This recipe also works well with goat and badger. We don't have badger here, but I plan to give this a go with wombat.
>
> Tallyho!

"Until the flesh melts"? Is Ed making a sly allusion to Hamlet's immortal "O that this too too sullied [or *sallied*, or *solid*] flesh would melt"? Or to "the melting pot"? "The Melting Pot" was a 1908 play by Israel Zangwill, an Englishman, who wrote, "America is God's Crucible, the great Melting Pot where all the races of Europe are melting and re-forming." I once interviewed Winona LaDuke, an *Ojibwa* activist who said of America, "I don't want it to be a puree. I want it to be a stew," an amalgam of complementary but identifiable ingredients. That is what the American English language still is, if we appreciate its particulars.

➤ free speech

According to *The New York Times*, a documentary titled *Shouting Fire: Stories from the Edge of Free Speech* includes an interview with the professor Ward Churchill, who lost his faculty position for making an absurdly callous statement about people killed on 9/11. "In a film in which the phrase 'free speech' is heard a lot," reports the *Times*, "Mr. Churchill gives the best assessment of it: 'If it comes at a price, it's not free.' "

Oh, yeah? Everything that has any impact comes at a price. If speaking freely didn't cost anything, everybody would do it—I mean, even nonanonymously, even elsewhere than the Web. You know what Mark Twain said: "It is by the goodness of God that in our country we have those three unspeakably precious things: freedom of speech, freedom of conscience, and the prudence never to practice either of them." There is even a certain justice, and a certain tempering (in the sense of toughening) in the fact that to get away with anything really telling in the way of free speech, even in the United States, you had best be *clever*.

➤ *frequent*

The adjective, as in "frequent-flier" (poor devil), came first. Odd for it to become (with the stress switching from the first to the second syllable) a verb. You wouldn't say to someone you have met in a bar or some other place of assembly, "Do you *often* here?" Some New York newspaper or good-government group might, however, have editorialized as follows:

> Let us be clear: we do not frequent prostitutes ourselves. We do not even seldom them. But we believe that Eliot Spitzer should have been retained as governor even if, for all we care, he had continued to occasional one or two.

➤ Frisian

I'm reading a *Harvard Magazine* article about recent genetic research
indicating that the Anglo-Saxon invasion of Britain displaced not only
Roman-Celtic civilization but also, as a result of widespread ravishment,
all Roman-Celtic Y chromosomes (except, for some reason, in Wales).
And I come upon a remarkable statement.

According to this article, one of the lands that the Anglo-Saxons em-
barked from on their way to Britain was "Friesland . . . and the language
spoken there is the closest living relative to English." Interesting. But
here's the remarkable bit, from Mark Thomas of University College, London: "Listening to a Frisian speak is like listening to somebody speak
English with a frog in their mouth."

Whoa! I would prefer "with a mouthful of frog," or some other way of
avoiding (ugh) "*their* mouth," but here is a more pressing issue: What does
English with a mouthful of frog sound like?

"Hello *ribbit* I'm Frisian"?

"Hel-*ribbit*-lo I'm Fris-*ribbit*-ian"?

Or am I on the wrong track here and Frisian sounds like English spoken in such a way as to avoid disturbing, or tasting, a springy green am-
phibian?

"H'o I'uh Frih'n"?

I think we can set aside the possibility that by "frog," Professor Thomas
means "French." So is he alluding to a figure of speech, so to speak? In
London, can a fetching-faced person who speaks with cold-blooded tongue
be accused of coming on "with a faceful of bunny and a mouthful of frog"?

Frogs, in their natural state, are far from frizzly. Yet both WIII and
Etymonline.com connect *frizz* and *frizzle* to an Old Frisian word, *frisle*,
meaning "curly hair." OED deems this etymology groundless: "the inter-
pretation of the ethnic name of the Frisians as 'curly-haired' being a mere
assumption." OED does give us a *nice* example of *frizz*: "Dr. Parr's wig . . .
swells out into boundless convexity of frizz"—Sydney Smith.

Chromosomes aside, here are some words that came into English from
Frisian, according to Etymonline.com: yet, *tusk*, *hoop*, *moor*, *rip*, *wall*, and
slobber. That last one might have a frog-in-mouth connection. OED quotes
Jonathan Swift:

But, why would he, unless he slobbered,

Offend our patriot, great Sir Robert.

(Some texts make that *slobber't.*) Sir Robert Walpole, chief minister of the British state (whose son coined *serendipity,* see **Google-logisms**), honored Swift with a dinner and took him aside to talk of Ireland. Swift believed Sir Robert to be no friend of Ireland and told him so. Sir Robert never had Swift over again. In the same poem, "On the Death of Dr. Swift," Swift quotes a criticism of Swift: "He never thought an honour done him / Because a duke was proud to own him." Swift, he went on to say of himself, "Would rather slip aside and chuse / To talk with wits in dirty shoes." Good for Swift.

What were we talking about? Oh:

> *frog*

An excellent word, up to a point. The *fro-* evokes propulsive force, but that hard-*g* ending leaves the frog gathered up unto itself—not so much "solid as a gob of mud," as in Mark Twain's description of the famous Calaveras County frog's *postlanding* posture, but rather all prepared to spring and yet unsprung. The Old English *frogga* was better: it let the frog go on and jump.

As John Ayto puts it, *frogga* "probably started life as a playful alternative to the more serious *frosc* or *forsc.*" Playful, shmayful—if we can't have *-ga,* we need, for sufficiently serious purposes of representation, that *g,* at least. German never put it in and is stuck now with *Frosch.* Spanish and Italian for frog, *rana,* is even worse. The French isn't bad, *grenouille*—it captures the leap, but maybe the suggestion of *whee* (or *ouiiii*) in there is a bit much. Something to be said, hopwise, for the Indonesian, *katak,* which however is too brittle. Slovenian *žaba,* Lithuanian *varlė,* and even Hungarian *béka* leave me cold.

Did you know there was such a word as *froghood*? Not that there's any reason there shouldn't be. OED quotes Christopher Smart, 1770: "Too hard for any frog's digestion, / To have his froghood call'd in question." It's from a fable mocking duelists—a mouse calls a frog a coward. They go at each other with swords. And a vulture,

> Quick to decide this point of honour,
> And, lawyer like, to make an end on't,
> Devour'd both plaintiff and defendant.

Not the earliest **lawyer joke**.

➤ *fudge*

Origin obscure, but the sound is rich. OED's first citation is from Oliver Goldsmith's *The Vicar of Wakefield* (1766): "The very impolite behaviour of Mr. Burchell, who . . . at the conclusion of every sentence would cry out Fudge!"

This usage, OED goes on, "seems from the context merely to represent an inarticulate expression of indignant disgust."

What's "inarticulate" about it?

➤ *full disclosure*

I kept seeing in newspaper and magazine articles—in which the writer felt obliged to divulge any possible sources of personal bias—sudden parenthetical confessions like "McQuorquedale's exquisite tact (full disclosure: her mother and mine share a nutritionist whose daughter and mine are in a playgroup . . .)."

So I wrote the following, which appeared in *The New Yorker* as "The Media Beat Goes On":

> As if "occupation, diarist" weren't cushy enough for tax purposes (theoretically you can write off *everything*)—and as if he had not already made an absolute enlighten-mint from his blockbuster hey-why-*not*-a-spiritual-memoir *Shoulda Woulda Buddha*—the hydratalkingheaded Kirbo Flange . . . who not so many years ago was regularly captivating some .5 percent of the adult Saturday-morning crowd with his mock-ironic (I guess) interactive audio art-talk series, *Like Watching a Kandinsky Dry* . . . now proposes to take his on-line journals public.
>
> Let's face it, our old friend Flange (full discolosure: Before surviving—by the skin of his botched-bleach-job teeth—the

"Content Blab" fiasco, before belatedly bagging the whole concept of telemarketainment, before embarking on his short-lived cable show *Behind the Insights*, which every week spotlighted a different pundit's assistant . . . on which I was to be showcased the week Hofstra-StrideRite pulled the plug, I being in those days a dewy-eyed layer of pipe for the Zeitmeister, oh yes, Warren DeCoverley With the Views . . . and *long* before anyone knew him as pay-per-view's Indecent Docent, Flange and my third ex-stepfather's sometime goodgal Fortuna Ruh . . . who may be recalled, through gauze, as Simplicity on *Simplicity Herself*, from which desultory natter-com I was once *literally* bumped by a *literal* dog-and-pony act, the pony, Toby, having made a name for himself on the Barnyard Channel, and there I am trying to establish myself as Mr. Mitch the Multimedia Maven when I am *literally* bumped out of the frame by this foreshortened *horse*, with a tiny vicious dog on its back, and the crew all guffawing because I wasn't union then and I suppose the pony was, people don't know what it was like on some of those bandwidths in those days . . . anyhoo, that dynamic duo co-scripted an odd sort of ink-sniffing old-media column in *Shafts*, a semimonthly, marginally postcoherent schlub-pub in large part underwritten by the As If Foundation, whose director, Simon Cork, was *subsequently* "deposed," as conspiracy buffs would have it, "in a palace [some palace] coup" which I—so I am told to my secret amusement—am widely suspected of having been a party to . . . this when yours truly was a downy-cheeked, very unpaid As If intern relegated to logging drafts of workshopped poop sheets, mind you . . . but even *had* I plausibly been involved—which is ludicrous on the face of it to anyone who has felt the chill of my absolute indifference toward persons who occupy what they themselves may consider to be positions of, how you say, clout—my views can hardly be regarded as compromised by any however-juicy *rumors* of my involvement given the fact that Alysse Letts, the Corkster's shall-we-say squeeze emeritus . . . whose own vaunted scruples did not prevent her, in one of her patented clit-lit-crit snits over Cork's supposed disrespect for *Modern Bride* Studies, from erasing his entire collection of bootleg Deborah Norville blooper tapes . . .

is after all the very person who, in her self-appointed capacity as the picture-your-ad-here conscience of the World Wide Web, and in the festering heat of her increasingly exaggerated recollection of a certain "incident" . . . let's just leave it that quite late one evening in my more flaneurial days I inflicted upon her frequent screening companion Mr. Hervé God-Forbid-Anybody-Should-Pronounce-It-*Harvey* DeLaBarbara what I have been advised by counsel to stipulate as "perceived physical discomfort" by dint of a simple whap on the upper arm that any halfway robust schoolchild would scarcely have registered let alone greeted with soap-operatic DeLaBarbarian howls of transparent anguish and much sloshing of Cosmopolitans and, I seem to recall, vintage back-issues of *Cosmopolitan*, which he was wont to carry around with him from *boîte* to *boîte* for reasons best kept to himself and a few faux-bosomy hangers-on of otherwise indeterminate nature . . . yes, *she* has taken it heavy-handedly upon her curiously assymetrical shoulders to pillory my offhand contribution to the Zeitmeister *Festschrift* e-conference as both "cankered" and "soft," although I might mention I have never been physically intimate with Ms. Letts ((not)) or any member of her rather glaringly permeable circle . . . which if I *had* been—under the transient sway of God can only imagine what sort of cheap subveterinary stimulants—and immediately and vocally regretted it, might not only explain my disinclination to bob and weave to the tune of her gala-hopping air kisses—she who is forever unpacking one's gender with the use of her cunning little satirical hand puppet Tex Tosterone, oh I'm so *unmasked*—but also just *might* account for the lady's need-driven characterization of my well-advised reserve toward her person as some sort of inverse acknowledgment of her being in a position to impact upon my critical reputation, when, sorry, Homey don't play that, as everyone who has really known me since I was **knee**-high to, I don't know, something very small with knees, must realize . . . *especially* in light of my recent demonstrable determination to hold to an unbending standard the increasingly reedy pronunciamentos of that watcher of watchdogs, my old mentor *manqué*, the aforementioned Zeitmeister, Swami-*meme*, who himself to his credit has always tended—with, as he would and indeed frequently does put it, "due reservations"—to acknowledge my own views with as much enthusiasm as anyone can expect the never-less-than-thoughtful, never-more-than-that-either masscommeister to muster these days in light of his actual age, his *regime* of questionably prescribed medications, his letter-from-Dad compositional style, and his tenuous pension-track niche in the dank, miasmal duodenum of the YahooSmithBarney media mini-Leviathan—itself a virtually owned subsidiary, not so incidentally, of Marco's Macrosystem Group, whose flagship yogurt-chain giveaway organ listed my Tuesday evening one-man pick'n'pan-slam in its "Hap'nin'" section for twelve straight weeks, even after the show folded in large part owing to the perpetually overstretched Marco's evident inability to correct one crucial typo without making several others . . . and yet it was Marco, ham-fisted typeface comic though he may be, who perhaps said it best—if only he knew!—late one Sunday-closing predawn when I logged on to vent and surf for context: *"Ve are too soon oldt undt too late schmardt"*) has lost his edge.

That exercise seems to have purged me of motivation to write a certain sort of thing.

➤ *fuss*

Perhaps, says John Ayto in his *Dictionary of Word Origins*, "simply ono-matopoeic, imitating the sound of someone puffing and blowing and making a fuss."

OED: perhaps "echoic of the sound of something sputtering or bub-bling, or expressive of the action of 'puffing and blowing.'"

Etymonline.com: "perhaps an alteration of *force*, or imitative of bub-bling or sputtering sounds, or from Dan. *fjas* 'foolery, nonsense.'"

We're talking **sonicky**. But people who are particular about how words are used are often dismissed as *fussy*. As in (OED), "habitually busy about tri-fles." Hey, sometimes it takes fussiness in that sense to clean up, tighten up, a mess of wordage, to render it relatively see-through and slick as a whistle.

OED quotes Leslie Stephen: "The butterfly . . . is much too fussy an insect to enjoy himself properly." That's very British, isn't it, "enjoy himself properly."

See **Dionysian, Apollonian, blended, briefly.**

➤ future, the, caught for the moment

David Carr, in *The New York Times*, on the introduction of the iPad: " 'Isn't this awesome?' Mr. Jobs says. It is, but everything looks good on stage. Nothing ages faster than the future when you get it in your hands."

➤ *fuzz*

OED: perhaps "imitative of the action of blowing away light particles." No one knows how, or whether, that sense is connected to the slang word for police (which goes back, in print, to 1929), but if *fuss* may be an alteration of *force*, why not *fuzz*? It's usually "the fuzz," as in "the (police) force."

g · G · g

Etymologically, *G-string*, a narrow nethergarment, leaves more than you might think to the imagination. We do know that the term goes back farther than the striptease, for "the strip and tease" has not shown up in print before 1930, and a writer referred to the string holding up an American Indian breechcloth as a *gee-string* in 1878. In 1885, *gee-string* was used for the string and cloth together, and in 1891 we read "Some of the boys wore only 'G-strings' (as, for some reason, the breech-clout is commonly called on the prairie)." The first recorded reference to a stripper's last vestige of modesty is John Dos Passos's *gee-string* in 1936. *G-string* took over after that.

So, *G* for a fiddle string tuned to G? Could be, but nothing about that string makes it more evocative of the loins than any other instrument string.

G for *groin*? In case ladies were listening? Originally, the English word for the area covered by a breechcloth was spelled *grinde* (not derived from *grind* as in the bump and grind, or as in all those songs about something the matter with the mill so I can't get no grindin'). *Groin* may have evolved under the influence of *loin*. Why not *L-string*, for *loin*, or *B-string*, for *breech*?

G for the exclamation *gee*? That euphemism for *Jesus!* or *Jerusalem!* has not been found in print earlier than 1895. But variations of *Geewhillikens!* go back to 1851; and *Jehoshaphat!*, sometimes spelled *Geehosofat!*, to 1857. The historical Jehoshaphat seems to have been a pretty good king of Judah, on the whole, except when he formed an alliance of necessity with Ahab, a wicked Baal-worshipping king of Israel. There is no reason for Jehoshaphat to be an expletive except for the sounds in his name. Many exclamations in English begin with the *j* sound: *jumping jiminy, jeepers, by jingo, by George, Judas Priest, Geronimo, by Jove.* At least some of these are thanks to Jesus and Jehovah, but there was no *j* sound, in words, in Jesus's day. His name in Hebrew was probably *Yoshua*. Romans called him *Yay-sus*. (The *j* sound came into English—from French, which later softened it into something like the *s* in English *exposure*—several centuries after Christ. The Old English word for Jesus was *healend*, one who heals, or the Savior. *Jesus* came in from French *Jesu* or *Iesu* . . . the *j* sound in itself has jiggy, jazzy jabber juice. See **ch** and **jump**.

Maybe a Native American was asked what he called the string that held up his *cache-sexe* and he replied, "Gee . . ." With "I don't know, what's it to you?" implied. Bottom line, we just don't know.

A more explicable term is *C-string*, as defined on **Wikipedia**: "As narrow as a g-string but without the band around the waist, leaving just a *C*-shaped piece between the legs held in place firmly by a flexible internal frame. Since there is no material around the waist, the C-string completely eliminates the panty lines which thongs and other underwear create. C-strings are also designed for use as beachwear, which reduces the tan lines that would have been left by the side straps of even a g-string."

What's next? The iString?

➤ *gag*

My old friend Robert Creamer, standard biographer of Babe Ruth and Casey Stengel, writes me of a wannabe gagster he knew when he worked in an ad agency right after World War II:

> He was a tall young New York Irishman about my age who was in charge of the steno pool. His stock-in-trade was a harassed look and a faint frown. What he wanted to be was a gag writer for comedians, and he would stop by my cubicle each morning to try his latest crop on me—without altering his harassed look and faint frown. He'd read one after the other of the four or five he had each day and would look up when he finished and say, "No good?" The gags were about as good as the stuff the current comedians were using, but I remember only two. One was, "I wear striped socks to make my feet look tall." The other was based on a New York City crackdown on subway

mashers in which cops disguised as young women would mingle with the crowds on subway trains. Jerry's gag was, "Don't cop a feel on the subway, you might be feeling a cop."

Even OED ventures that *gag*'s original meaning, to choke, would appear to be "imitative of the sound made in choking." So how did *gag* become associated with comedy? Before it meant a professional jokester's one-liner, it meant a hoax, a trick, a lie, a tall tale. Makers of silent films referred to their carefully constructed stunts and illusions as gags; these became known as sight gags when movies added sound.

The connection that leaps to mind, and that OED allows to be possible, is that the trickster's *gag* is related "to the notion of thrusting something down the throat of a credulous person, or testing his powers of 'swallowing.'" ("Sayyy, is this some kind of gag?")

"On the other hand," OED goes on to suggest, *gag* "may be of onomatopoeic origin (cf. GAGGLE) with the original sense of 'unmeaning chatter.'" Onomatopoeic in either case. And why on the one hand or the other? Both connections might apply. Another word for empty talk is *guff*, and people say "I'm not taking any more of your guff." Everyone seems to accept that the word *guffaw* is an attempt to capture the sound of a belly laugh; maybe it also captures an ejection—*phaugh!*—of someone else's guff.

Then there's the spit take, and people who speak of something so hilarious it made them laugh till water (or worse) came out of their noses. *Yuk* meaning laugh is also *yuck* the sound of disgust (or vice versa). *Chuckle* comes from Middle English *chukken*, to make a clucking noise, but it's close to *upchuck*. *Cackle*, though also chicken-imitative, resembles *kaka*. *Giggle*, which the OED calls echoic, doesn't really sound like giggling, which is more *hee-hee-hee*, but it brings us back around to *gaggle*, which is imitative of geese, who are famous for their excretory powers. Maybe laughter is the propulsive release of something stuck in one's craw—*craw* meaning the crop of a bird, or by humorous or derisive transference (OED), the stomach of a person. I'm forcing some of these connections, but give me credit for not trying to squeeze in *foie gras*.

The striped socks gag just made me smile, but I liked it. Wonder what happened to Jerry.

> ## garden path phenomenon

An example: "The young man the boats."

You're going along for a moment there thinking you're reading about a young man, and then you realize: no. You're reading that the boats are manned by the young.

Here is a much juicier example, from a review, by Janet Maslin in *The New York Times*, of a memoir by Barbara Walters:

> Ms. Walters is not specific about her age (or about the
> youth-preserving surgery of anyone other than Roy Cohn, the
> young Ms. Walters's weirdest suitor), but she will acknowledge
> this much: She's old enough to have had the daughter of one
> of the Three Stooges . . .

WHAT? WHAT? Which one? Surely not Curly! Good God, how can such things be? And . . . well, you *could* say Roy Cohn was weirder than, okay, Moe, but . . .

But you read on, and you discover that Barbara Walters is "old enough to have had the daughter of one of the Three Stooges as a childhood friend."

Oh. Here's another one, Joyce Carol Oates in *The New York Review of Books*:

> To watch a boxer seriously training (as I once watched the
> twenty-year-old heavyweight contender Mike Tyson at his
> Catskill camp preparatory to his defeat of Trevor Berbick in
> November, 1986) is to realize firsthand how contrary to nature
> boxing actually is, how one might argue that when practiced
> on the highest levels, the discipline of boxing bears . . .

Whoa! Mike Tyson got in shape by boxing *bears*? That *is* unnatural. Kangaroos are one thing, but . . .

But you read on, and you realize that Oates is saying "boxing bears more relationship to a shrewdly cerebral contest like chess than to anything like streetfighting."

Oh. But you have had (and you'll have it forever) the image of Barbara Walters bonking heads with, say, Shemp, and somehow from that union . . .

And you have the image of Tyson biting Smoky's ear. I don't say you want those images. I do say no one can take them away from you.

The garden path is not confined to print. On NPR I hear a biologist say, "It travels on fishermen's feet," and I snap to attention. A mythical beast of some kind, it must be, that travels on fishermen's feet, looks out at the world through the eyes of a Indian scout, and its hands are those of an obstetrician.

But no. In a twinkling, because I have snapped to attention, I realize that what the biologist is discussing is just terrible algae, popularly known as "rock snot," which is being spread among the nation's trout streams by the feet of anglers. I'm not dismissing rock snot as a problem. I'm just saying it's not what I thought it was there for a moment.

See **typos, going with them** and *page turning*.

➤ gender neutrality, absurd

When you're referring to a dog, whose sex (you don't have to say *gender* when talking about dogs) you do not know, I can see why you (I wouldn't) might refer to him or her as *it*. But surely the couple in this item from the *Rocky Mountain News* deserved a *his* and a *she*:

> A male chow mix laid [yes, should be *lay*, but never mind that] down in the middle of a busy street this morning to keep watch over its companion, a female German shepherd mix, after it was hit and killed by a car on Chambers Road near East 52nd Avenue.

It? You're going to call each of those dogs *it?* And thereby not only render them underromantic but also leave some confusion as to which one was hit and killed? *What kind of person are you?*

➤ *ghostwriting*

Why do people resist the notion that the author of something wrote it? In *The Facts on File Encyclopedia of Word and Phrase Origins*, Robert Hendrickson baldly asserts that "Mark Twain wrote most of Ulysses S. Grant's autobiography." That's a shame, because Grant was a heroic hands-on writer.

Twain published and promoted Grant's memoirs—so generously and well that the royalties enabled Grant's widow to live comfortably the rest of her days—but Grant wrote the book himself, while mortally suffering from cancer eating away his mouth, tongue, and neck.

In *Grant and Twain*, Mark Perry writes that Grant's military aide, General Adam Badeau, and Grant's son Fred, both of whom were authors themselves, provided Grant with considerable research assistance, and at the end of a long writing day they would discuss with him what he had written. Badeau had been reluctant to get involved in the project, having already produced his own account of Grant's campaigns, using Grant's records. "I had looked forward to going into history as his mouthpiece and spokesman," Badeau wrote, "and, of course, if he wrote a new work himself my special authority would be superseded."

The *New York World* reported that Badeau was ghostwriting Grant's book. Grant and Twain were convinced that Badeau had planted that rumor, to which Grant issued a point-by-point denial. Badeau wrote to Grant offering to ghostwrite the rest of the book, for more money than he had been getting. Grant fired him: "You and I must give up all association so far as the preparation of any literary work goes which bears my signature." Badeau wrote back: "I have no desire, intention or right to claim authorship to your book. The composition is entirely your own. What assistance I have been able to render has been in suggestion, revision or verification."

"That seemed to end the matter," writes Perry, except that "while Twain could never prove it, Badeau was probably the person responsible for the rumors that soon began circulating . . . that in fact it was not Grant, or even Badeau, who wrote Grant's memoirs—but Mark Twain."

The truth is that Twain, who had invested most of his own fortune in the printing, marketing, and distribution of the book, was impatient for Grant to turn in the manuscript of volume two, but Grant kept *fuss*ing with it. As publisher, Twain sighed. As writer, he knew how Grant felt—except for the cancer—at this stage of a book. "He is going to stick in here and there no end of little plums and spices," Twain wrote approvingly to William Dean Howells.

Four days before he died, Grant dictated, in a whisper, his last revisions. After looking them over as transcribed to paper, and touching them up here and there, he put down his pencil, satisfied. Then he wrote a note to his doctor. Knowing he was incurable, he said, "I first wanted so many days to work on my book so the authorship would be clearly mine . . . There is nothing more I should do to it now, and therefore I am not likely to be more ready to go than at this moment."

Twain was fixated on Grant. He imagined having met Grant in battle, sort of, and he boasted of having cracked Grant up with a joke at Grant's expense, in a speech honoring Grant. If Twain had contrived to write most of Grant's book, in Grant's clean, relentless style, he would have left behind some hint of having done so.

In Twain's last book, *Is Shakespeare Dead?*, he argued that someone else, Sir Francis Bacon, wrote Shakespeare's plays, since Shakespeare himself lacked formal education and was not a celebrity in his own hometown. Twain derided the "thugs"—that is, the scholars—who continued to believe that Shakespeare *did* write his own plays. In *Is Shakespeare Dead?* Twain pointed out that Samuel Clemens, too, lacked schooling, but he *was* celebrated in his hometown. So, bottom line, Samuel Clemens did write Mark Twain.

If there is an Elysium, Twain and Shakespeare by now may have tried to write a play together, and fallen out over it. And Francis Bacon may be constantly having to tell people, even in the VIP area, "Listen, *I* never claimed I wrote Shakespeare. Why does no one ever ask me about what I *did* write?"

Then again, I hear of scholars today claiming authorship of their graduate students' work. Some medical professors even sign their names to scientific papers written by ghostwriters paid by pharmaceutical firms. According to *The New York Times*, the drug company Wyeth engaged the ghostwriting company DesignWrite to produce medical-journal articles favoring Wyeth's drugs. Then those articles were run past doctors who agreed to be purported to be the authors of them. One gynecologist—whose actual work, I stipulate, is far more valuable to society than mine—could see nothing wrong with this practice. She had *read* the paper, after all, and agreed with it, and therefore was able to say with a clear conscience, "This is my work, this is what I believe, this is reflective of my view."

No. You may believe it, it may reflect your view, but it's not your *work* unless you wrought it. For his part, the president of DesignWrite wrote, or at least signed off on, the statement that DesignWrite "has not, and will not, participate in the publication of any material in which it does not have complete confidence in the scientific validity of the content, based upon the best available data."

That's some piece of wordsmithing right there. Doesn't "has not . . . participate" make you cringe? Would you write, "I have not, and will not, tell a lie"? Or, alternatively, "I have not told, and will not, a lie"? When you could write, "I have not told a lie, and will not tell one"?

And what's up with those three *in*'s? It's not a matter of simple overindulgence in *in*. Sometimes people liberally sprinkle several short words into a sentence, in hopes that one of them will fall into the right slot. A case in point is the excess of *is*'s in the following statement by the fine young Red Sox pitcher Jonathan Papelbon, as quoted by the Associated Press, with regard to the 2009 pennant race: "That's what is the hard part about it is to realize that early on in the spring is not what it's all about."

He's a ballplayer, and he's talking. Someday, when he's ready to tell his life story in, say, *Coming Out of the Pen* (the bullpen, that is), he will hire a ghostwriter to sort out his *is*'s. But a *writing company*, presumably by *design*, wrote, of itself, that it "has not, and will not, participate in the publication of any material in which it does not have complete confidence in the scientific validity of the content." If I were a company's president, I think I would refer to the company as *we*, but never mind that. A company might straightforwardly write of itself that it "has not participated, and will not participate, in the publication of any material in whose scientific validity it does not have complete confidence." But when a company writes that it "has not, and will not, participate in the publication of any material in which it does not have complete confidence in the scientific validity of the content," forget about ghosts. That company has stirred form and content into a whirl of syntactical dust. No wonder so many people doubt authorship today.

➢ *gikl*

When a toddler I knew many years ago saw a shining light, he would point to it, beam at it, and say in a definitive tone, "Gikl." An instinctive **portmanteau** of *glitter* and *sparkle*? Or had he precociously got hold of some ancient linguistic root? The original pronunciation of English *light* was more like the German *Licht*, and lots of *gl-* words relate to shining—*gleam*, *glow, gloss, glare, glisten,* and *glow,* which OED connects to the Teutonic root *glô-*. OED also includes the obsolete word *blik,* to shine, which goes back to Old Teutonic and has cognates in many languages, including the Dutch *blikken,* to twinkle.

OED recognizes no *gikkle* or *gickle* or indeed any word beginning in *gik-* or *gic-,* but Urbandictionary.com has a *gikkle* entry, attributed to someone going by "Theeph." The definition is icky and unrelated to *gikl,* but the whole entry is worth quoting, I believe, for the sake of its remarkable narrative twists:

GIKKLE

A much cuter way of giggling. The *kk* must be whispered in the back of your throat for ultimate effect. Takes practice.

Angry mob: *We gonna mess jOO!*
John: *Is't possible?!*
Stu: *We are lost!*
John and Stu exchange conspirital grins
John and Stu: *gikkle!!*
Angry mob: *Awwwwwwwwwwwww!!!!*
Angry mob turns on itself

➤ *gillie, girl*

When I went to Iceland in the summer of 1972 (to cover the Fischer-Spassky chess match, which is another story), I had heard about the salmon and I had heard about the women. I was thirty and effectively single for the first time since college. The salmon were said to be plentiful, the women active.

I liked Icelanders in general: open, unfancy people, two or three of whom paid me the compliment of addressing me in Icelandic, thinking I was one of them. Then when they found I was American they went on amicably in English as if I were one of them anyway.

I particularly liked a wistful-looking, bright-lipped young divorcée in a low-cut fiftiesish party dress I met at a Saturday night dance at the Saga

Hotel. I escorted her home and traced a finger across her low-cut line, and she looked detachedly down at her bosom and said the neighbors would be watching to see when I left. I persuaded her to look out the window with me and see that no lights were on up and down the street.

"But mine," she said.

She looked me in the eye with feeling that was stronger than mine, and wasn't for me.

There, I bet any neighbor who may in fact have been watching would have observed, goes a wistful-looking guy.

Let me remind you that I was in Iceland as a journalist. In one aspect of that capacity, three other journalists and I met three Brennivín-drinking women (Brennivín is a kind of schnapps) and accompanied them to the apartment where they lived. With one of them, I wandered out back. We lay down in a little pup tent, which seemed odd. She said she didn't approve of capitalism. I said I didn't either, all that much. She said she was a Stalinist. That stumped me. Leninism, I might have been able to embrace for the evening, but—and then she asserted without changing tone that she was pregnant. We were lying side by side, looking up. "Why . . . ," I said, "do you have this tent?"

Silence. No spark. We went back inside, where two of the other three correspondents were visibly fading, and the third, who was British, was gamely singing a song involving knickers. The other two women were expressionless. The pregnant Stalinist surveyed the company dourly and said, "You don't know what to do with girls like us."

I know, now, that *girl* is an etymological mystery. Not to mention a Rorschach test. John Minsheu in 1617 derived *girl* from the Latin *garrula*, garrulous, on the notion that young females talked so much; or alternatively from *girella*, a word for weather vane, on the notion that young females changed as the wind blew. Neither of those derivations has stood the test of time. Anatoly Liberman concludes that *girl* may well have arisen from among a number of Germanic roots that began with hard *g* or *k*, ended in *r*, often took a diminutive suffix *l* or *le*, and "denoted young animals, children, and all kinds of creatures considered immature, worthless, or past their prime."

At any rate, *girl* originally meant a child of either sex. No one knows why it became female. Not until the sixteenth century does OED find men using the word to wax eloquent over female charms. In about 1520:

For by god it is a prety gyrle
It is a worlde to se her whyrle
Daunsynge in a rounde.

In 1593: "I saw one Lasse farre comelier than the rest, / A peerlesse peece, an heart-delighting gyrle."

Sounds great in poetry, but we hardened journalists returned to the Saga Hotel unlucky. The question that sticks with me is this: Was that pregnant Stalinist looking (in or out of that tent) for a deeper commitment? Or, maybe, a shallower one? In the latter case, I'm kicking myself—except how superficially can you respond to someone, Stalinist or not, who is in the family way?

The next morning I went salmon fishing, on the Grimsá River north of Reykjavik, and met another girl.

With the light tackle we were using, you can't horse a salmon in. It can break your hook, your leader, your line, or your rod if you ever once say, "Now listen, stop that foolishness, come on here to me." You must pay long, scientific court, working the fish against the current, gradually cadging line bit by bit. When a salmon first takes the hook, it is likely to lie there in the water, waiting for you to do something wrong. You may have to throw rocks at the fish with your free hand before it will deign to move. To a fish like that an old worm fisherman like me is inclined to say, "Well, if you don't want to do this, let's forget about it. Go *jump* a falls, and I'll sit here and watch."

Which is what I spent a lot of time doing. I had often heard about salmon fighting their way upstream, but I'd never realized what a feat it was. They don't usually make it up an eight-foot waterfall in one leap. Sometimes they get halfway up and hang there in the torrent, fighting against the water and the rocks with a *flippety-flip* sound that is clearly audible above the rush—then somehow they double-clutch and nose ahead into a route that carries them higher, and then they meet more resistance and are borne precipitously down and maybe back over a couple of smaller falls they've already negotiated. Reminded me of writing. Battling your way up one sentence, and another one, and another one, and losing that one and finding another way up so that reading it all can be like going *with* the flow.

Salmon is probably from *salire*, to leap. As salmon beat on against the current, they are preyed upon by seabirds that follow them in from the ocean. A local man told of seeing a bird dive, sink its talons into a salmon's back and then, unable to carry the fish away, tow it with great effort to the bank. That sounded more natural to me than flailing around with a tiny fake insect bearing some grandiose name—a Blue Charm, a Black Doctor, a Hairy Mary, a Thunder and Lightning—at the end of lots and lots of line.

But there was no saying that around the star of our party, an internationally renowned angler. He showed me his six-and-a-half-foot, four-ounce rod, his number six fly line, and his six-pound test leader, with which he was resolved to catch twenty- and thirty-pound salmon. That struck me as no more feasible than trying to pick up Princess Di on a bicycle, but I didn't say anything. He pointed out that the rod was impregnated with Bakelite resins. The reel, he said, had been handmade of missile alloys by a jeweler on Long Island.

"Did you soak it in formaldehyde to get it into the country?" I asked. My understanding was that in order to keep salmon disease out of Iceland, all foreign fishing gear had to be thus sterilized before customs would let it in. I meant my question to be deflating.

"No," he said, "I had a surgeon friend put it in his autoclave." He winked at our gillie and she smiled.

Gillie is an old Gaelic word. Originally it meant a lad, or an attendant upon a Highland chief. In the nineteenth century it began to mean a sort of caddie for hunters or fishers. For a gillie to be female is unusual. Gunna was nineteen, a sturdy blond farm girl who trained Icelandic ponies. When a twelve-pound salmon got off the hook of a woman in our party and started flopping around in an inch or two of water, Gunna came running through the shallows and dived on the fish as if it were a loose ball.

I liked her a lot. She reminded me of girls I used to run around with when I was nine, but I noticed her soft green eyes more than I noticed theirs then. She had them only for the MF, as I will call the master fisherman.

I stood out in the icy river in borrowed hip boots for a while, casting badly yet hooking several salmon, which, since I would lose patience, would unhook themselves. I caught a pound-and-a-half sea trout, a lively but relatively simple soul that reminded me of many other nice fish I had met. And then I stood high on a riverside bluff, looking out at lava slopes the color and texture of old elephant skin, surrounded by various shades of aquamarine sky, grass, river, spray, and light rain, watching the MF do his stuff.

He played one eighteen-pounder for an hour. "You must keep the balance nearly equal," the MF announced as he did so, "or the partnership will be dissolved." He tried to keep the fish in the middle of the river, but it worked its way into the shallows, where it got more oxygen and became exhilarated, took off again, jumped and twisted in the air, and the MF kept with it.

"Edge pressure," he called out in a professional tone. He was maintaining traction on the corner of the salmon's mouth, keeping the fish off balance, its head against the current. Finally MF was within ten feet of his opponent. He got down on his knees and crept in, gaining line, trying to remain low because if the fish saw him, he said in his running commentary, it would be exhilarated again.

I doubted this. But sure enough, the salmon stuck its head out of the water, evidently got a look at the MF, and took off across the surface like a speedboat. A wonderful move, to which the MF was equal. He stood and gave just the right amount, held, and began to close in again. Disdaining gaff or net, he got the fish to where he could see it swimming near his feet, then crouched for several minutes, holding his rod high with one hand and extending the other hand over the water.

Then he made his grab, stood up straight, and presented something long, still, and whitish that extended from his waist to his ankle. Holding the salmon up by the tail stretched out its spinal column so that the fish couldn't move at all, while the MF rapped it behind the head—on the brain—with a rock.

I went down and saw the fish lying on the shore, looking like a single, stout, silver-and-grey muscle with a tail, an eye, and a strong, underslung jaw. Silver scales lay around loose, scattered by the coup de grâce. The main thing that occurred to me about this salmon, however well caught, was that it was dead.

But hey, that was what we were there for, and Gunna regarded the MF with admiration. That night in the lodge, the MF favored her casually with his attention, and she smiled.

The guy—believe me when I say this—was not right for her. Okay, he could fish. Would you want your daughter or your little sister or just a young woman who was a friend of yours to tumble for a guy—one more than twice her age—because he could *fish*? After dinner I stayed up until it was just the three of us. Until three a.m. Finally Gunna gave me a put-out look and went to bed. Then after a while the MF, looking *almost* ruffled, went up to his room. I waited another half hour, and then I went up to mine.

The next morning, back out on the river, the MF ignored Gunna. "Let's go over there," I said to her. "It's the best place to watch 'em jump."

Well, the MF had no need for a gillie—in the daylight—and I was a member of the party. Coolly, Gunna climbed with me to a fifteen-foot cliff overlooking a deep pool above sheer, narrow eight-foot falls and below that, in sequence, a shallow pool, a wider, six-foot falls, another deep pool, and a broad stretch of rapids.

On the lower levels, the fish were visible only when they jumped or tore across the top of the water. At the big falls and in the pool beneath it, you could see one jumping and hitting midway up the falls and scrambling against the water and the rocks at once. You could see one hitting just short of the top, being flung back end over end and falling with a smack like a person doing a belly flopper. You could see one shooting up in a greyish streak, losing his keel and sliding back down on his silver side; and then see black flashes of him boiling around in the crush at the bottom. Away from the foam, in the quieter parts of the middle pool, you could see lots of them waiting, looking much softer—a pale catfish grey with pastel splotches. Fins trembling.

"I've never seen so many salmons!" Gunna exclaimed. "Salmons *with* salmons!" And then she gave me a nudge with her elbow, pointed to the uppermost pool, and whispered, "There is a *big* one."

An evocative cry. It took me back beyond all fishing to the girls I used to catch bumblebees with, out of honeysuckle bushes. "There's a big one!" they would say, and I would calmly screw open my mason jar, at the ready. But this was more exciting. I tried to make corner-of-the-eye contact with Gunna.

Then, oddly enough, the big one took my fly.

I had cast my Thunder and Lightning and let it drift just below the surface of the pool. What the heck. Now a salmon had it, a much bigger one than any the MF had caught, and we weren't going to have to throw rocks at it to get it moving. It was tearing around the pool; I set my hook just by jumping in surprise; the fish was heading downstream with it.

And Gunna and I were standing fifteen feet above, on a tricky lava cliff, with our hip boots on. We were going to have to work our way down and around the rocks and into the pool and who knew where after that. It was like a dream in which you try to run under a perfectly thrown pass and find yourself standing in a canoe drifting rapidly the opposite way. The fish was determined, it was clear, to shoot the rapids back down, all the way to the ocean if necessary, and there I was trying to catch up with it, tentatively holding some wild notion of its life in my hand.

I once rode an amusement-park ride that revolved, rotated, dipped, rose, and oscillated along seven different vectors simultaneously. I once untangled a six-month-old boy from an earphone cord while trying to keep his left hand out of the pudding and his mashed-potato-coated right hand off my suit on a dinner flight in heavy turbulence while fending off his almost equally food-covered two-year-old sister from the other side. But I have never been involved in such a multifariously lively operation as the one that took place that day on the Grimsá among me, Gunna, the cliffs, the falls, and that salmon.

Gunna kept trying to grab the rod. I wouldn't let her. We clambered over the lava, nearly pitching ourselves right down in there among the salmon several times. We scrabbled along ledges—she guiding my steps and crying out advice, I striving to play the great fish neither too tight nor too loose—for four or five full-to-overflowing minutes. As we scrambled we watched our fish sprawl down the upper falls and disappear into the pool below and then reappear in a flash over the next falls and into the next pool and then into the rough water at the lowest level.

Where it got off. Suddenly. I had ceased to flow, had become too literal, too direct or maybe too abstract—had thought, "Now, surely, even though I seem to be dancing, which seems to be good, I should be pulling in"—and the salmon got a fix on my Thunder and Lightning and spit it out. I had a loose line.

I assume the salmon was relieved. Though now he had to work his way back up the falls.

I was exhilarated. Towed by the fish into richer air.

Gunna didn't say anything when I beamed at her.

I didn't know what to say. We climbed back up to the lip, to the ledge right next to the top of the highest falls. I reeled in my Thunder and Lightning, which looked ravished. We were close enough to kneel and reach in and feel the cold water surging down, so I did.

And just then another big salmon plopped right up onto the ledge beside me. I swear. It had misjudged its bias and precipitated itself out of the water.

It flopped around, not much better at walking than I was at fly casting. I gave the silver-scaled meaty flash a little grab or nudge with the first two fingers of my right hand—it was something like standing on a football sideline and "catching" a player who has burst out of bounds and is braking, spinning his wheels, trying to reverse so as to get back into the thick of things. I could, physically, have seized the salmon and flipped it up farther ashore the way a bear fishes, but I didn't. Neither did Gunna. We watched it flounder—no, not flounder, watched it salmon—on the rocks between us. On its fourth flip, the salmon seized itself by its bootstraps, heaved itself sideways, landed in the corner of the falls, and astoundingly slid *up* and over the lip, upriver and out of sight. Off to spawn. Imagine a poured-out goldfish slipping back into the tank along the stream, against the flow, of the pouring water.

I gave Gunna an elbow nudge.

"What would we have said we caught him on?" I asked.

"A Hairy Mary," she said, giving me a smile, finally.

➢ *glass*

George Orwell, a great prose stylist, is often quoted as having said "Good prose is clear as a pane of glass." In fact, in "Why I Write" (which the excellent, highly readable linguist Geoffrey Nunberg calls the most widely cited of all twentieth-century essays on English), Orwell wrote: "Good prose is like a window pane."

Orwell was certainly speaking in favor of clarity, and against worn-out phrases "tacked together like sections of a prefabricated hen-house" (hear, hear!), but he was too judicious to present a pane as purely transparent. The earliest panes of glass, prized today if you can find them, were by no means invisible. And even today, to try getting a windowpane utterly clean is to court despair—go for that last little streak on the inside and you realize it's on the outside, and when you go out and get it, you see a fingerprint on the inside. There's a reader-writer metaphor in there somewhere; I'm not going to try to buff it up any further.

The word *glass* derives from the same root as *gold, arsenic, melancholy, gall, Hare Krishna, glimpse, glide, zloty, glare, gloss, gloaming, glitch,* and *glib.* If you're glassy-eyed, your soul is not exactly visible, is it? In "through a glass, darkly," *glass* means a mirror. I heard once of a man who was killed when the mirror over his bed fell on him. Imagine a last moment of seeing yourself descending, in great alarm, upon you.

See **puppy**.

➤ *Gmail?*

No. Should be *G-mail.* As in *G-man, G-spot* (*Gspot*? Come on), and *G-string,* not as in *Gstaad. Gmail* looks like someone sat on Warren Harding's middle name.

➤ *gnat*

Chambers says this is ultimately related to *gnaw.*

A *gnatling* is a small gnat.

At Answers.com, we are told that "a gnat usually reaches a length of 4 cm (2.114 in.) and a wingspan of approximately 6.23 cm (3.415 in.)." Call that the average gnat? That is a *huge* gnat. Information drawn from a pest-management company. Scare tactics, if you ask me.

➤ *Godwottery*

"An affected or over-elaborate style of gardening or attitude towards gardens," says OED. From "My Garden" by T. E. Brown: "A garden is a lovesome thing, God wot!" (*Wot* an archaic word meaning *knows.* OED, however, seems to say proper present third-person singular would have been *wots* or *wotteth.*)

➤ going global

Alan Furst, a highly regarded novelist of international intrigue, was quoted in *The New York Times* as saying that his books "should read like books in translation—it's translator's English." That remark brought me down. Global markets driving out local flavor. I prefer what I. B. Singer told *The Paris Review*, that the modern Yiddish writer "was brought up with the idea that one should get out of Jewishness and become universal. And because he tried so hard to become universal, he became very provincial." My ambition is to write American English like a native.

➤ *golf*

The brassie, the spoon, the mashie, the niblick, the cleek. All gone! You can hear all those old clubs rattling about in the golf bag of history. According to *The Historical Dictionary of Golfing Terms* by Peter Davies, *cleek* is an old Scots word for "crook, walking stick with a hook." The light narrow-bladed iron in question "was sometimes also spelled *click*, and so associated with the sound of the impact of club on ball." *Niblick*—referring to the original stubby-headed wooden version of this club—probably meant "short-nose" (*nib* being an old Scots word for "beak"). With a niblick you could root a ball out of a bad lie like a pig snouting up truffles, and put a solid lick on it.

Those clubs' modern equivalents are just woods (made of steel or titanium) and irons, with numbers. Where's the romance there? Where's the onomatopoeia?

Did you know that the real name of actor Jeremy Irons is Stephen F. Randall III—that he took his stage name from a golfing friend of his father's who wouldn't use woods? If you did know it, forget it, it isn't true. It's a bit of misinformation I gleaned from Lycos.com, a self-described "information fusion machine" that I found by Googling "Jeremy Irons golf." My thinking was, there must be a joke there somewhere. And ironically enough, there was: Lycos cites as its source a website that turns out to be entirely tongue in cleek. I mean cheek. In fact, the actor was born Jeremy John Irons.

His sister, according to nndb.com, is Felicity Irons. If you were writing a golf novel, that would be a good name for a golfer with perfect pitch and chip. But who would believe it? Robert Frost wrote of his fellow poet Edward Arlington Robinson, "His life was a revel in the felicities of language." Has anyone ever reveled in the felicities of, say, the sand wedge? At any rate, Jeremy's sister, according to nndb, is not a golf pro but a "rush weaver." Weaves rushes. Jeremy's father's name, though, is Ping.

No, I made that up, the father's name. I'm reaching, I'm pressing. I'm trying to revel in golf language, and all I am doing is foozling.

To *foozle*, of course, is to bungle a shot. *The Historical Dictionary of Golfing Terms* leaves the etymology of *foozle* at "origin unknown," but WIII raises the possibility that *foozle* may come from the German dialect verb *fuseln*, "to work hurriedly or poorly."

Which is what I'm doing. Pressing. Getting frantic. Jeremy Irons jokes!

So. Let me do a little waggle here. (*Waggle*, referring to a preliminary flourishing of the club before grounding it, goes back at least as far as 1890. Before that, did people not waggle? Did they call waggling something else? We don't know.)

To *sclaff* is to unintentionally hit the ground before the ball. The very sound of it jangles my wrists.

Divot is just an old Scottish term for a chunk of turf. Roofs used to be made of them. *Taking* a divot, however, does not imply that you can carry it home with you, to start a new lawn with, or a roof garden.

A *chili-dip* is a mishit somehow evocative of the fact that when you try to dip up a lot of chili with a taco chip, you don't get a lot of chili. On your taco chip. Should've gone with the 5-iron.

Start over. Shift weight back and forth. But no *happy feet*. Let the club swing itself. Yeah, right.

I won't try to tell you that just as baseball is a four-pointed pastoral journey from home back on around to home again, golf is a reenactment of the eternal quest for beachfront property. What with the sand and all. No. My game is not philosophy. It is words.

Take *golf*. You may have assumed that the the word was *flog* backward, as in self-flagellation. Or a compression of "*Gosh all Friday*" or some stronger oath. But no, the Scots probably borrowed the word from the Dutch, who played some comparable game (only without that essential Scottish contribution, the hole) that involved hitting a ball with a *colf*, or *kolf*: Dutch for "club." *Kolf* sounds like hitting, all right, but it's too close to *sclaff* for my comfort. Then too, *golf* introduces a strong hint of *gulp*. Not to mention the vast *gulf* between that pretty green up ahead and where you are standing.

After a number of *strokes* (defined by OAD as "a sudden disabling attack or loss of consciousness caused by an interruption in the flow of blood to the brain"), we have reached that green. And must *putt*. Which is not, ideally, the same as *punt*. The roots of *putt* are the same as those of *put*, as in "Just put that down anywhere." Chambers says the golf term was probably associated, back around the fourteenth century, "with earlier *putting*, now known as *shot putting*." And indeed it may be as hard to get a golf ball into a four-and-a-quarter-inch hole as to fit a sixteen-pound ball of lead into it. But of course *putt* rhymes not with *foot* (as does *put*) but with *but*. As in, "I had the break figured perfectly, but . . ."

Speaking of putts, and the anxiety of confronting a necessary short one, the nervous condition known as *yips* is "probably imitative of jerky motions caused by tension," says AHD. Tommy Armour is sometimes credited with coining the term. "Once you've had 'em, you've got 'em," he said. Yep.

Bogey is a word that managed to turn a relatively easygoing concept into a demon. In the late 1800s, holes and courses, began to have target scores by which a player could be judged. *Par*, deriving probably from the financial term *par value*, was pretty much perfect. An unofficial, less demanding standard, which a good amateur should be able to equal, came to be called *bogey*: the bogeyman of should-be-able was breathing down the amateur's neck.

Birdie probably came from "a bird of a shot," *bird* meaning something like *hell*. An *eagle* (unless it is breathing down your neck) is better than a birdie. A double eagle, three under par, is called an *albatross*, which may seem odd, since shooting that bird at sea is regarded as disastrous luck. Shooting one on a golf course just makes everyone else hate you.

The origin of *tee* is a mystery. It doesn't have to do with the little wooden deal's shape, because the original tees were small mounds of sand. Dust to dust, tee to trap. The man for whom the *mulligan* was named is identified in various stories, but none is confirmable—perhaps because, although many a *duffer* (origin also obscure) would be happy to claim the indulgence, no one ever wanted to claim the honor. It would be like saying, "You'll concede me that eight-footer, I assume, for I am the eponymous James Elmore Gimme."

When Mary Queen of Scots, who had grown to womanhood in France, returned to Scotland and hit the *links* (from the Scottish for "ridges, hummocks"), she called the boy who carried her clubs a *cadet*, rhyming with *pâté*. Her countrymen heard it as *caddie*. The derogatory term *cad* seems to have come from *caddie*, possibly owing to the snobbish assumption that anyone who schleps is low and ill-mannered.

It isn't usually a caddie, however, who resorts to the use of a *foot wedge*: a stealthy lie-improving kick.

Time to move on. *Fore!* (Which means "look out ahead." More helpful, from the standpoint of those being shouted at, would be *Aft!*, meaning "watch your back.") Let us thrash forward wielding our *blasters* and *baffies*.

Damn. Those, too, are obsolete words for approach-shot implements. Wielding *irons*, then. So cold, so clinical. As if you knew precisely what will become of the ball after you hit it with a given iron, even if you hit it right. According to WIII, the word *iron* is etymologically akin to the Sanskrit for "he sets in motion, swings" and the Latin for "wrath." There should be a club called the *wrathie*, especially designed for wrapping around a tree.

> *gollywaddles*

Sometimes one is tempted to despair of the level of reasoning on the U.S. Supreme Court. In 2008 *The New York Times* reported on the Court's discussion of whether "fleeting expletives" could legally be televised:

> "Why do you think the F-word has shocking value or emphasis or force?" Chief Justice Roberts asked Carter G. Phillips, a lawyer for Fox Television Stations, which had broadcast some of the offending language. The chief justice answered his own question: "Because it is associated with sexual or excretory activity. That's what gives it its force."
>
> Justice Antonin Scalia added that this was the reason people "don't use *gollywaddles* instead of the F-word."

Poppycock. Any number of terms associated with sexual or—and I love this expression—"excretory activity" are quite inoffensively speakable, not only on TV but in a Supreme Court session. For instance, *pregnancy* and *restroom*, or for that matter *sexual* and *excretory*. What gives *fuck* its force is the combination of its meaning and its kinephonic value. Probably the word is used more often ("Where the fuck has Grandma's strudel recipe gone?") with no connection to sex. But the *f*-word in any context evokes naked flesh smacking together. Its rude, explosive soft-*f*-to-hard-*k* sound—soft *f*, *uh* as in *thrust*, and *k* (see *K*)—and the way in which it surges through the oral apparatus make it a gratifying epithet to utter and often a frightening one to hear. It may not require any imagination, but it means business. Who would exclaim, "My gollywaddling printer is out of gollywaddling ink again!"? Perhaps Ned Flanders, the Simpsons' irrepressibly euphemistic next-door neighbor.

➤ *Google-logisms*

Marty Mazzone, in a query to *Harvard Magazine*'s "Chapter & Verse" department, writes: "My mother used to say, as fast as she could, 'The high uffum buffum and the compound presser and squeezer and the beefer dog trim.' At least, that's what we think she used to say. She would never repeat it for us on the spot. Can anyone identify the origin of this very strange, unGoogle-able phrase?"

Shouldn't that be *unGooglable*? As in *unbunglable*: "The gang thought their caper was unbunglable, but . . ." Maybe not. "The average person will find watermelons unjugglable." Doesn't look right, does it? "Eventually, over the years, one's hips become, to all intents and purposes, unwigglable." Ugh. "Nothing befuddles her. She is unbefuddlable." No. English is not primarily what is known as an *agglutinative* language, in which words are strings of distinct elements that naturally hook together, like Lego blocks. English does have agglutinated words, for instance *dog-catch-er*, but the elements of English are so diverse that its bits don't necessarily groove on one another.

A little Googling establishes that *Googleable* is most common on the Web. OED, as of this writing, does not recognize any Google-based word except the verb *Google*, first noted (in the participular form *googling*, with quote marks around it and a question mark after it) online on August 1, 1999, three years after Google began as a Stanford University research project called BackRub.

Mazzone's mom's "phrase" (a sequence of phrases, actually) is Google-able now, of course, because Googling *uffum buffum*, or *beefer dog trim*, brings up Mazzone's query. To call something unGoogleable in print is self-refuting.

Googling *uffum buffum* brings up something else: the sad story of Robert Buffum, who in 1863 was presented with one of the first Congressional Medals of Honor, and congratulated in person by President Abraham Lincoln, for his part in the hijacking of a Confederate locomotive, the exploit that inspired Buster Keaton's great movie *The General* and the Disney version, *The Great Locomotive Chase*. Eight years later, Buffum ended his life by cutting his own throat, in an asylum for the criminally insane.

Fellow soldiers said Buffum was a "small, bony" man, "argumentative and stubborn," "morose and downright garrulous," with "quick moving arms," "little bony arms, which were more like hand-spikes than arms." According to the Googleable book *Here Rests In Honored Glory* by Andrew J. DeKever, Buffum was "a family man and a committed abolitionist but also a whiskey-drinker . . . An avid fan of Shakespeare, he was known not only for praying and swearing at the same time, but also for engaging his comrades in 'absurd, pointless arguments,' such as when he tried to convince friends of his that a black hat was actually white."

Before they could get the captured locomotive into Union territory, Buffum and his comrades were captured and crammed into various fetid holes so stifling they could scarcely draw breath. Expecting to be hanged, Buffum prayed characteristically: "Lord, we are taught to pray for our enemies, therefore we pray Thee to have mercy on those god damned rebel sons of bitches, for they know not what they do."

After escaping once but being caught (he was said to be nimble and nervy, but not a good runner), Buffum was released in a prisoner exchange. He returned north a hero, which meant that people kept buying him a drink; and psychologically unfit for regular duty. He went AWOL. His new commander said, "His character is that of a jayhawker [see J], filibuster, and guerilla with a slight sprinkle of the horse thief." (*Filibuster* in those days meant a freebooting soldier who engaged in unauthorized warfare, bordering on piracy, against another state.)

Mustered out of the army, Buffum shot a man for saying Lincoln should be hanged. That man survived and didn't press charges, but Buffum spent time in an asylum in Worcester, Massachusetts, where conditions may not have been much more humane than the Confederate lockups. He got out, made enough money to buy a house for his family by helping to promote a comrade's book about the locomotive heist, and then shot another man to death, which is why he was in the asylum where he killed himself.

Had it not been for Mazzone's query, and my dissatisfaction with the word *unGoogleable*, I doubt I would ever have stumbled upon Buffum. There should be a word for . . . Wait a minute, let me check . . .

There is, in the chatosphere, such a word: *Googledipity*.

In English ("humble.life" quoting "gord," December 2005): "Found this as a result of 'Googledipity' while looking for something entirely different."

And in German ("Daggio" to "Brianna," December 2007): *"Also bisher fand ich Sie besser, aber wenn Sie schon bei so einfachen Begriffen wie 'Lost' versagt, dann gehe ich lieber zu Googledipity."*

Which may be translated as "So far I've found you better, but if you've already failed with simple terms such as 'Lost,' then I'd rather go to Googledipity."

Brianna's response to this is: ":rofl: Googledipity! :biggrin:"

Which of course means, in any language, "Rolling on the floor laughing. *Googledipity*! There is a big grin on my face." (The grin might also be represented by :D—tip it to the right and the colon forms eyes, the D a lopsided grin—which has been voted the most hated emoticon.)

Brianna goes on to wonder, *"Habt ihr mal Googledipity bei Google eingeben? :biggrin:"*

Which means, "Have you suggested 'Googledipity' to Google yet?"

Daggio does not respond to this question, perhaps taking it as rhetorical.

Serendipity was coined, in 1754, by Horace Walpole, the essayist and historian whom Lord Byron in the following century called greater than any living writer, "be he who he may." Walpole said he was inspired by a fairy tale about three princes from Serendip (a former name for Sri Lanka) who "were always making discoveries, by accidents and sagacity, of things they were not in quest of." As far as Googling can tell us, *Googledipity* was coined by "gord." But thanks to Mama Mazzone, I was first to define it on Urbandictionary.com. Example: "I Googled 'Lincoln' to find out about Town Cars, and found out we had a president by that name. Sheer Googledipity."

My mother sang "Chickery chick, cha-la, cha-la" around the house. Never knew where it came from. Just now Googled it. Novelty song, Sammy Kaye, three weeks at number one, *Billboard*, 1945.

See **Gmail?**

➤ *grammar/glamour*

The next time someone tries to tell you that grammar isn't glamorous, you can point out that *glamour* is a corrupt form of *grammar*. In the Middle Ages, *grammar* tended to mean learning in general, which to unlearned folk included the occult. By way of Scottish, the supposed magic-spell aspect of scholarship became *glamour*, as in "cast the glamour over her." Robert Burns in 1789 wrote of

> Ye gipsy-gang that deal in glamor,
> And you, deep-read in hell's black grammar,
> Warlocks and witches . . .

I'm always surprised when regular people think of glamour as reputable, rather than chi-chi. Of course I'm from Georgia, come from Methodist parents, and appear on National Public Radio, so I wouldn't know glamour if I stepped in it, but if *glamour* insists on ending in -*our*, it ought to go ahead and turn French and rhyme with *amour*. Note that it can't hold on to that *u* adjectivally: *glamorous*.

➤ *granular*

Jean Strouse on *granularity*: "I like this relatively recent addition to our vocab (the word isn't new, just the use, as in getting down to a granular level of detail). I said to a friend yesterday that the guy we were discussing doesn't 'get granular' about his work."

I concur—I mean, about the word, I don't know who the guy was, except that his name is legion. *Granular*, evoking both granules and grain as in the grain of wood or stone or skin . . .

You want to read a great quote? James Agee in *Let Us Now Praise Famous Men*, on coal oil:

> This "oil" is not at all oleaginous, but thin, brittle, rusty
> feeling, and sharp; taken and rubbed between forefinger and
> thumb, it so cleanses their grain that it sharpens their mutual
> touch to a new coin edge, or the russet nipple of a breast erected
> in cold.

Granular in itself is a granular word, which sounds like it ought to sound. *Gl-* words are *glib, glossy, glitz, glop,* and, yes, well, okay, *glory.*

Gr- words get us down to hard texture, the **nitty-gritty**.

In *Word Origins, and How We Know Them,* Anatoly Liberman writes that *gr-* has tended, in fact, to appear "in numerous words whose meaning can be understood as '(to produce) a nonsonorous sound (of discontent).' An association between *kr-, khr-,* and *gr-* with a growl or low roar is universal." Citing the terrible man who shouts "Goroo, goroo" at David Copperfield, Ayto goes on to say that "*Gr-* made people cower in the nineteenth century, as it did in the days of Grendel and the 'grinning' warriors of old." (To grin was originally to show pain or anger by baring the teeth.) A more directly relevant value of *gr-* to *granular* is, as Ayto points out, the sound of a grinding wheel.

Nobody ever said getting granular was a day at the beach—oh, wait a minute.

"A friend of mine," adds Jean Strouse, "now talks about manularity, as in doing the dishes by hand." I'll say this: writing is manual work. Maxim Gorky wrote of Leo Tolstoy, "Sometimes, when talking, he would move his fingers, and gradually close them into a fist, and then, suddenly opening them, utter a good full-weight word."

➤ *growsome*

There's a likable old word, meaning apt to grow or conducive to growth. OED cites an 1863 Staffordshire source, "Our pig is such a growsome little thing; it will eat anything"; and an 1877 Lincolnshire one, "It's growsome weather noo."

h · **H** · h

If letters were people, I could see bony *H* hanging out with round *O*. Oh. Ho. Hohoho. H_2O. *H* as bred-to-be-upright Prince Hal. *O* as eternally globular old Falstaff.

How fitting, then, that someone designing a new typeface will customarily begin with capital *H* and capital *O*. Designer Tobias Frere-Jones in *The New Yorker*:

> Just drawing the *H*, there are a number of choices to make. How substantial? How wide? Are there serifs, and, if so, how broad, how thick? When you get to the *O*, you have to decide how heavy the heaviest part of the letter should be. There are reasons it can't be the same as the *H*. If the heaviest part of the *O* is the same as the heaviest part of the *H*, the *O* will look too thin, because the *O* reaches its heaviest weight only for a moment, whereas the *H* gets to hold that maximum weight all the way to the top. Also, if you draw the capital *H* and *O* at the same height, that *O* will look too short, so the base of the *O* has to fall a bit lower than the *H*, and the top has to rise a bit higher for them to seem compatible.

> ➤ Haskell, Eddie

American television has produced many indelible characters—Urkel, Paulie Walnuts, Roseanne Roseannadanna, Dan Rather, Bubbles on *The Wire*—but only one stone archetype. Eddie.

➤ *head*

Originally, in Old English, this word was *héafod*, pronounced more or less *heh*-uh-vud. Perhaps we have all known mornings when that felt about right. Even the modern *head*, pronounced *hed*, is heavy compared to French *tête*, Italian *testa*, Spanish *cabeza*, or Latin *caput* (which by the way is not related to *kaput* meaning finished but does happen to be *Tupac* backward). Even German *Kopf* has more bounce than *head*. Why does such a potentially uplifting part of the body rhyme with *dead* and *lead* and *dread*? It is no inducement to thinking. "Why don't you use your head?" parents say.

"Don't want to. Want to use my hips," b'dumpadump.

Head does, however, have gravitas. That's why it's hard to hold up.

Why do we say that someone fell "head over heels," when that is the upright order of things? Ernest **Weekley** called the phrase "a curious perversion" of the Middle English "heels over head."

While "head over heels" may be illogical, it has the right rhythm. Let us ask ourselves why.

We say *tip-top*—see **blob**—instead of *top-tip* because *top* has a broader, heavier sound: *top-tip* is top-heavy, about to topple, and we don't want that in *tip-top*. We do want it in *head over heels*, and *head* is heavier than *heels*.

Here's a consideration: "I'm head over heels in love" connotes falling forward, headlong. "I'm heels over head in love" suggests feet slipping out from under, causing a person to fall backward. Doesn't it?

I know this: "head over" is faster to say, more sudden, less deliberate, than "heels over." "Let's not have Amy and Ed over" tumbles out. "Let's not have the McNeils over" requires careful articulation.

Eelzover is an interesting sound—"I'll have two eels over easy," "This dream feels overdetermined"—but it doesn't turn over readily, like *eddover*, like an easy-cranking car. "Now the back wheel's over my leg"—the tongue must pick its way through. Compare: "Let's move your bed over next to mine." "The trail led over the hill."

At the phrase's end, on the other hand, *heels* works well. The long vowel (*wheee*, *eeek*), the liquid *l*, the buzz at the end—it sprawls. Well, it doesn't exactly sprawl, because nothing sprawls like *sprawl*, but *head* at the end would jam on the brakes; *heels* evokes extended loss of control. *Head over heels* is fun to say.

The tongue hath its reasons that reason doth not necessarily know, until reason takes into account the physicality of the tongue, without which, where would reason be? Oral gratification trumps logic. That's one reason our heads feel like *héafods* some mornings.

➤ headlines

There is something about a good news*paper* headline that I fear will not be perpetuated online. Here is a great headline from the nonvirtual *New York Times*:

GERMANY, FORCED

TO BUOY GREECE,

RUES EURO SHIFT

What that is, is a triumph of compression. But headlines can be more alluring than that. In the paper-and-ink *Berkshire Eagle* I read:

COCONUT-CARRYING OCTOPUS FOUND

And I do want to know about the octopus (which, *Current Biology* reports, has been filmed collecting coconut shells for shelter—"the first evidence of tool use in an invertebrate animal"), but I also love the headline itself, which fits its four-column space, to a *T*, and is metrically gratifying. Let's see if we can't incorporate that headline into a verse form discussed in *Alphabet Juice*, the double dactyl:

Higgledy-piggledy,
Current Biology
Now is reporting, to
Plaudits all round,

Divers have proof of in-
Vertebrate tool-use: a
Coconut-carrying
Octopus found.

And how about the poetry (without going into the meter, which is essentially iambic, with a variant first line) of this headline from *The New York Times* (over a story suggesting that it is too soon—as always—for New York's National League baseball team to feel good about itself):

METS, MISSING LEADERSHIP,

ARE WISE TO TEMPER JOY

"Are wise to temper joy." Where are you going to find language that poetic anymore (not in contemporary poetry, surely) except in headlines? Yet headlines tend to be stereotyped as superficial hypery!

So often, a headline is anything but sensational. This was the *lead* headline in *The Berkshire Eagle* one day in 2010:

COUNTY

WELLNESS

LAGGING

➤ *hiccup*

OAD's definition seems fine, if a bit over the top, until the last word: "an involuntary spasm of the diaphragm and respiratory organs, with a sudden closure of the glottis and a characteristic sound like that of a cough." A cough? To me a hiccup sounds more like a reaction to being clotheslined (to use the felicitous football term for running into a forearm with your Adam's apple), only somewhat more upbeat. AHD's definition is better: "A spasm of the diaphragm resulting in a rapid, involuntary inhalation that is stopped by the sudden closure of the glottis and accompanied by a sharp, distinctive sound."

Sometimes *hiccup*, pronounced the same way, is spelled *hiccough*. If the *gh* were intended to be pronounced as in *ugh*, there would be some **sonicky** justification for this, but anything that looks like it ought to be pronounced *hih-coff* is a denial of basic onomatopoeia. I don't think anybody quite articulates a *p* in hiccupping (the French go *hoquet*, Danes *hikke*, Walloons *hikéte*, Swedes *hicka*, the Dutch just *hik*), but the lips do come together at the end, as if preparing to form a *p*. There is something to be said for *up* in that a hiccup makes your torso bounce.

Walter W. Skeat in his discussion of this "spasmodic inspiration" alludes to the expression "a hacking **cough**" (also to *hitch*—a hiccup is a hitch in one's oral getalong) but as to the spelling *hiccough* he is firm: "seems to be due to a popular etymology from *cough*, certainly wrong; no one ever so pronounces the word."

Some hiccups might have more of a *higg* sound to them. Skeat points out that the Welsh have a word *ig* meaning sob.

Why not *hickup*? Too quick. We are familiar with *pickup, stickup, lick up, brick up, trick up, **prick** up*, but I don't think there's another word in English with *-iccu-* in it. (A mysterious tenth-century *sticcum* crops up in OED's entry on *ice*, but it warrants neither its own entry nor credit as an ancestor of the American colloquial *stickum*, which OED first finds in print in 1909.)

Note that when two hard *c*'s come together in a two-word phrase—*public cup*, say, or *static cling*—they don't run together. Each is sounded separately. So *-iccu-* educes a mental hic'cup. Previous attempts to get *hiccup* right were *hickock* and *hicket*, both of which Skeat thinks were "better forms" than *hiccup*. But there's no glottal hitch in those *ck*'s. And *hiccet* would look like it should be pronounced *hik-set*, maybe, and *hiccock*—well, that might not be bad. Etymonline.com says all of these forms replaced Old English "*aelfsogoða*, so called because hiccups were thought to be caused by elves." We know today, of course, that they are caused by Wiccans.

Just kidding! If Wicca were a corporation, we might suspect it of spelling itself funny to attract attention. But Wicca the neopaganistic sect, also known as the Old Religion, comes by its name traditionally, *wicca* being Old English for wizard. Male wizard, actually. The female was *wicce*, which in modern English would not look like anything.

➤ *hippopotamus*

From the Latin for horse and river, but you don't have to know that to enjoy saying the word while thinking of or looking at the animal in question. *Hippopotamus* sounds appropriately ponderous, not to mention hippy and bottomous. French *hippopotame* is too perky, if you ask me.

➤ *hopefully*

One can see why a public official would like to say, "Hopefully, the ecosystem will not collapse" instead of "I hope the ecosystem will not collapse." The latter is more straightforward. It is more nearly responsible. Yet it sounds relatively wishy-washy. In the *Idaho State Journal* of August 20, 2009, an Idaho Fish and Game official, when asked whether hunters would be able to track down wolves by tapping into the frequencies of their radio collars, responded as follows: "I don't think so. I hope not. I don't know if that would be considered fair chase. I'm pretty sure that would be against the law."

For his own job-covering sake (and maybe even, who knows?, the wolves') he would have been better off saying, "Thinkfully, no. Hopefully not. Nonknowfully, that would be considered fair chase. Pretty be-fully sure, that would be against the law."

So, go ahead, make your peace with *hopefully*, but don't come complaining to me when a publisher sends you this rejection:

"Regretfully, our dog ate your manuscript. Mournfully, your manuscript killed him. Doubtfully, you can write anything now we will read with pleasure."

➤ *humble*

Almost inevitably, a person who has just been given grounds for feeling high pride, in public will instead profess to be humbled. "Thank you, Mr. President," said Sonia Sotomayor when nominated for the U.S. Supreme Court, "for the most humbling honor of my life." Jerry Lewis, in his acceptance of a lifetime-achievement Oscar, went, not surprisingly, farther: "My humility in this moment is staggering." There may be cases, then, where it is humility that goeth before a fall. But I am content to believe that the average person cannot possibly comprehend the *titanic* humility a Jerry Lewis can feel.

About *humble* there is something aw-shucks and down-to-earth. Like *humus*, earth, *humble* comes from Latin *humilis*, lowly. But no one is likely to say, when honored, "I have never been so humiliated." *Humble* has a homey sound—*hum, bumble*. The bumblebee was originally called a humblebee.

But David Simon, auteur of the great TV series *The Wire*, says that "to give a humble," in Baltimore law-enforcement parlance, is to arrest some-one—whose offense had otherwise been too routine to warrant his being charged—because the perp presumed to give the officer a dirty look: "He eye-fucked me so I gave him a humble."

➤ hunch

A fine example of a **sonicky** word, and there are scientific grounds for say-ing so. IN BATTLE, HUNCHES PROVE TO BE VALUABLE ASSETS was the headline of a story in which *The New York Times* reported, unsurprisingly, that in combat you often don't have time to think; you have to react to subtle cues. "As the brain tallies cues," the *Times* reported, "it may send out an alarm before a person fully understands why."

And how do hunches manifest themselves in the body? That question was addressed by a 1997 experiment in which people chose cards based purely on hunches. When a hunch was coming on, "their bodies usually tensed up—subtly, but significantly." Subtle tensing was quantified, in this case, by "careful measures of sweat," but I can recall, from tense situations, the physical tensing, or coiling, that comes with the flash of how to react.

The noun *hunch*, meaning a premonition or an unreasoned basis for action, derives from the verb to *hunch*, which means, according to AHD, to "bend or draw up," to "assume a crouched or cramped position." Pro-nouncing the word *hunch* tenses up the whole vocal apparatus.

➤ hyphen

Far too much hyphenation goes on in popular media today. On *The Huffing-ton Post* we read of a senator "worried about the supposedly-lax" language in a bill, and another who "would support a less-restrictive proposal." Huffpo, again: "The president's actions in the wake of the BP disaster has been a case-in-point." (Subject-verb disagreement there, too.)

The New York Times: "220,000 voters the G.O.P. can ill-afford to lose" and "to venture into even-deeper waters."

A post on the Romenesko news-of-the-media site: "I was pretty-much broke at the time."

Andrew Sullivan's website quoted Barack Obama: "I believe that change comes not from the top-down, but from the bottom-up."

AP photo caption: "California quarterback Kevin Riley hands-off to tailback Jahvid Best."

I despise every one of those hyphens (except mine in *news-of-the-media*). They form clumps. It's as if perfectly functional individual words can't be trusted to stay on track unless they are forced to hold hands.

I can't believe that any stylebook sanctions those hyphens. It is standard practice, however, to underhyphenate when an expression of more than one word is joined to another word. For instance, in Ron Powers's estimable biography of Mark Twain, someone is referred to as "a little main chance-struck." Surely that needs to be "main-chance-struck." In *Paste* magazine, we find a "Jack Kerouac-by-way-of-Tom Waits tune." That looks like someone named Jack Waits whose middle name is Kerouac-by-way-of-Tom. And how about this, from the *Times*: ". . . plans to open seven gyms in the area for high school-aged basketball players." School-aged players who are high? (This was the *Times*'s attempt to improve upon LeBron James, who had announced on Nike's website his plans to open such gyms for "high-school aged" players. LeBron's version is better, but it suggests players who have become aged in high school. Why not "high-school-aged players"? Or, better, "high-school-age.")

Somewhere online I came upon this dictum from a New York University editing workshop: "The hyphen has no analogue in speech; it is punctuation created purely by the needs of print." That makes no sense. All punctuation was created "by the needs of print." And a hyphen is, or should be, audibly significant, nearly as vocal as a comma. Surely NYU can hear the difference between the *stuck-up* in "You're a stuck-up little snob" and the *stuck up* in "You're stuck up," or "You stuck up a bank?" In *stuck-up*, there is more stress on *stuck*, a bit of a push, so that it catches onto *up*. In *stuck up*, the stress is equal between *stuck* and *up*, so the two are distinct. In its original Greek form, the hyphen was probably an indication (Chambers) "that two notes were to be held or blended together in music." In print today, the hyphen betokens a quickening that pointedly connects two words into one.

A hyphen is something you need to get a feel for. The great radio comedian Fred Allen, whose voice was notably nasal, once wrote to Groucho

Marx that he was "taking a refresher course" in "nose oratory." Eschewing capital letters, as he was wont to do in correspondence, Allen went on: a "problem that confronts the man who talks through his nose is the hyphenated word. saying the word quickly, one part can come down each nostril. the catch is how to handle the hyphen. it takes quick thinking to . . . decide instantly which way you will tip the hyphen to have it tumble out of the nostril you have chosen."

i · I · i

In electronics (iPhone, iMac, iPod, iPad), little-letter *i* has come to loom larger than any capital *I*. *The New York Times* quotes David Sloan, producer of a TV program called *i-Caught*, which exploits video clips sent in by viewers: "the 'i' is emblematic. It stands for information and the Internet. It also stands for the first person, . . . active, user-generated content that's catching something of the moment. Who'd have thought one little skinny lowercase letter could mean so much?"

"The small-'i' trend," says the *Times*, "seems to have begun in earnest with the arrivals in 1995 of iVillage.com, a Web site aimed at women, and in 1996 of the iMac computer from Apple. 'I guess I could say, "Ay, ay, ay," but flattery is a beautiful thing,' said Deborah I. [note middle initial] Fine, president at iVillage Properties in New York."

This, on the *Times*'s part, is a terrible lapse in phonetic spelling. Obviously what Ms. Fine said was "i-yi-yi."

The reporter (or copy desk) may have been thinking of *aye*, which Etymonline.com calls "perhaps a variant of *I*, meaning 'I assent,'" or of the Middle English *yai*, meaning "yes"; or that *aye* may derive from the other *aye*, which means "always, ever." Both those *aye*'s are pronounced like *eye*, as in "Aye, aye, sir." But "Ay, ay, ay" is A, A, A.

See **A**.

➤ *ingenuity*

Etymologically, *ingenuity* ought to mean ingenuousness: candor, artlessness. Instead, it means ingeniousness: cleverness, imaginative skill, which is pretty much the opposite.

Before we dare to imagine how such a thing can have happened in an upstanding language such as English, let's look at the core that *ingenious* and *ingenuous* share. Many English words incorporate this *gen*, whose roots relate to birth—*generate, congenital, genesis*—and by extension to kind or nature—*genus, gentry, gene*. According to Etymonline.com, the early meaning of *ingenuous* evolved from "with the virtues of freeborn people" into "honorably straightforward." (More recently, perhaps owing to a rise in cynicism, or to the dramatic influence of *ingenue*, we are likely to think of *ingenuous* as meaning about the same as *naïve*—which also derives from *gen* via Latin words meaning innate, natural.)

Ingenious, on the other hand, comes from the Latin for "gifted, with inborn talent."

But people have for centuries confused *ingenuous* with *ingenious*. As a result, *ingenuity* long ago came to mean ingeniousness. And however ingenious we may be, there's nothing we can do about that now.

We can, however, slip into our loose-speculation shoes and try to figure out what caused the confusion. To the eye, *ingenious* and *ingenuous* look a lot alike, but to the ear, *i/u* isn't the only difference. The *e* in *ingenious* is long, forceful, as in *genial, genius, genie, gee!* (The *i*, which sounds like a long *e* itself, seems to bring out the beast, so to speak, in the preceding *e*.) The *e* in *ingenuous* is short—soft, we might call it, as in *gentle*, or reassuring, as in *genuine*, or anyway impartial, as in *general, gender*. This difference between the *e*'s is appropriate to the different meanings.

But then when you try to turn *ingenious* into an *-ity* noun you get *ingenity*. Now the *i* following the *e* is pronounced *ih*, not *ee*, and *ingenity* wants to rhyme with *serenity, amenity, lenity*. The *e* that was *ee* becomes *eh*.

On the other hand, when you turn *ingenuous* into an *-ity* noun, you get *ingenuity*. The stress shifts from the soft *e* to the oomphy *u*. "Ooo! What ingenuity!" sounds in accord with "Gee! That's ingenious!" The ingenuity of the ingenious tongue and ear defy etymological consistency.

(If *ingenious* had been *ingeneous*, the noun could have been *ingeneity*, as in *homogeneous* and *homogeneity*. But *ingeneous* might have been reduced to *ingenous*—as *homogeneous* has largely been replaced, in popular usage, by *homogenous*. The influence of *homogenize* has probably had a lot to do with the latter shift, and there's no such word as *ingenize*. Visually, though, *ingeneous* might have been too close to *igneous*, which has to do with fire.)

➤ *"Is the pope fallible?," alternatives to*

Has a cat got a climbing gear?

Does a fat dog fart?

Would a fifty-pound bag of flour make a big biscuit? (No good anymore, been co-opted by TV commercial.)

Does the pope wear a funny hat?

See **zythum**.

➤ *itch*

This seems such a natural word, you'd think it occurred early on to Adam. But at one point in Middle English it was *yekth*, and an old Scots form was *yuke* or *yeuk* ("When I get that dry yeukin' in my thrapple"). OED's first citation of the intransitive verb *itch* as we spell it today is from Shakespeare, *Troilus and Cressida*: "I would thou didst itch from head to foot, and I had the scratching of thee." Quite possibly a romantic sentiment, between the two lovers. But no, it's Thersites—"I would make thee the loathsomest scab in Greece," he continues—exchanging insults with Ajax.

Here's a poignant note: in one form or another, according to OED, *itch* goes back to circa 1000, but *scratch* didn't arise until the sixteenth century! Sure, before *scratch* there were *scrat* and *cratch*, both of which carried the meaning of *scratch*—but the violent, aggressive meaning. Not until the sixteenth century does OED find an example of *scrat* meaning to scratch for pleasure, "To rub lightly with the finger-nails, etc., to relieve itching or the like." By that time, *scratch* was taking over. OED says *scratch* was probably a "confusion" of *scrat* and *cratch*. Okay, I'm going to get romantic again: Don't you think maybe the *s-* from *scrat* softened *cratch*, and the *-ch* from *cratch* connected *scrat* to *itch*? The language itched, and itched, and finally found its *scratch*.

Oh, *thrapple* is throat.

j · J · j

On the face of it, "naked as a jaybird" is a mystery. Some of our pinker feathered friends might evoke human nudity, but you'd have to really want them to, and surely you don't. "Barefooted as a yard dog" speaks for itself, but a jaybird looks overdressed if anything.

First of all, why *jaybird*? A jay is already a bird. Is there a parallel in *tuna fish*? No, *tuna fish* applies specifically, as AHD puts it, to "the edible flesh of tuna, often canned or processed." I don't know what other processed form of tuna there is, than canned. Liquified and bottled? But never mind that. Is *tuna fish* some kind of crazy euphemism, so we don't have to say "tunaflesh sandwich"? No. We don't say "salmonflesh croquettes." (Germans do however call pork *Schweinefleisch*.)

You know how I think *tuna fish* arose? I can't prove it, but see if this doesn't make sense: a parent opens a can of tuna. A child looks inside and says, "What is *that*?"

Parent: "Tuna."

Child (backing away): "What . . . is . . . tuna?"

Parent: "It's fish! Don't worry about it!"

But we're talking primarily about *jaybird*, here, and I don't know anyone who has eaten, or been served, jaybird in any form.

So. Where does *jay* come from? AHD and many other sources (OED, though, says origin obscure) assert, or suggest, that (like *martin* and *robin*, from those English personal names), it's from the Latin personal name Gaius. Even if this is so, nobody calls a robin a robinbird. Nor is *jaybird* like *johnboat* or *tomcat*, because *john* doesn't stand alone as a boat, nor does *tom* (quite) stand alone as a cat. *Jay* does stand alone as a bird, without the *-bird*.

As to the derivation of *jay*, I don't see how etymologists can ignore the fact that the blue jay's most common cry, according to the *Sibley Guide to Birds*, is "a shrill, harsh, descending scream *jaaaay*." Granted, a blue jay by the same authority can go *toolili* on occasion, and *shkrrr* when attacking a raptor.

And a Steller's jay most commonly emits "a harsh, unmusical, descending *shaaaar*" and sometimes "a rapid, popping *shek shek shek shek*" and "a clear *whidoo.*"

And a western scrub jay "a harsh, rising *shreeeenk*" and a *wenk wenk wenk* or *kkew kkew kkew*, also "a harsh, pounding *sheeyuk sheejuk*" and "a low chuckling *chudduk.*"

And a Florida scrub jay "a distinctly lower, harsher, flatter, less rising *kreesh*" and "a low, husky *kereep.*"

And a Mexican jay "a rather soft, musical, rising *zhenk* or *wink.*"

And a green jay "a harsh, electric *jeek jeek jeek jeek*" and "a high, mechanical *slikslikslikslik*" and "a nasal *been*" and "a high, nasal *unneeek-neek* or *grreen-rren*" and a "drawn-out clicking *ree urrrrrrrr it.*"

And a brown jay "an intense, clear bugling *keerg* or *paow.*"

And a pinyon jay delivers "a soft, conversational series *hoi hoi hoi . . .* or single *hoya*" and "a series of harsher rising notes *kwee kwee kwee . . .* and loud, clear, nasal *waoow.*"

And a grey jay "generally soft, whistled or husky notes . . . from clear *weeoo* and *weef weef weef weef* to musical, husky *chuf-chuf-weef* and very rough, dry *kreh kreh kreh*" (also "a screeching *jaaay* reminiscent of," and in fact perhaps imitative of, a blue jay).

So, what, it's a coincidence that blue jays go *jaaaay*? They found out they were called jays, so they started calling *jaaaay*?

I don't know. I do know that, based on years of observing blue jays whether I wanted to be observing them or not, that if a jaybird were naked, it would strut around ostentatiously representing nudism. Telling all the other birds—squirrels, even—*they* should only look so good so naked. A jaybird is naked as in the expressions "naked aggression," "naked power," "naked censorship" (as opposed to subtle governmental pressure on the media), "naked avarice." Expressions that, come to think of it, we don't hear much anymore, perhaps because people are jaded.

Does *jay* have intrinsic value? It has the abruptness of *Hey!* or *Say!* It's at home in hip-hop culture: *Dee Jay, Jay-Z, Jay Smooth, Dr. Jay's, triple j, Jay Rock, Jay and Silent Bob Strike Back*, and so on. Then, until he died of "cocaine toxicity with alcohol as a contributing factor," there was punk rocker Jimmy Lee Lindsey Jr., who performed as Jay Reatard.

A jay is a joint, and *vajayjay* is slang for *vagina*. A *popinjay*—the English adaptation of, ultimately, Arabic *babgha*, which was probably imitative of the bird's call—is a parrot and by extension a vain, gaudy person. A *jay-hawker* was a guerrilla/pillager in Bloody Kansas before, during, and after the Civil War; presumably the free-state cutthroats in question came on as bold as jays and as deadly as hawks. (Today, they might drink Jäger-meister.) Before it managed to wedge its way into the English alphabet, the very letter *J*, which was often represented as an *I* but with the soft-*g* sound, was regarded as a crass interloper. OED quotes this sixteenth-century huff: "Now as concerning *I* consonant, which oftentimes vniustly vsurpeth the sound and place of *G*: me thinke it hath small reason: or rather I may say it is verie absurd, and much against both Art and reason."

Probably owing to jaybirds' uncool image, in the United States beginning in the nineteenth century, *jay* meant hayseedy, hicky, bumpkinish, ill adapted to urban ways—as in the Irving Berlin song, sung by Jimmy Cagney as George M. Cohan in *Yankee Doodle Dandy*, "Forty-Five Minutes From Broadway": "Oh what a fine bunch of rubens, / Oh what a jay atmosphere." Hence *jaywalker*, a person who has no more sense than to walk out into traffic. Today in Manhattan, hip pedestrians jaywalk advisedly, going not by lights but by their feel for street flow, but try that in Dallas and you'll get a ticket. (God knows Dallas is jay.)

➢ Jack

The quintessential English male nickname. On both sides of the pond we use it generically, as in *I'm All Right, Jack*, "Hit the Road, Jack," jumping jack, every man jack, lumberjack, steeplejack, you don't know jack, jack-of-all-trades, Jack Frost, jack-o'-lantern, Jack the Ripper, Jack and Jill.

Jack is the common man, and by extension a nonroyal face card, or a mechanical fellow laborer: a jackknife, a jackhammer, or just a jack. Here's a democratic tip of the hat to a nation that calls its flag the Union Jack.

How *Jack* arose as a diminutive of *John* is not clear. It may have been influenced by *Jacques*, which however is the French equivalent of *James* (from which we get *jimmy*, as to jimmy a lock). It is clear that *jack* has a snappy charge to it, from the energizing *j* through the fast bright *a* to the quick stop of *ck*.

Money is jack, and in baseball a home run is a jack, from the verb to *jack*, as in "jack it out."

I hope some of you out there are old enough to remember Jack Benny. On radio and TV, he portrayed himself as a skinflint. He once asked his factotum, Rochester, who is sharpening a pencil, "Roch, would you mind sharpening that in the fireplace?" Benny was born Benjamin Kubelsky. He was still unestablished in show business, and was calling himself Ben K. Benny, when he joined the navy during World War I. In those days, all sailors called each other "Jack." That's how he came up with his stage name. Jack Benny. It's as bouncy as Bob (born Leslie) Hope, Bing (born Harry) Crosby, or Jim Dandy.

➤ *jejune*

An inapt-sounding word, since it means barren (or as OED puts it expansively, "Unsatisfying to the mind or soul; dull, flat, insipid, bald, dry, uninteresting; meagre, scanty, thin, poor; wanting in substance or solidity") and has *june* in it. Jejunity may, regrettably, be bustin' out all over, but you don't want to think about a jejune bride.

Well, *jejune* was borrowed from Latin *ieiunus*. Latin had no *j*. Latin's *i* was originally a *y* sound. *Yeyune* sounds more like *jejune* ought to.

The pronunciation of *jejune* given in Chambers, *jijün*, is a rare occurrence of five dots in a row.

➤ *joke, linguists', which I don't get either*

From Geoffrey K. Pullum at *Language Log*, the linguistics blog:

> Q: Two linguists were walking down the street. Which one was the specialist in contextually indicated deixis and anaphoric reference resolution strategies?
>
> A: The other one.

➤ juice

The word *juicy* would be juicier—over-the-top juicy, too literally mouth-watering—if it were *jucious*, as in *luscious*, *delicious*, *scrumptious*, *lubricious*, *squishy*, **supercalifragilisticexpialidocious**. Early English spellings of *juice* (when *i* could stand for a *j* sound) include *iuyshe*, *iwisch*, *iuwys*, and *iwse*. All were attempts to adapt French *jus*.

Jus just wouldn't work in English, because of children.

"Drink your orange jus."

"Yuck. Rhymes with—"

"Don't say it!"

Hence the *-uice*, which looks odd the more you stare at it, but it's like the *-uit* in *fruit*, the *-uise* in *bruise*. We must concede to French *jus* a juicier *j*. But *juice* will do, by golly, *juice* will do. Sometimes I squeeze a little more out of it by saying "j(y)oose," to rhyme with *deuce*.

See **Dionysian, Apollonian, blended, briefly** and **-sh, sh-**.

➤ jump

Good basic English word. How would you define it? And can't use your feet. OED is on it:

> To make a spring from the ground or other base by flexion and
> sudden muscular extension of the legs (or, in the case of some
> animals, as fish, of the tail, or other part); to throw oneself upward,
> forward, backward or downward, from the ground or point of
> support; to leap, spring, bound . . .

You think that's that? No, OED knows there's a distinction to be made:

> . . . to leap with the feet together, as opposed to *hopping* on one leg.

Okay. But was *jump* with us from jump, or the jump, or jump street, that is to say from the jumping-off point, the get-go, the beginning? No. There was *leap*, there was *spring*, but there was no *jump* until the sixteenth century. And no one knows where it jumped in from. John Ayto in his *Dictionary of Word Origins* says "etymologists fall back [so to speak] on the notion that it may originally have been intended to suggest the sound of jumping feet hitting the ground (the similar sounding *bump* and *thump* are used to support this theory)." The *ump* part, yeah, but how about the *j*? Maybe intended to suggest the kind of kinetic energy that gets words like *jab* and **Jack** and *jig* and *jerk* and *juke* under way?

And *leap*, somehow, is relatively high-flown. Would *leap ball* or *leap blues* or *leap cut* or *leap shot* or *leap start* have the requisite charge? *Spring* is tight, all right, and yet it borders on the lah-di-dah. Feeling springy and feeling jumpy are different things. We needed *jump*. So we summoned it from our vocal apparatus.

k · **K** · k

When, ironically enough, people are treating *fuck* as ineffable, they speak of "the *f*-word," of "effing." But a great deal of the word's *kick* is in its final letter. Try saying, "What the fub?" or "Let's go somewhere and fud" or "I will fuff you up" or "We fummed ourselves silly" or "Fur 'em if they can't take a joke" or "When desperate housewives fuv around, they don't fuv around."

And in *West Side Story*, the delinquents did not sing, "Officer Frupfe, frupf you."

➤ *kick*

John Ayto in his *Dictionary of Word Origins* calls this "one of the mystery words of English. It first appears towards the end of the 14th century, but no one knows where it came from, and it has no relatives in the other Indo-European languages."

Well, it sounds right. Its first uses in English are attributed to the dissident Catholic theologian and translator John Wycliffe, or people associated with him (called Lollards). In a tract published around 1380, the author tells "secular lords" they should get right with Jesus, because (my modernized paraphrase) "It is too hard to kick against the spur—you should know that this harms you. For it takes away soul-help from you and your people." Around 1382, Wycliffe and his circle produced the first English translation of the Bible. In the ninth chapter of Acts, Saul is on his way to Damascus, bent upon arresting any Christians he can find there, when a blinding flash of light brings him to his *knee*s, and a voice asks, "Why persecutest thou me?"

"Who that?" asks Saul.

"I am Jesus whom thou persecutest; it is hard for thee to kick against the **prick**s." By "hard for thee" is meant "hard *on* thee." In other words, when you kick back against the prick of a spur or a goad—as is the natural reaction of a horse or an ox—you just make it worse for yourself than if you go along with the divine guidance that the prick represents. Christ has been prodding Saul into becoming a Christian himself, and to fight back is folly. Saul converts on the spot and goes on to become the Apostle Paul.

Did Jesus use words like *kick* and *prick*? Maybe not. The foregoing direct quotations are from the King James Version, which retained the Wycliffian "kick against the pricks" expression. The Wycliffe version was a translation of the Latin Vulgate version, *durum est tibi contra stimulum calcitrare*, the antepenultimate word meaning a cattle prod, sometimes used against slaves, and *calcitrare* (from which English gets *recalcitrant*) meaning, according to *Cassell's Latin Dictionary*, "to strike with the heel, kick" or "to resist obstinately" or "to writhe the feet about, at death." Heel in Latin was *calx*, spur was *calcar*, so *calcitrare* derives from the way animals, not humans, kick, except when humans are riding an animal and wearing spurs.

The Vulgate version, in turn, was a translation of Erasmus's version of the original Greek, where the word for "pricks" is a word usually translated as "goads." But in earlier Greek manuscripts, the expression "kick against the pricks" does not occur at that point. It does occur in chapter 26, verse 14, where Paul, in chains, is describing to the Roman governor Agrippa his conversion, and he says that Jesus spoke to him in Hebrew. Since versions of "kick against the pricks" had popped up in classical literature since well before the birth of Christ, Paul may have been departing from direct literal quotation to use an expression that Agrippa would understand.

Within a few years after the Wycliffe Bible, a very different character from St. Paul, Chaucer's Wife of Bath, asserted on the road to Canterbury that it is wise to flatter a woman, not reprove her, because anyone, if scratched on his or her sore spot, will kick. The first use of *kick* as a noun was "Kicke of an horse."

So kicking begins as knee-jerk bucking or payback, instinctive, quick: *kick*. Over centuries the concept has expanded—to kick the bucket, to kick someone in the pants, to kick a ball, kick as the recoil of a rifle, kick as a jerk or jolt, and kick as (OED) "a strong or sharp stimulant effect, . . . a thrill, excitement, pleasure."

Louis Armstrong, when Murray Kempton told him how much he liked his record of "When You're Smilin'," replied, "I was working the house band at the Paramount when I was young. And the lead trumpet stood up and played that song, and I just copied what he did note for note. I never found out his name but there was kicks in him. There's kicks everywhere."

➤ kiss

William Makepeace Thackeray, in *Pendennis*, pointed out that this word, used to represent both "the salute which you perform on your grandmother's forehead, and that which you bestow on the sacred cheek of your mistress," is of four letters, "not one of them a labial." A labial is a letter whose utterance requires complete or partial closure (and generally some pooching) of the lips: *p*, *b* (*buss*, *baiser*), *m*, *w* (note the air-kiss sound, *mwah*), *f*, *v*, and the rounded vowels, basically *o* and *oo*. That's why *smooch* (compare German *schmusen*) is better. Even for your grandmother, though for her you might want to cut it off at *smoo*.

See *ch*.

➤ kludge

Here's a word that gets computer people's *juice*s flowing. Though *kludge* may date farther back in oral culture (see online discussion at Michael Quinion's World Wide Words), OED calls it "J. W. Granholm's jocular invention." In a 1962 article, "How to Design a Kludge," in the computer magazine *Datamation*, Granholm defined *kludge* as "an ill-assorted collection of poorly-matching parts, forming a distressing whole." Granholm said it "derived from the same root as the German *Kluge* . . . , originally meaning 'smart' or 'witty,'" and "eventually came to mean 'not so smart' or 'pretty ridiculous.'" Granholm added that "the building of a Kludge . . . is not work for amateurs. There is a certain, indefinable, masochistic finesse that must go into true Kludge building."

According to Quinion, *kludge* "is used in computing and electronics . . . for a hastily improvised solution to some fault or bug, but doesn't seem to have moved much outside those fields, if at all."

It should do. Whether pronounced *klooj*, as dictionaries have it (roughly following the German), or to rhyme with *fudge*, it's **sonicky** enough, and it certainly applies to a great many things besides computers. Granholm, known outside the OED as Jackson Granholm, had a long career in aerospace and electronic physics. On the side he wrote frequently about "things that were basically silly in the computing world," as he put it in an interview. He would "take a five-page IBM press release and edit it for content and end up [with] two lines."

The "many idiocies welded into" computer programs that Granholm pointed out in that interview included the weird-looking numbers at the bottom of a bank check:

> I reach in my checkbook and take out a check and it's got magnetic
> character recognition on the bottom . . . And every bank in the
> world has that, and they have that because Bank of America footed
> the bill to do it, really, and then sold the project to General Electric.
> So the whole world uses magnetic ink. Optical recognition was just as
> well-developed, in fact came along before magnetic ink character
> recognition was done. And if that were used, we could use an
> ordinary typographer's font . . . readable by any human being as well
> as any machine, and we would have eliminated the cost of magnetic
> ink, special type fonts, and revision of printing technology in order
> to have checks processed by a machine. It didn't happen that way.
> And it's never going to go back. The stupidity is wired in now.

Granholm, who grew up in Puyallup, Washington, was an Army Air Force officer in World War II, therefore familiar with a wide range of kludges. In 2000 he published, in the UK for some reason, a lively memoir, *The Day We Bombed Switzerland: Flying with the US Eighth Army Air Force in World War II*. He was appointed defense counsel in the court-martialing of two young pilots who happened, by mistake, to bomb Zurich. A remarkable aspect of the trial is that the presiding judge was Colonel James Stewart, who behaved in that real-life situation as you would expect one of the characters he played in the movies to do. He was fair minded, unpretentious, and smooth. When the corporal charged with recording the complex testimony began to sob softly, Stewart said, "Just a doggone minute here! Let's just hold it up here a bit. This poor lady is snowed with all this big technical talk. Yeah, yeah, that's all right dear. Just take your time."

➤ *knee*

From a PIE root *g(e)neu-*, whence French *genou*, Italian *ginocchio*, and, in English, *genuflect*. John Ayto in his *Dictionary of Word Origins* adds *genuine*, from the ancient custom of a father's acknowledging a newborn as his own by placing the infant on his knee. But now I see that OED and Chambers both throw cold water on this notion, which was the only reason I got into *knee* in the first place.

Seems like it should be an interesting word. Popular song from 1918: "Would You Rather Be a Colonel with an Eagle on Your Shoulder (Or a Private with a Chicken on Your Knee)?" In England at about the same time, the song "Knees Up, Mother Brown!" urged the lady in question to cheer up and dance, giving rise to the term *knees-up*, meaning a party.

To "give a knee" to a boxer, in England in the nineteenth century, was to serve as his second—the boxer would sit on second's knee between rounds. When an American football quarterback "takes a knee," he is semi-kneeling immediately upon receiving the ball from his center, downing the ball because his team is ahead with seconds to play and the clock will continue to tick.

Eh.

Knee and *gnu*? No. *Gnu* is probably from the *Hottentot*. But then *Hottentot* is considered (OED) "both archaic and offensive; the word *Khoekhoe* . . . is now usually used in its place." *Hottentot* may have come from a Dutch word meaning stammerer, stutterer—typical imperialistic insensitivity. To be fair, that can work both ways. According to Dennis Tedlock, editor of *2000 Years of Mayan Literature*, the name *Yucatán* came about when a Spanish explorer asked some locals what the name of that area was, and he misheard what he took to be their reply. "What they actually said was *k'iut'an*, which means, 'The way he talks is funny.'"

According to OED, to *kneeify* meant "to make a knee of," that is, "to attach (the toe of a shoe) to the knee by a chain, as was the fashion" in the fourteenth century. From *The Tragedy of Richard II*: "This chayne doth (as it were) soe tooefy the knee, and so kneefye the tooe, that . . ." Oh, never mind.

There is no English word for the back of the knee. How about *eenk*?

➤ *knickers*

Short for *knickerbockers*, trousers gathered at the knee, named for the **knee** pants in George Cruikshank's illustrations of Washington Irving's satirical *History of New York, . . . by Diedrich Knickerbocker* (1809), which proved so popular with New Yorkers of Dutch descent that they began to call themselves Knickerbockers, which is why New York City's pro basketball team is the Knicks.

Irving got the name from his friend Herman Knickerbocker. Dutch *knikkerbakker* means "marble baker." As a young girl, my friend Marianne Swan, born and reared in Holland, played with marbles made of clay. The *kn* in *knikkerbakker*, I am advised by her husband, Jon, "would not be an *n* sound that smothers the *k*. The *k* would be present and accounted for. Washington Irving's *Knickerbocker* loses that sound, as does *knickers*, which in Dutch slang are called turd catchers. Our Icelander friend told me of how that language, basically Old Norse, preserves the *k* sound in its *knee* and *knife* words, but you combine the *k* and the *n* in your nose, like a controlled **sneeze**."

In England, of course, *knickers* are panties. Dating back to when they were knee length. Now try not to think of *naughty* and *nookie*.

➤ *knickknack*

Often spelled *knicknack*, occasionally even *nicnac*, but I'm for preserving the four *k*'s. *Nicnac* would suffice to fix the pronunciation, but I like to sense unvoiced *k* sounds in the background. The echoic word *knack*, as in (sixteenth century) "make a fillip or knack with the fingers," betokened a sharp rapping noise. (The onomatopoeic *fillip*, first cousin to *flip*, is when you bend a fingertip back with your thumb, generate tension, and release, to flick a booger or some other tiny object at someone or to tap smartly against someone or something: "Hee . . . gives the cup a phillip to make it cry Twango," 1619.) We might imagine Fred Astaire dancing and singing "Knack knack knack on wood."

That *knack* may have been the precursor of *knack* meaning trick, trinket, or delicacy and, as we use the word today (OED): "A 'trick' of action, speech, etc.; a personal habit of acting or speaking in a particular way."

Knickknack is a reduplication with a quicker vowel in the first part, for rhythm's sake, as in *click-clack*, and "This old man, he played one, he played knick-knack on my drum." You know that clickety instrument "the bones"? It has been called "a pair of Knick-knacks."

The knickknack we know today is a gimmick, trinket, kickshaw. Note all the *k*'s. Knickknacks tend to be clicky little things on the shelf.

1 · **L** · 1

This letter ought not to be so angular; the *l* sound goes with long, slow, flowing, relaxed, languourous lolling. Certainly there was nothing cut-and-dried about the old unit of measure, the ell. The foot, the yard, the inch, the cubit varied, but the ell was all over the place. Originally it represented an arm. Or just a forearm. The English ell was 45 inches, the Scots one 37.2, the Flemish one 27, we are told by OED, which then cites a period authority as saying that in Scotland an ell was either 42 or 38, and another that 50 English ells were equal to 102 Danish. I don't think we can find in those numbers the answer to whether the Danes or the Scots had shorter arms. Than each other. Or than the English.

Why should we care about the ell? Well, it's related to our elbow, isn't it? The *el-* means arm, the *-bow* means bend. Or if you go back farther, according to John Ayto, the *el-* comes from a PIE root (which also gave us *ulna*, the longer forearm bone) meaning bend, so an elbow is a bend-bend proposition (unless you happen to catch one in the head), which fits right in with this little festival of flexibility.

laughing, in letters

Her laugh is a raucous *Ha!*, as if an *H* and an *A* had collided in midair.

—Tad Friend in *The New Yorker*, on Phyllis Diller

laughs, textual

I have watched humorous authors, in performances geared to the selling of their books, getting laughs by batting their eyes, mugging, hopping like kangaroos. If the material is good enough, none of that is needed. And it's false marketing: those laughs are not going to be there in the text some few kind souls in the audience (maybe) will shell out their hard-earned dollars for. At any rate, selling the material in this way offends against a long tradition of authorial straightface. Which can be effective. Mark Twain's casual-seeming pretense was to address an audience in utter earnestness, even solemnity. With friends, he went perhaps farther. "He always appeared to be pained in a gentle lovable way if his listeners smiled," said J. M. Barrie, "and it almost broke him up [today we would say "broke him down"] if we laughed."

➤ lawyer joke, earliest

OED cites this proverb from 1553: "The lawyer never dieth a beggar. The lawyer can never want a livyng until the yearth want men." But maybe that's a joke on men. Saint Ives, or Yves, who devoted his life to representing the poor and is sometimes called the patron saint of lawyers, died in 1303. The following is said to have been inscribed on his tomb: *Sanctus Ivo erat Breto, Advocatus et non latro, Res mirando populo.* "Saint Ives was a Breton, an attorney, but not a bandit—a thing astonishing to the people."

Or we could go with this improved version (if I do say so myself) of the looser, rhyming translation by E. Cobham Brewer in *Brewer's Dictionary of Phrase and Fable*:

> Ives, from the land of beef,
> A lawyer and not a thief!
> Beyond most folks' belief.

Maybe in part a Breton joke. I don't know enough about early fourteenth-century Breton stereotypes—beefeaters?—to be sure. I can pass on to you a contemporary Cape Breton joke. Cape Breton is a Nova Scotian island. Apparently Cape Breton jokes are popular in Canada.

In an art gallery in Toronto, an obvious out-of-towner is looking at a portrait of three naked men side by side. They're black all over except the middle man's penis is pink. The gallery owner assumes that the visitor is baffled by the painting, so he goes over and kindly fills him in:

"You see, this is a depiction of the sexual emasculation of African Americans in a white-dominated society."

"Nope."

"Ah. . . . Or, it might also be seen to reflect the objectification of gay men in society today, because of course—"

"Nope."

"Excuse me?"

"No African American, nor gay man either."

"I see. Perhaps you could tell me how you can be so sure of that."

"Watched it being painted, back in Cape Breton. Those are three Cape Breton coal miners, picking up extra money posin'. And the one in the middle went home for lunch."

➤ ling, lit, don't invite 'em

In a 1971 *New Yorker* profile of Noam Chomsky, Ved Mehta asked Chomsky why linguists write so awkwardly. He replied:

"The ability to use language well is very different from the ability to study it. Once, the Slavic Department at Harvard was thinking of offering Vladimir Nabokov an appointment. Roman Jakobson, the linguist, who was in the department then, said that he didn't have anything against **elephant**s but he wouldn't appoint one a professor of zoology."

See *upaya*.

➤ looks, poetic

"The first words Dylan Thomas said to me," the poet David Waggoner said to me, "were 'I'm only a poet when I'm writing poetry. The rest of the time—Christ, look at me.'"

➤ *lunge*

From French *allonger*, to lengthen. First taken into English as the fencing term *allong*, which English improved upon—*lunge* is more sudden, more thrusty. The *l* is good, the *-ge* is good. Lose the *al* and change the *on* to *uhn*. Voilà.

➢ *-ly*

My friend the biographer Jean Strouse has a problem with *leisurely* used as an adverb, as in "He walked leisurely down the street," which, she says, "makes you want to say 'He walked leisurely-ly down the street.' So I use it only as an adjective ('He walked in a leisurely way down the street')."

I know what she means. But I have come around to liking "walked leisurely down the street," maybe because thinking about it—taking on board a sort of adjectival-adverbial **wobble**—slows me down, appropriately. To me the adverbial *leisurely* is akin to the *lively* in "Step lively" or "Look lively." You could say that the latter *lively* is an adjective, as in "Here come the media—put on your wig and look lovely. And try to make Daddy look life-like, at least." But when you tell someone to look lively you are telling him or her to get cracking, not just to appear a certain way.

At any rate, I concur in Jean's recoil from *leisurely-ly*, or even *leisurelily*. Chambers says forms such as *earlily* and *lovelily* "are still found in the 1600s . . . , but are now considered ungraceful, except for an occasional use of *friendlily*." I don't feel friendly toward *friendlily*, even. For one thing it looks like "my friend Lily," and the only Lily I know, I don't see often.

Ghostlily, *motherlily*, *manlily*, *beastlily* are all dictionary-approved but prohibitively awkward, as is, in another way, *lily-liveredly*. *Lilylikely*, though . . .

"She lay palely, lilylikely, upon her laid-out lover's breast." Not bad.

For that matter, awkward can be infectious:

"Bah," he said woollily.

Must you murder people so grislily?

"Coochy-coo," he said touchy-feelily.

He proceeded wobblily along.

In American English, at least, there seems to be no way to say something along these lines: "For the nine months I carried you, growing inside me, no charge," Tammy Wynette sang motherlily.

WIII has no space for either *motherlily* or *fatherlily* and brands adverbial *motherly* archaic and adverbial *fatherly* obsolete.

OED calls adverbial *motherly* "now rare," but cites an example as recently as 1997: "touched her lightly, motherly, as she passed through." Aww. For adverbial *fatherly*, OED has noted nothing since 1853: "The sky . . . That great smooth Hand of God stretched out / On all his children fatherly."

Willy-nilly (from "will he, nill he" or "will ye, nill ye," meaning whether he or you intend to or not) is already an adverb, as in "The earth is drifting willy-nilly toward shriveling up like a roasted peach," so let's not even consider *willy-nillily*.

But a band whose lead vocalists are actors lip-synching to recordings made by real vocalists might be said, suggests Jean Strouse, to perform Milli-Vanillily.

m · **M** · m

It's the first letter that Helen Keller, who was struck permanently deaf and blind at the age of nineteen months, learned to pronounce. She was ten years old and had been mute. Her principal teacher and eventual life's companion, Annie Sullivan, had connected her to language and the world by spelling things out in her palm with fingertips three years before, but Helen remained incapable of oral speech until another teacher, Sarah Fuller, "passed my hand lightly over her face," as Keller would recall in *The Story of My Life*, "and let me feel the position of her tongue and lips when she made a sound. I was eager to imitate every motion, and in an hour I had learned six elements of speech: M, P, A, S, T, I."

Four years later, when she was fourteen, she and Mark Twain began a long and highly conversant friendship. "He made me laugh and feel thoroughly happy," she wrote, "by telling some good stories, which I read from his lips." She would put her forefinger to his lips, her thumb to his throat, and her middle finger to his nose. "His voice was truly wonderful. To my touch, it was deep, resonant. He had the power of modulating it so as to suggest the most delicate shades of meaning, and he spoke so deliberately that I could get almost every word with my fingers." In all she wrote twelve books. Twain called her and Napoleon the two most remarkable people of the nineteenth century. "I suppose there is nothing like [our friendship] in heaven," he wrote to her, "and not likely to be, until we get there and show off. I often think of it with longing, and how they'll say, 'there they come—sit down in front.' I am practicing with a tin halo. You do the same."

➤ mediablur

It is summer of 2008 and I am in an airport, trying to read a story in—I mean *on*, on my laptop—the online *New York Times* about the rare white Chinese river dolphin. It has finally been driven "functionally extinct" after surviving for twenty million years. I would like to feel outraged about this. But I can't focus, for all of the other . . .

I can almost make out what CNN is murmuring, the Arctic or maybe Iraq will melt by 2040 . . .

. . . almost make out what a teenager is whining through studded lips into her cell phone—something involving the term *shazbot*, which according to Urbandictionary.com (I looked it up) is "an exclamation of displease-ment" coined by Robin Williams on *Mork and Mindy* . . .

. . . almost make out the announcement of what is causing the latest extension of our flight delay (either "weather" or "whatever").

And look! The people in—I mean *on*—the news and the people sur-rounding me are running together!

That shifty-eyed man over there may be a defector oozing polonium, that glazed-looking youth may be on the verge of keeling over from taco-related *E. coli*, that haunted-looking woman may be the notorious one, poor anonymous soul, who was reportedly kicked off her flight early in the week for lighting matches to cover her toxic farts. I feel for her. Shouldn't planes have a farting section?

And shouldn't airports have a reading section? In the midst of this low-decibel bedlam, how can anyone concentrate long enough to read anything?

Maybe, up there on the TV screen, I can keep up with the crawl. Got . . . to . . . focus . . . on . . . the . . . crawl . . .

The crawl says: 60 percent of Americans polled would be "enthusiastic or comfortable" with a presidential candidate who is female or black.

That's good. We should not rule out candidates categorically. Ah, but someone has popped onto the screen who is wearing a Cautionary Look.

Wait a minute! Is that not the same bland necktie . . . the same bland jacket . . . the same bland *face* of the man who was trying surreptitiously, just moments ago, to blow his nose into *USA Today* over there by the recycle receptacle? Now he's on TV? My bearings all shot, I lurch over closer to the screen. There must be a message in this. Maybe this man is cautioning me not to get on this plane.

No. He's cautioning us all—all of us worldwide—to be skeptical of poll results: "People tend to tell pollsters what they think they want to hear."

I recoil from the screen, from the notion that a scientific sampling of the American people, too, can lie.

Maybe it's not true. How, after all, can we know for sure? From polls?

What if a pollster were to ask me, "Do you think people tell pollsters what they want to hear?" Having heard the news, I would have to say yes. Which would not be what the pollster would want to hear.

A conundrum. But what is this on the screen? It's a dolphin. A dolphin in China. Evidently, one as-yet-unextinct dolphin remains. But—this dolphin has an enormous human arm thrust down its throat! It's not enough that they're overfishing dolphins to extinction, they're torturing the last survivor? Is there at long last no decency . . .

When I lurch back toward where I can make out what CNN is saying, CNN has broken for commercial. *Shazbot!*

Wait. I have brought up CNN online. It's all right, this dolphin story. It's *good* news. The dolphin I saw was one of two *blue* dolphins who were choking on plastic they ate off the side of their aquarium pool. No medical instrument known to man could access the blockage. So, for a change, something sensible was done. A media figure was summoned:

The world's tallest man. All seven foot nine of him. And he came, from the flock (of what, yaks?) he was herding in Inner Mongolia. The great long fingers of the great long hand at the end of his great long arm reached in beyond the dolphin's gag reflex, seized the bit of plastic, and brought it out!

Consider the uncheesiness of the world's tallest man. He could be abiding here in this airport flock, in the course of touring as a paragon, being herded hither and yon across waves of indistinct communications. But no, there he was in Mongolia, sticking to his herding, the work he knows best (must be yaks, sheep would not be enough of a challenge for him).

My laptop interrupts—*urgent, battery running low!* On-screen CNN is putting forward a product that will give me a hand—*no, go away, don't need it*—with my erection. The previously dysfunctional man's newly rosy wife there, didn't I sit next to her between here and Cincinatti? She wasn't rosy then; our eyes never met; nor do I want them to now.

Another announcement: my flight is delayed again, this time, as best I can make out, "for equipment." The man who just sat jiggily down next to me, plugged into his iPhone, doesn't realize—I assume he doesn't realize—surely he doesn't realize—that he is humming.

Come get me, world's tallest man.

➤ *me*-fear

Charles Hoyt is the author of *Witchcraft* (Southern Illinois University Press) and "a descendant of Susanna Martin who was hanged as a witch for walking through a Salem rain without getting her feet wet." He played piano with Louis Armstrong, Jack Teagarden, and Eddie Conlon. He has this interesting theory about what he calls (and I concur) "the vile misuse of *I*," as in "They took my wife and I to the movies":

> This, I believe, is not only false gentility, but an example of *me*-fear; *me* is the badge of early childhood, and like other childish things, it becomes embarrassing. I recall vividly the fate of a colleague of mine, in 6th grade: having muttered something like "Me 'n' Jim went down to the store," he was immediately crushed by our teacher: "Oh, ho! *Me* went to the store, me did!"

Me-fear is not a universal condition, certainly not in professional football. Rex Ryan, coach of the New York Jets: "I'm man enough to be me." Terrell Owens, the noted National Football League pass catcher: "I love me some me."

I am told on good authority that a guy on a reality TV show once referred to "Gretchen and I's relationship."

➤ memory, institutional

My friend Veronica Geng told me that when she was an editor at *The New Yorker*, the magazine published a short humor piece of hers not close to the front, as was the usual practice, but farther back, in one column down the middle of a single page. The week that issue came out, there appeared at Veronica's office doorway the magazine's longtime City Hall reporter, Andy Logan. Veronica did not know Ms. Logan well, but she knew how deeply woven she was in *The New Yorker*'s fabric. Born Isabel Ann Logan, she had taken "Andy" while at Swarthmore, in tribute to the *New Yorker* pillar E. B. White, who had been called Andy since college because everybody named White who went to Cornell when he did was called that in honor of somebody, I forget who, named Andy White. Logan had been a *New Yorker* writer since 1942. All this aside, Veronica thought Andy Logan was cool.

And now here she was to fill Veronica in on the background of her piece's placement in the magazine: the rarity of that placement, the editorial thinking that must have gone into it, and the tradition it perpetuated. The first piece so published, Logan informed her, was back in the late thirties, a few years before Logan came to *The New Yorker*. It was one of several brief humorous sketches by John O'Hara about a character named Pal Joey.

Veronica would of course be aware, Logan went on, that O'Hara had gone on to expand those sketches into a novel, which inspired a Rodgers and Hart Broadway musical, best known for including such standards as "Bewitched, Bothered and Bewildered," and a movie starring Rita Hayworth, Kim Novak, and Frank Sinatra—by no means at his best—in the title role.

Then Logan paused, said "God *damn*, I'm interesting," and disappeared.

➤ metanarrative, pig and possum throwing

Like, the cultural assumptions underlying a story. Black-and-white movies don't mind coming right out with these. Victor Mature, a crook, to Brian Donlevy, a cop, in *Kiss of Death*: "Your side of the fence is as dirty as mine." Donlevy: "With one difference. We hurt bad people, not good people." The movie, a good one, colors outside those lines in various ways, and its crowning glory is Richard Widmark as the leering evil guy Tommy Yudo, whose chuckle is like a snarl. But the moral framework is there, so we can enjoy the kissing and killing and so on.

In the postmodern era, we are meant to go "Yeah, right" to moral frameworks—to be radically skeptical of metanarratives. And whoops-a-daisy. According to **Wikipedia** (which is good enough for me when it comes to something like this):

> Thinkers like Alex Callinicos and Jürgen Habermas argue that
> [Jean-François] Lyotard's description of the postmodern world as

containing an "incredulity toward metanarratives" could be seen as a metanarrative in itself. According to this view, post-structuralist thinkers like Lyotard criticise universal rules but postulate that postmodernity contains a universal skepticism toward metanarratives; and this "universal skepticism" is in itself a contemporary metanarrative. Like a post-modern neo-romanticist metanarrative that intends to build up a "meta" critic, or "meta" discourse and a "meta" belief holding up that Western science is just taxonomist, empiricist, utilitarian, assuming a supposed sovereignty around its own reason and pretending to be neutral, rigorous and universal. This is itself an obvious sample of another "meta" story, self-contradicting the postmodern critique of the metanarrative.

That would *seem* to cover everything. But. What if, for the life of you, you can find no metanarrative? Some years back I wrote a book about being a Southerner in the North. As I trudged from city to city trying to induce people to buy that book, I was called upon to explain what non-Southerners regarded as characteristically Southern phenomena. In Wellesley, Massachusetts, a lady handed me a printout of this article:

MAN FINED FOR TOSSING PIG
OVER HOTEL COUNTER

AP

WEST POINT, Miss. (Dec. 6, 2006)—When pigs fly, indeed. Kevin Pugh, 20, of Cedar Bluff, has been fined $279 for tossing a pig over the counter at the Holiday Inn Express in West Point on Nov. 12. Pugh pleaded guilty Tuesday in city court to a charge of disturbing the peace.

West Point Police Lt. Danny McCaskill has said Pugh didn't know the employees of the hotel. There was no evidence intoxication was a factor. No one was hurt, including the pig, officers said.

"This was the silliest thing I've ever seen," McCaskill said. "Almost every officer we had was involved because the incidents kept happening at different hours."

McCaskill said Pugh was accused of walking into the hotel and throwing the 60-pound pig over the counter.

"He said it was a prank," McCaskill said. "It must be some redneck thing, because I haven't ever heard of anything like it." McCaskill said there have been four late-night incidents involving animal-tossing at West Point businesses. Twice a pig was tossed and two of the incidents involved possums.

All four of the disturbances took place between 2 a.m. and 4 a.m., McCaskill said.

Pugh is accused in a second animal-throwing incident at a Hardee's restaurant. He has pleaded innocent to disturbing the peace in that case.

"Why would they do that?" the lady wanted to know. I had the feeling that if Wellesleyans had a clear-cut second-person plural she might have said, "Why do *you-all* do that?"

I was tempted to make something up. This man undoubtedly belongs to SPOT, I could have told her. Society of Pig and Opossum Throwing. They do a lot of good things, too—raise money for new fire engines and so on. And most of the throwing is ceremonial and open to the public. They throw pigs and possums back and forth to each other, and it is something to see, especially the catch-and-release action, which must be accomplished in one motion so the tossed animal will not get its bearings and bite the receiver. "*Hot possum*," they will cry, or "*Hot pig.*" Up North, I believe the game is watered down to "hot potato," which is a good indication of the difference between North and South. But some SPOT members, if they don't get to bed early enough, are bad to indulge on occasion in what might be seen as extracurricular pig or possum throwing.

But saying that would have contributed to misunderstanding between the regions. I assured the lady that this story, to the best of my knowledge, was an isolated instance, or, okay, a series of isolated instances, not amounting to a trend or custom. She wasn't satisfied. She looked at me as though she felt I was covering something up. Maybe I should have just said, "*Y'all* don't ever pay a hotel bill that way in Wellesley?"

Truth is, I was curious about the story myself. So I did some Googling.

That news story, it turns out, circulated internationally. Here is the Romanian version:

PORC ARUNCAT INTR-UN HOTEL

Oana OLARU

Kevin Pugh, in vârsta de 20 ani, din Cedar Bluff a primit o amenda de 279 dolari pentru ca a aruncat un porc in hotelul Holiday Inn Express din West Point, informeaza site-ul abclocal.go.com. Pugh a pledat vinovat pentru deranjarea linistii publice, iar in urma incidentului nimeni nu a fost ranit, nici macar porcul.

Din declaratiile politiei, se pare ca Pugh a intrat in hotel si a aruncat pur si simplu un porc de 27 kilograme la receptia hotelului. Locotenentul Danny McCaskill a declarat:

"A fost cea mai mare grozavie pe care am vazut-o vreodata. Acuzatul spune ca a fost o gluma, insa nu inteleg ce fel de gluma e asta, pentru ca nu am mai auzit niciodata de asa ceva." Locotenentul a mai declarat ca nu e prima data când in orasul West Point au loc astfel de incidente: de doua ori s-a întâmplat sa se arunce porci, iar in alte doua incidente au fost aruncati oposumi, si toate acestea s-au petrecut intre orele 2 si 4 dimineata.

And here, the Slovenian:

ČEZ PULT JE VRGEL ŽIVEGA PRAŠIČA

Zanimivosti, 6:11 7.12.2006

Američan Kevin Pugh je moral plačati 279 dolarjev kazni zaradi kaljenja miru, ker je v nekem hotelu v recepciji čez pult vrgel prašiča.

Policijski načelnik Danny McCaskill je povedal, da 20-letni Pugh ni poznal zaposlenih v hotelu, prav tako pa ni bilo nobenega dokaza, da bi bil pijan.

V incidentu ni bil ranjen nihče, niti leteči, približno 30 kilogramov težki prašič.

"To je najbolj smešna stvar, ki sem jo kdaj videl," je priznal

McCaskill in dodal, da je Pugh prašiča vrgel zaradi šale. Policija je tisto noč, ko se je to zgodilo, med drugo in četrto uro zjutraj naštela še štiri podobne izgrede, v katerih so eno osrednjih vlog igrale leteče živali: dva prašiča in dva oposuma.

Pugh je sodeloval tudi pri metanju nebogljenih živali v neki restavraciji, vendar tega prekrška ni priznal in se bo moral zagovarjati pred sodnikom.

Evidently the word for "possum" is similar in Romanian and Slovenian, but "pig" appears to be quite different in the two languages. Romanian for "lieutenant" is "Locotenentul," which I like. I can't tell whether the words for "redneck" or "silliest" are in there or not. I don't see anything like "Mississippi," so Romanians and Slovenians may not associate pig and possum throwing with the South particularly. They might even associate it with the West Point in New York where our elite army officers are educated. That would be unfair to the army, but a break for Mississippi.

No Kevin Pugh is listed in the Cedar Bluff area, according to Information, so we may never know what motivated him in these acts.

Or I should say, "in this act," because we don't know that he was the perpetrator of more than the one throwing. It is even possible that no possums were thrown, since you'll notice that the story says only that possums were "involved." Which is not to imply that the possums were the brains behind any of these incidents. I once asked Basil Clark, who organized the Possum Growers' Benevolent Association in Clanton, Alabama, whether a possum was intelligent.

"He is if he has to be," said Clark. "He'd rather just mosey along."

When all is said and done, however, I wonder, myself, what Mr. Pugh was thinking, other than just "Pig . . . hotel desk . . . hot damn!" I believe we may speculate. You notice that no animal-throwing incident is said to have occurred in a locally owned hotel or restaurant. According to the town's website, "The charm of West Point will hold you spellbound, as you stroll along her quaint downtown sidewalks. . . . West Point captures a simplicity of life rarely found in today's fast-paced society." She has been named, according to the website, "one of the 'Top 100 Small Towns in America.'"

Might Mr. Pugh have been protesting the intrusion of chain genericism into such a genuinely local locale? I don't know that Hardee's serves anything really vile, like reconstituted chicken meat, but maybe they don't get their beef from nearby farmers, and I do know that there is nothing less reconstituted than a live possum. And in the absence of evidence to the contrary, we may assume that the thrown pigs were local.

Or Mr. Pugh may have been being postmodern. Here is as far as I got a couple of years ago on a think piece about how the South might save America from where it was headed:

> In 1979 Jean-François Lyotard defined the postmodern condition as "incredulity towards metanarratives." Since then a metanarrative has infected the world's only superpower, the United States. An imperialistic good-versus-evil metanarrative has drawn the nation into a preemptive war halfway around the world. It is a cheesy, treacherous metanarrative, which has proved more than a match, however, for snarky incredulity. Is there an alternative metanarrative to be forged, or at least a grittier incredulity?
>
> If so, it will come from the Southern United States, from whose cultural debris the cheesy, treacherous metanarrative has been forged.

Here's what I had in mind: down-home Southern values and feistiness, which I felt had been perversely evoked by the Bush administration's jingoism ("git those evildoers before they start blowing up our church suppers" summoning us to a big crazy mess of a war), might somehow erupt into . . .

Into something . . . better. I have a hard time sticking with a think piece for very long. But I'll say this: I can't see that this animal-throwing story fits any metanarrative at all.

Unless. There is one possibility. I am by no means implying any sort of complicity here. But it just could be that the metanarrative of the animal throwing is an effort to establish, internationally (and credibly, as far as I'm concerned), that there is a police lieutenant in West Point, Mississippi, who is not a redneck.

➤ *me-time*

As of this writing, neither OED nor WIII online defines this term. I suppose it has arisen too recently, and also perhaps—not that your typical lexicographer is dour anymore—a touch too ickily. But the number-one Urbandictionary.com definition, "A euphemism for masturbation," overstates the case.

Wiktionary.org at one time defined *me time* satisfactorily: "a period during which someone relaxes by doing something he/she enjoys." This is an excellent example of the advantage of using *he/she* (better, *he or she*) instead of the (ugh) singular *they*. "A period during which someone relaxes by doing something they enjoy" would not do, because the point of me time is precisely *not* to do what *they* or even *we* want to do.

But note how odd that looks: "the point of me time is. . . ." Even odder would be "Sometime I got to get me some me time." I agree with Urbandictionary.com that this term calls for a hyphen.

➤ *mimi*

A colloquial French term for a little kiss, and, by extension, *mon mimi*: "my sweetie."

➤ *mixed metaphor*

Nice example in *The Borzoi Handbook for Writers*: "You can't sit on your hands if a recession is coming because you don't know where the bottom is."

➤ *modernism/postmodernism*

I will not go deeply into this distinction, because anyone who cares about it knows much more about it than I do, probably, and certainly thinks so. But I will say this: nobody ever talks about postmodern life. And I will quote this from John Lanchester's novel *The Debt to Pleasure*: "Modernism is about finding out how much you could get away with leaving out. Postmodernism is about how much you can get away with putting in."

I quote that, for one reason, because I think "how much you could get away with" is an element of the arts that is too seldom brought to the fore. I mean, when critics or foundations write about someone's getting away with presenting, say, a rotting shark or a roomful of peat moss as art, do they never *chuckle*? Give one another a high five? Surely they should, if anything, *whoop*. Do they never say, even to themselves, "Love this crazy shit"? Maybe they do, in their own circles; but by the time their comments reach me, their mode is straight-faced, hushed-tone analytical. You'd think art was a public service. And so it is, but not because of its gravity. Because people enjoy, whether they want to admit it or not, successful rascality. Thank goodness for Philistines—you can get a rise out of them.

➢ *mouse*

As recently as 1982 (which, come to think of it, isn't all that recent), *The New York Times* had to explain what a computer mouse was. "Instead of typing commands or code words to request information, users can point to words or symbols on the screen . . . through manipulation of a hand-held device known as a mouse." The inventor of the mouse was Douglas Engelbart of Stanford. In 1965 he and his colleague Bill English, who had constructed the prototype mouse from Engelbart's designs, mentioned the device by its rodental name in print for the first time, according to OED: "Within comfortable reach of the user's right hand is a device called the 'mouse' which we developed for evaluation . . . as a means for selecting those displayed text entities upon which the commands are to operate."

At various sites online, under "Mother of All Demos," you can check out Engelbart demonstrating, in 1968, a number of technologies, experimental at the time, that we have come to take for granted: interactive text, e-mail, hypertext, and the mouse—all in the interest of "helping humans to operate within the domain of complex information structures." At one point he says, "You have a [tracking?] device called a mouse. . . . I don't know why we call it a mouse. Sometimes I apologize. It started out that way and we never changed it." *Apologizing!* Apologizing for the mouse! It's like Eve saying "We call it a 'baby,' I don't know, someone will probably come up with something more technical, but it made that sound, *ba-ba*, when it was being relatively bearable—we didn't want to call it *waaaaaaaah*." According to **Wikipedia**, Engelbart never made any money off the mouse because his patent lapsed before mouses, or mice, became commercially available.

These days the mouse may be on its way out, but its realm has greatly expanded. If you Google "mouseover mouseout," as my sister, Susan, the computer person suggests, you get for instance this severely underhyphenated excerpt from an instructional site:

> **Mouse Events.** The mouse events are by far the most important
> events . . . We'll go through all mouse events: mousedown, mouseup
> and click, dblclick, mousemove and finally mouseover and
> mouseout . . . Finally the Microsoft proprietary mouseenter and
> mouseleave events . . . You'll see the events that take place in the
> textarea . . .

By "severely underhyphenated," I mean: *mouseenter?* That looks as though it should be pronounced mow-seenter. *Mouseleave?* What language is that from? Maybe you'd say moo-se-lay-av-eh. *Textarea?* Ugh. I guess we're in a *textarea* right now. Feh. It looks like it should be pronounced tex-ta-ria; a shopping mall in Lubbock, maybe.

➤ *music*

The verb *muse*, to reflect to oneself, goes back to the Old French noun *muse*, muzzle or snout, which gave rise to the Old French verb *muser*, to ponder—literally, to stand there with one's nose in the air. Etymologists disagree whether a clear etymological connection can be made between that *muse* and the Muses, Greek goddesses of the arts, but *Muse* certainly inspired *music.*

Can we assume, however, that a person who is good at music is good at other arts, for instance writing? As the least musical member of a notoriously challenged rock-and-roll band of authors, the Rock Bottom Remainders, I may be biased. But I don't think many *great* writers have been known for their musical talent. James Joyce had a fine tenor voice, we are told, but then he was Irish. So was the late lamented Frank McCourt, but I was once present on stage (in a vague capacity) when Frank sang one Beatles song as the rest of the band, the Remainders, played another, and the discrepancy—or I should say, the *nature* of the discrepancy—was not readily apparent.

Flannery O'Connor was no nightingale, either, nor even a listener of note. "All classical music sounds alike to me," she said, "and the rest of it sounds like the Beatles."

At a concert, Samuel Johnson was clearly musing to himself, or attending to his own Muse, instead of listening to a virtuoso violinist. A friend urged him to observe how difficult the performance was. "Difficult do you call it, Sir?" replied the doctor; "I wish it were impossible." On another occasion a harpsichordist, after playing brilliantly, asked an unresponsive Johnson whether he was fond of music generally. "No, madam," Johnson replied, "but of all the noises, I think music is the least disagreeable."

"Music, I regret to say," said Vladimir Nabokov, "affects me merely as an arbitrary succession of more or less irritating sounds."

None of those three great prose stylists can be accused of having a tin ear. Sad as indifference to music is, it does remove the temptation to enhance, self-amusingly, one's own keyboard performance by humming along, so to speak. Tone and rhythm have to be there in the letters on the page.

A certain old person of Tring,
When someone asked her to sing,
    Replied, "Ain't it odd?
    I can never tell 'God
Save the Weasel' from 'Pop Goes the King.' "

—Anon.

n · N · n

Might I suggest, without being branded as a nut or a crank, that *n* carries a negative value? There are of course some upbeat *n*-words: *new, natural, nimble, neat, nectar, neighborly, noble, normal, nourish, nugget, nurture, nuzzle.*

But weigh those against *no, not, none, nyet, nicht, nein, non, neither, nor, in-, un-, anti-, under, nag, narc, narcissism, narcosis, narrow, narwhal* (the *nar-* part is from Old Icelandic for corpse, a reference to the animal's color resembling that of a drowned person), *nasal, nasty, natter, naught, naughty, nausea, Nazi, needy, nefarious, negligent, nerd, nettle, neuralgia, neuter, never, night, necrology, nefarious, niggle, ninny, nit, noir, noisome, noogie, noose, nosy, notorious, noxious, nudge, nudnik, nugatory, nuisance, null, numb,* and *nut.*

Also weigh, against the stylishness of **snazzy** and the sweetness of *snuggle* and *snookums,* the following *sn-* words: *snafu, snag, snail, snake, snallygaster* (a legendary huge reptilian bird of prey), *snap, snarf, snarky, snarl, sneaky, sneer, snicker, snide, sniffling, sniffy, snigger, snipe, snippy, snit, snitch, snivel, snob, snockered, snollygoster* (a wily, unprincipled politician), *snooker, snoop, snooty, snore, snort, snotty, snout, snub, snuff.* Many of those words' derivations are nasal, even if not obviously—*snitch* for instance was originally a slang word for the nose, and *snit* comes from *snort.* I submit to you that pronouncing *n* evokes, however distantly, a wrinkling of the nostrils. As in *stink, stench, dung, rank, rancid, funky, skunk.*

Or should I go snaffle myself?

➤ name, fictional, too often taken for granted

Humpty Dumpty maintains, in *Through the Looking Glass,* that he is the master of words, but he's at the mercy of his own name: Humpty is his character and Dumpty is his fate.

➤ **names, common but relationship straining
(I would imagine)**

At one time, according to the popular press, Taylor Lautner, a young male actor who has achieved phenomenal popularity by playing a cuddly were-wolf, was the real-life boyfriend of Taylor Swift, a young female singer whose own phen. p. derives from her performance of cuddly country music.

But what did they call each other? Was one of them, to the other, "Tay," and the other, to the party of the first part, "Lor"?

Pet names, of course; you would have to nail down a couple of those (and perhaps resent, sometimes, the *necessity*). But while it is all very well, at a peak of passion, to be addressed as "OH! PUMPKIN!," there is nothing quite so reassuring as being invoked by one's own name at such a juncture. And if we're both named Taylor . . .

Let's not intrude into real lives. Let's take an imaginary couple, straight or gay, who are both named Pat. "OH! PAT! OH MY SWEET PITTY-*PATTY.*" Won't the Pat who is crying out feel just the least bit self-referential, and won't the other Pat wonder how primarily he or she is in fact the Pat that the other Pat has in mind? Especially if the Pat who is *not* crying out is at something less than a peak of passion.

There must also be awkward social moments. I don't suppose Taylor and Taylor ever needed to introduce each other to anyone, but how about Pat and Pat?

"I'd like you to meet . . . Pat."

Do you see what I mean?

➤ **names, funny**

Why is *Muncie* a funny name for a town? Because it falls between *munchy* and *mincy*? It's obvious why Fort Mudge is a funny name for a town: it rhymes with **fudge**. To my knowledge, nothing rhymes with *Muncie*, unless you force it:

> To a fretful young lady from Muncie
> An angel made an Annunci-

Atorial visit.

"All right, what is it?"

She snapped, and . . .

. . . we are left hanging.

➤ names, good ones

Dr. Wild Willie Moore, blues sax player.

Jerome Cotchery, New York Jets wide receiver.

O. J. Mayo, Memphis Grizzlies guard. The initials stand for Ovinton J'Anthony. His fan site is OJMayonnaise.com.

➤ names, not so good

Cleveland Browns linebacker D'Qwell Jackson.

Professed scientist and healer (who was paid more than $100,000 by the Los Angeles Dodgers to send the team positive energy from his Boston-area home) Vladimir Shpunt.

➤ names, unexpected

Desiree Fish, an American Express spokeswoman.

The Newark Eurekas, a nineteenth-century baseball team.

➤ negative, double

Say I say to you, "I can't get no satisfaction." You will not think me illiterate. You will know, I assume, that I am adopting the grammar of the Rolling Stones song. (Ask your parents. Okay, grandparents.) To mean that I can't get any.

You might answer, "I can't see why not." Is that a double negative? Not in any negative sense. It's a semicontradiction of my remark, but it doesn't contradict itself. It means something distinct—not the same as "I can see why not," which would be insulting.

You might answer, "No you can't." The import would depend upon rhythm and tone. "No. You can't," is a straightforward, rather deflating confirmation. "*No* you can't" might be a sarcastic contradiction along the lines of "*Yeah* [i.e., "Like hell"] you can" if I had said "I *can* satisfy your mama."

But. If you say "I can't neither," you are not using English well. If you say, "Nobody can't get none, no more," a quadruple negative, you are calling too much attention to yourself.

And there are subtler double negatives for which nothing can be said. I don't remember what I clipped this sentence from, but it still annoys me: "The nosy and stern-but-loving materfamilias is a venerable character that never seems to lose its usefulness, if not its charm." What that means to say is, "always seems to retain its usefulness, if not its charm."

And here is Jay Leno: "I'm sure you heard those rumors that NBC is talking about canceling our show. You know what that means? I didn't sleep with any of my staff for nothing." Listening, we might not have wondered how those negatives are wired together. Even in cold print, we see what he means, because we are aware that David Letterman did jeopardize his talk-show security, briefly, by sleeping, fairly extensively, with some of his staff. But Leno's literal meaning might be "Not for nothing did I sleep with any of my staff" or "I refrained from sleeping with any of my staff for nothing"—both of which seem to say, "I slept with only those members of my staff who compensated me for doing so."

Would there have been a crystal-clear way of putting Leno's joke? "My refraining from sleeping with any of my staff was all for naught." I didn't say funny, I said crystal clear.

➤ *nice*

This is an easy word to use, approvingly (I have often done so in this book), and yet there is something unreliable about it. According to OED, the development of its meaning "from 'foolish, silly' to 'pleasing' is unparalleled in Latin or in the Romance languages." Along the line of that development lies, on the one hand, the expression "'nice' girls didn't used to compete with each other in getting lipstick on boys' private parts" and, on the other, the obsolete sense of *nice* as wanton, lascivious: Antony, in his cups the night before battle, assures Cleopatra that although people may have mocked him "when mine hours / Were nice and lucky," he will henceforth "set my teeth."

In December 1970, President Richard Nixon sent an eleven-page single-spaced memorandum to his closest aide, H. R. Haldeman, conveying how upset he was that his staff had not established an image of him as warm and caring. "There are innumerable examples of warm items," he wrote. For instance, he had been "nicey-nicey to the cabinet, staff and Congress around Christmastime," had treated not only cabinet but subcabinet officials "like dignified human beings and not dirt under my feet." He emphasized, however, that all White House promotion of this "warmth business" should stress that it wasn't being promoted by the White House, and that the president (Nixon referring to himself in the third person) "does not brag about all the good things he does for people."

Lots of things wrong there ("warm items"!), but what stands out is the use of *nicey-nicey*, which fails as a synonym for *warm* in part because it rhymes with *icy*. Distinctly enunciated, *warm* is orally enclosing, like a sip of wine taken in and rolled around; *nicey* entails a wince and a hiss.

Nice works best, in fact, in its mostly obsolete meaning of precise or even finicky, which survives in *nicety* and "a nice distinction." When you add the *-y* and double it, you're pushing *nice*'s sonics too far. (I'm not sure how Nicely-Nicely Johnson, in *Guys and Dolls*, fits in here, but the *l*'s make a difference.)

Chilling *nice*'s are spoken in the movie *Revolutionary Road*, when the Leonardo DiCaprio character finds to his astonishment, after a night of vicious marital discord, that his wife, played by Kate Winslet, is calmly, submissively fixing him breakfast. Although her expression appears to be frozen—and she will kill herself, in administering a home abortion, after he leaves for work—he says, in a genuinely relieved yet walking-on-eggshells tone, as he finishes his eggs, "This was really nice. I don't know when I've had a nicer breakfast."

➤ *nitty-gritty*

Online I came upon a dumb British discussion deploring the tyranny of "political correctness" as reflected in a police constable's assertion that in police work *nitty-gritty* had been banned as racist. The expression, according to a story in the *Daily Mail*, was "said to have its origins in the 18th Century slave traders' phrase for the debris left at the bottom of a slave ship after a voyage. A visit to the hold was described as 'going to the nitty-gritty.'" What's offensive is the knee-jerk anti-PC faux etymology there, not the good **granular** term *nitty-gritty*.

But even an eminent linguist can find extraneous stink there. Anatoly Liberman knows a lot more about etymology than I do, but in his book *Word Origins, and How We Know Them*, he writes (in an aside from a bracing appreciation of **sonicky** *gr-* words) that "dictionaries pass by the obscene origin of *nitty-gritty*."

No. Yourdictionary.com (citing *Webster's New World College Dictionary*) does in fact say "orig. black slang: rhyming euphemism for *shitty*," but that doesn't ring true. Black slang, to be sure; but that derivation sounds more like Cockney rhyming slang than anything ebonic; and the way *nitty-gritty* has been used down through the years evinces no fecal influence. "Perhaps ultimately connected with *nit* egg of the louse, and *grits* finely ground corn," says Chambers. Okay, and how about the grit in sandy soil ("I believe I will dip my pink-and-white body in yon Roman tub," says W. C. Fields in *My Little Chickadee*. "I feel a bit gritty after the affairs of the day"), and in "the hard, gritty facts," and in "true grit."

And in *Grit* magazine, which deals with fundamentals. Its March/April 2010 issue featured an article titled "Behold the Hoe! An ancient tool becomes the go-to item for any gardener." A sidebar carried this quotation from Henry David Thoreau:

> I once had a sparrow alight upon my shoulder for a moment,
> while I was hoeing in a village garden, and I felt that I was more
> distinguished by that circumstance than I should have been
> by any epaulet I could have worn.

I am aware that "the shit" is hip for "the real thing," but never in my life have I heard or read anything called shitty except something that was a poor excuse for whatever it was supposed to be. OED's definition of *nitty-gritty*, though abstract, is palpably sound: "The most important aspects or practical details of a situation, subject, etc.; the harsh realities; the heart of the matter." Scratching your head, digging in dirt, yanking on a wrench, you can get a feel for *nitty-gritty*.

The last sentence in OED's lengthy discussion of the letter O's development is this: "The fancy, frequent in authors of the 16th and 17th centuries, that the shape of the letter O represented the rounded shape of the
mouth in forming the sound can be seen from the history of the letter to
be without foundation in fact."

Oh, I don't know. David Sacks, in *Letter Perfect: The Marvelous History of
Our Alphabet From A to Z*, which came out in the twenty-first century,
writes: "O is the only letter whose name creates its shape, however imper-
fectly, on the speaker's lips." Sacks studied Greek and Latin at Oxford,
and is also the author of *Encyclopedia of the Ancient Greek World*.

And in its recounting of O's history, the first thing OED, itself, says
about the sound of O is: "From Greek times downward, this letter has regu-
larly represented some variety or varieties of mid or low back vowel, usually rounded."

According to WIII, *rounded* in this sense means "produced with rounded
lips, labialized," and *round* means "to make (the lips) more or less round
and protruded by lessening the distance between the corners of the mouth
(as in the pronunciation of \ü\"), which is to say, oo. Which is two o's.

Coincidental? Maybe. The oldest ancestor of the O was a Semitic representation of the eye. It had a guttural sound, unspellable in English. The
Greeks didn't need that sound. They had a short-*o* sound, for which they
chose the O sign, and called it omicron, or little o. They also had a long-*o*
sound, for which they fashioned an O with a gap in the bottom and two big
feet sticking out on the sides, and called it omega, or big O. "Just possibly,"
Sacks says, the Greeks' "marriage of shape O and sound 'o' was prompted
by the letter's shape, which suggested the shape of a speaker's mouth saying 'o.'"

If you don't believe *that* Sacks, how about Oliver Sacks? He wrote about a novelist who woke up unable to read (able still to write, but not to read anything including what he had written, because unable to recognize letters). According to Sacks, a certain area of the brain—damaged in the novelist's case by a stroke—"appears exquisitely tuned to the act of reading," that is to say, the act of recognizing and appreciating letters. But that area "could not have evolved specifically for this purpose," because the human capacity for writing did not emerge until "little more than five thousand years ago—far too recently to have occurred through evolution by natural selection."

What researchers have found, writes Sacks, is that neurons dedicated to letter recognition have been "recruited" from parts of the brain that evolved eons earlier to serve the obviously essential purpose of object recognition. "The world of objects must be learned through experience and activity: looking, touching, handling, correlating the feel of objects with their appearance." Researchers at Caltech who "examined more than a hundred ancient and modern writing systems" concluded that the shapes of letters "share certain topological similarities." These researchers hypothesize that the shapes of letters, in all languages, "have been selected to resemble the conglomerations of contours found in natural scenes, thereby tapping into our already-existing object recognition mechanisms."

So.

See **arbitrary**.

➤ *oaf*

Originally this meant a child whose deformity was explained by its having been left by elves, in place of the real child. An elf-left child.

➤ OED and me

Readers of *Alphabet Juice* may recall my disappointment at having leafed through the entire AHD and failed to find myself cited as a user of any word at all, even though I am a member of that dictionary's Usage Panel. Well, I realized recently that a person can seek himself digitally. And oh, baby.

I'll have you know that I am among the online Oxford English Dictionary's acknowledged users of *thing*. In connection with "any old thing," colloquial U.S., but still. Words don't get much more essential than *thing*.

I am also to be found in the definition of *psychopathology*, more precisely, *psychopathologist*: "Don't give any more interviews. Unless it's to a licensed psychopathologist."

I pop up in *portray* (derivative: *portrayable*), and *Panamanian*, and the prefix *over-* (*overmellow*, shared with Tennyson), and *outslick*.

The English language, I realize, is not all about me. But I can feel that my work has not been entirely in vain, knowing as I do now that I have provided a certified example, for the ages, of *outslick*. Along with Erle Stanley Gardner, the *Pittsburgh Courier*, a book titled *The Life*, and *Boxing Monthly*, I have got your *outslick* covered.

Then too I have a piece of *nut* (*nut-cutting*), and *no more*, and *'mongst*. Indulge me a moment on *'mongst*. When it comes to *'mongst*, I am in there amongst such *'mongst* users as Christopher Marlowe, Milton, and Mark Twain—and my *'mongst* is the only *'mongst* after 1907!

I'm in on *maid*, too, not to mention *mad* (with Shakespeare for God's sake and Noël Coward and Oliver Goldsmith and St. Thomas More), and *Mace* (the verb), and *kiss and tell*.

And *involve*. "I was not horny or crazy enough to get involved with a Klanswoman even if I weren't already in love . . . with a Maid of Orleans whose cause I believed in"—that brief passage, from my novel *First Hubby*, got me into *maid*, too. Two OED cites from one sentence!

And *fink*, and *feel-good*, and *affecting*.

Seventeen in all. I used these words, and they stuck. I'll probably never catch Tennyson's 4,739. All the same, I am deeply **humble**d. I want to thank the Decatur, Georgia, public school system, which so often required me, so many years ago, to "use each of the following words in a sentence."

➤ off-off rhymes

oodles/bloodless

firefly/briefly

mysterious/my serious

sausage/assuage

shapelier/Montpelier

laundress/undress

heartthrob/bathrobe

ominous/nominees

voodoo/video/voh-doh-de-oh-doh

boat ramp/ boa tramp

alumni/aluminum

forebearing/furbearing

knits/stink

Off-off limerick:

"Yes!" he affirmed, feeling bubbly,
"That is, I mean to say, probably,
    Or possibly so.
    I wouldn't say *no*.
Which is not to say that I'm wobbly."

➤ *Ojibwa/Chippewa/Anishanabe*

European explorers spelled the name of this Native American tribe many different ways. *Achipouá, Anchipawah, Cheppewes, Chiappawaws, Dshipowe-hága, Etchipoës, Gibbaways, Icbewas, Jibewas, Ochipay, Odgjiboweke, Ojeebois, Ojibaway* (Lewis and Clark), *Ojibua, Otchipoises* (LaSalle), *Otjibwek, Ouchipawah, Outchibouec, Shepawees, Tsipó,* and *Uchipweys* are just a few.

To the rapids near where the tribe lived, Frenchmen gave the name Sault Ste. Marie (*sault* being French for tumbling, leaping rapids), so another French name for the people was *Saulters.* English speakers mistranslated that into Jumpers or Leapers, and were no doubt disappointed when the Ojibwa didn't leave the ground any more notably than anyone else. Champlain called them *Cheveux-relevés,* because they wore their hair up.

Iroquois, on the other hand, called them *Dwakanen*, which sounded to Europeans like it should be spelled *Doewogannas* or variations thereof. Dakotas called them *Lyohahanton(wan)*, with lots of diacritical marks that I can't find in my computer, meaning "those at the waterfall." One English speaker rendered that as *Hahatona*, another as *Ra-ra-to-oans*. Other tribes called them *Baawitigong*, or *Pouichtigouin*, both of which meant "those at the rapids." Or so I understand.

The matter is still not entirely settled. In English, *Chippewa* took hold, and it still appears in dictionaries as an alternative, but in the mid-1800s *Ojibwa* or *Ojibway* began to be preferred, especially in Canada, as phonetically correct. Some contemporary members of the tribe—for instance, the activist Winona LaDuke, with whom I went wild-rice gathering in 1996 (see *fox*)—prefer *Anishinabe*, which means "original people." OED uses *Odjibewa*.

Mississippi is an Ojibwa word. It means "big river." *Chicago* is said to come from an Ojibwa word meaning "at the skunk place" or "place of the bad smell."

English gets *totem* from an Ojibwa word, either *nindoodem*, "my totem," according to AHD and OAD, or *ototeman*, "his totem," according to WIII. RHU offers a more extended derivation that clarifies, somewhat, the discrepancy. OED points out that "Rev. P. Jones (a native Odjibewa)" in 1861 rendered it *toodaim* . . . , while the Abbé Thavenel "gives the simple form as *ote*, 'the possessive of which is *otem*.'"

The word *chipmunk* is from either the Ojibwa *ajidamoon* or the Chippewa *atchitamon*, meaning in either case "one who comes down trees head-first."

Explorer: "I say, what is that little animal coming down the tree there? Chipper little fellow."

Local person (thinking, "As any fool can see"): "*Ajidamoon*."

Explorer: "I see. A chipmunk. Picked up the *chip* part right off, if I do say so. Not much resemblance to a *monk*. But I suppose, if you don't look too close . . ."

It used to be correct for English speakers to call Inuit people what the Ojibwa called them: *Eskimo*, meaning "eats it raw." *Inuit*, in Inuit, means "the human beings." The verb *intuit*, "to know intuitively," from a Latin verb meaning "to look at," has nothing to do with any of this.

See **ouistiti** and **knee**.

➤ *omen*

When a bald eagle, carrying a deer's head, fails to clear a power line, caus-ing a power outage and killing the eagle—what is the word for that?

Not *myth*, *allegory*, or *fable*. This eagle story is different from Icarus fly-ing too close to the sun, so that his artificial wings melt, or Hemingway's Old Man, trying to get back to shore with a fish bigger than his boat.

This eagle story is not fictional. It actually happened, in January 2007, in Juneau, Alaska. An explosion! Ten thousand people's lights went out! A repair crew sped to the site! And there lay a deer's head and a dead eagle.

The eagle had evidently picked up the head from a nearby landfill. (Who *throws away* a *deer's head*?) The eagle, said a spokesman for Alaska Electric Light and Power, "got ahold of a little bit more than he could handle."

An *omen*. ("Several etymologies of the Latin word have been suggested," says OED, "none of which seems more likely than the others.") Yes. But an omen of what?

Clearly the eagle is America (the eagle in that song, "Let the Eagle Soar," that John Ashcroft used to sing, remember him?), writing a check with its talons that its wings can't cash. And the power outage is, **well,** loss of power.

But what is the deer's head, exactly?

Before we decide what the deer's head represents to us, let us consider what it represented to the eagle. Was the eagle going to eat that deer's head? Or was he going to hang it on the wall of his eyrie?

"This would have been a major score," said the AEL&P spokesman, putting himself in the eagle's shoes. "That eagle would have been the king eagle of the Lemon Creek group."

The eagle wasn't flying too high, for horizon expansion's sake, like Icarus. The eagle wasn't trying to preserve a hard-earned product of his labor, like Hemingway's fisherman. The eagle had found a trophy.

A trophy that was too big for him. And when you get right down to it, a trophy that was trash. Presumably some human hunter, or more likely his spouse, had finally gotten it out of the house. Even if the eagle had managed to get home with it, the other eagles would have busted his chops:

"Oh, a deer scrap. How long did you have to chase that deer before you threw him down and ripped his head off?"

Not simply a trophy, then, but an oversize, cheesy trophy.

The secret word must be *hypertrophy*, which means exaggerated, abnormal, generally unhealthy development or growth, as of an organ or an enterprise.

Steroids . . . obesity . . . banking bubble . . . housing bubble . . . excessive CEO compensation . . . two wars at once lasting on and on and on . . .

If the eagle came to warn us, it came too late. An after-omen.

See **metanarrative**.

➤ *onesies*

I was wondering, why does *The New York Times* have a "ThursdayStyles" section? Do people in stylish circles dress in a particular way on Thursday? Indoor work clothes I guess, but if you don't find out what to wear until the week is almost over. . . . Maybe it's to prepare people for casual Fridays, but that's not the impression I got, thumbing through it.

If I had been reading *on* Nytimes.com, I would not have ventured into "ThursdayStyles." And the phrase "funereal onesies" would not have jumped out at me. But I was reading *in* the actual newspaper, so there it was, "funereal onesies." What in the hell. Was this some sort of reference to our all dying alone? In "ThursdayStyles"?

No, the story was about how "the skull motif" had taken hold in fashionable clothing. There was a photograph of a funereal onesie. (That's how I assumed the singular would be spelled, much as I preferred *onesy* because it looked like an **off-off rhyme** with *Jonesy*.) A little black one-piece garment, a leotard, with snaps on the bottom. This onesie was emblazoned with a grinning skull wearing a black cap, and the words "The Misfits Fiend Club."

Setting aside the funereal aspect, I found *onesie* provocative. For one thing, it doesn't look like English. But then *one* doesn't look like it ought to be pronounced *wun*. *One* is from the same PIE root—*oi* or *oi-no*—as *only* and *alone*. Perhaps there's an inkling of *w* there—in French *oi* is pronounced *wa* (with singular intimacy in *moi* and *toi*), and Chambers cites an extension, *oi-wo-s*, as the ancestor of certain other languages' versions of *one*. But that's a stretch.

Let us turn to AHD, which says, "Over time, stressed vowels commonly become diphthongs, as when Latin *bona* became *buona* in Italian and *buena* in Spanish." Ah. As so often, we are brought back to the mouth. *Twenty-wun* and *gimme wun*, or for that matter *only wun*, vocalize more smoothly than *twenty-on* and *gimme on* and *only on*. Beginning in Wales and the west of England, *one*'s pronunciation evolved, according to AHD, from *on* as in *only* to *oo-on* to *woon* to (around 1400) *wun*. According to Chambers, *one* was only occasionally spelled the way it was pronounced—the pronunciation *wun* "is first referred to by a scholar in 1701; earlier grammarians give to *one* the sound that it had in *alone, atone, only*, and the . . . suffix *-one*," as today in *acetone*. By the time grammarians' ears caught up, it was too late to change the spelling. (In certain other British dialects, *one* is or has been pronounced *yahn* and *eena*. See the wonderfully baffling rundown on *eena*, as in *eena meena mina mo*, in Anatoly Liberman's *Analytic Dictionary of English Etymology*. He says that in Yorkshire *eena* is still used, instead of *one*, for counting sheep.)

That wasn't the only way I found *onesie* provocative.

"What you doing?"

"Lying in bed."

"What you wearing?"

"Oh, my onesie."

Imagine my chagrin when I Googled *onesies* and found that a onesie was infantwear. You couldn't tell that from the *Times*'s picture, which displayed the onesie, out of scale, next to a skull-motif bikini bottom. The accompanying story never mentioned the onesie. Come to think of it, I believe what first brought my attention to this matter was my impression that the bikini bottom was the onesie.

But okay, a baby thing. The snaps are so you can get at the baby's diaper. *What kind of people put a grinning skull on their baby?*

For that matter, *WHAT KIND OF FAMILY NEWSPAPER RUNS A PICTURE OF A BABY THING NEXT TO ONE OF A BIKINI BOTTOM?*

But wait. My wife tells me that a friend of ours, a grown woman, wears onesies. Adult sizes are getting harder to find, but she tracks them down. "That's her underwear. I'll ask her about it."

"No," I say. "Never mind."

➤ *ooze*

Is this a great word, or what? It didn't happen overnight. Going back to Old English, attempts to capture it, as noun and verb, include *wase, waise, woise, woyse, woze, woose, woes, wozy, oous, oes, owes, oase, ouze, owze, oose, owse,* and *oaze.* West Frisian tried *weaze.* Something to be said for the *w,* which was abandoned in the sixteenth century, but it came in handy in the nineteenth, when O. Henry was the first to publish *woozy.* And we wouldn't have wanted *ooze* to get confused with *woo*—as in pitching it, for instance. (Nobody knows where *woo* came from.)

Chambers relates *ooze* to *virus.* Neither OED nor any other source I have found is willing to suggest that there is anything **sonicky** about it. Come on!

Louis Armstrong on one of the pleasures of life at home in Queens, New York: "A *Garage* with a magic up and down Gate to it. And of course our Birthmark *Car* a Cadillac (Yea). The Kids in our Block just thrill when they see our garage gate up, and our fine Cadillac *ooze* on out."

➤ *ouistiti*

While looking at *squ-* words on OED (see **squelch**), I found, under *squiff* (a contemptible person), this quote from a letter written in 1939 by Ezra Pound: "that squiff, that femme ouistiti and lowest degree of animal life (apart from Cambridge Eng. profs)."

What in the world, I wondered, is a *ouistiti*? OED prefers *wistiti* and calls it a South American monkey or marmoset, named (as so often happens) for its call. Who first used *wistiti* in English print? Of all people, Oliver Goldsmith, in his *History of the Earth and Animated Nature* (1776): "Of the sagoins with feeble tails, there are six kinds. . . . The third is the Wistiti; remarkable for the large tufts of hair upon its face, and its annulated tail."

What did dotty but sweet-natured Oliver Goldsmith (see *Alphabet Juice*) have in common with certifiably insane, fascism-loving Ezra Pound? Why would anyone use this monkey or marmoset as an insult? Because of its feeble tail? The game was afoot!

In OED I looked up *sagoin* and several other terms that arose in that connection, and all I learned was that Goldsmith was a pioneer mentioner of monkeys across the board. The marakina, the sapajou . . . It's not that he was an *expert* on monkeys. Goldsmith was a man who wrote for a living. Aside from the aforementioned *History of the Earth* and so on, and his several abiding imaginative works, Goldsmith produced *The Bee* (essays), *The Grecian History*, *An History of England in a Series of Letters From a Nobleman to His Son*, *The History of England*, *The Memoirs of a Protestant Condemned to the Galleys of France for His Religion*, *Miscellaneous Works*, *A Survey of Experimental Philosophy*, a biography of a famous fop, and on and on and on.

I Googled *ouistiti*. The first thing that came up was a photograph of several beaming naked people riding bicycles, led by a woman with very large breasts. Do algorithms have a weakness for cheap *-titi* jokes? After that came photos of monkeys or marmosets looking much more elegant than the nude bikers. I couldn't see that it would be so insulting to be called a wistiti. They're not suspending themselves by their tails from trees, but they're not sitting buck naked on bicycle seats, either.

I Googled on, and the nudists were explained. In France, to smile while posing for a photo, which the nudists were demonstrably doing, you don't say *"fromage."* You say *"ouistiti."* In *Pardon My French, Unleashing Your Inner Gaul*, Charles Timoney writes that if you say *ouistiti* "in a flat English accent reminiscent of the cartoon dog Droopy, you will look thoroughly miserable," but if "you say it enthusiastically in a strong French accent, the two last syllables force your mouth sideways into a broad grin." Just like *cheese*.

A literary madman (*fou littéraire*) named Claude-Charles Pierquin de Gembloux theorized that people and animals originally spoke the same language. By way of rather oblique proof, he produced a glossary of words used by the ouistiti. For instance, he maintained that when a ouistiti goes *"Irouah-gno,"* it means (as Google translates, poorly, from Gembloux's French) "I have a terrible emotional pain, save me, save it for me." Whereas *"O coco"* means "terror deep," and *"Q uouééé"* is a ouistiti's way of saying "suffer with despair at what we can not escape."

Then I found where Pound might have picked up the word. In his 1921 translation of Remy de Gourmont's *The Natural Philosophy of Love*, we read that "the vagina is more or less closed by a membrane, which the male penis tears in first encounter, in . . . certain small monkeys, the marmoset, certain carnivore . . . The maidenhead is, therefore, not peculiar to human virgins, and there is no glory in a privilege which one shares with the marmoset." The word Pound translated as "marmoset" in that distinctly unappealing passage is *ouistiti*.

From there the trail of Pound and the *ouistiti* got even less pleasant. Possibly the person Pound was insulting was Marcel Proust, whom he calls a *ouistiti* by name in another letter. Proust was gay (so the *femme* might be meant to apply) and half Jewish. In the thirties, shortly before being elected the first Jewish president of France, Léon Blum was beaten nearly to death by anti-Semites and called, by another French politician, "a ouistiti of the ghetto."

The push-button Google translation of that politician's diatribe is lousy, but the nastiness of what he called Blum comes through: "Grumpy Little Girl vivisectionism the early days of birth, marmoset ghetto of twit who is not even from us." In *ouistiti* the polyglot Pound may have been resorting to a common French ethnic slur of the time. He was living in Italy, where he made pro-Fascist, Jew-hating radio broadcasts during World War II. He was captured by American troops, thrown brutally into a literal cage, charged with treason, judged incompetent to stand trial, and sent to a mental hospital for twelve years. After his release, he told Allen Ginsberg, in an interview, "The worst mistake I made was that stupid, suburban prejudice of anti-Semitism." Suburban, is it? Sub-something, anyway.

But it's a pretty little animal (except in the squinchy, beady-eyed face), the ouistiti. A series of popular French children's books chronicle the adventures of a ouistiti (a *mignon*, or cute, ouistiti) named Sapristi. *P'tit ouistiti* is sweet to the tongue. So is *ouistiti* neutral? Only in the sense that *sweet* is. You can call someone "Sweetie" sweetly or meanly, and either way, the *we/wee/oui/tweet/twee/teeny* in there evokes a squeeze.

➤ *outdo*

"You've outdone yourself" strikes me as a dubious compliment. An editor told me that once about a book review I'd written, which, to be sure, was deftly turned, but I had to wonder: Hadn't he for God's sake ever read the much better stuff I'd been doing over several decades? Also, to outdo my-

self would be to perform over my head, to reach a fortuitous level I'd be lucky to reach again. Wouldn't it?

I am not usually this **touchy**.

➤ *ox*

This strong, stolid animal might feel better about his loss of testicles, and his consignment to hard labor, if he knew that no other animal has everything (at least in terms of tick-tack-toe, football plays, and, yes, kisses and hugs) summed up so **succinct**ly in its name.

p · P · p

This is one of the first alphabet sounds a baby can make, and you can tell it pleases the baby. No wonder it looms so large in the arts:

Pap, Huck Finn's reprobate father.

Pep, Nathanael West's nickname (because he tended to lack pep).

Willie Pep, the great featherweight fighter.

Pip, the hero of *Great Expectations*. That novel's other memorable characters include Aged P., Mr. Wemmick's aged father (the *P* is for *Parent*), who though stone deaf has a propensity for social cheerfulness. "All right, ain't you, Aged P.?" Wemmick will ask the dad, who will reply, "All right, John my boy, all right!" Says Pip, of a meal with the Wemmicks, "We ate the whole of the toast, and drank tea in proportion, and it was delightful to see how warm and greasy we all got after it. The Aged especially, might have passed for some clean old chief of a savage tribe, just oiled."

Then there's Pip in *Moby-Dick*, the diminutive, jolly-bright black youth who can't resist jumping into the water when they've got a whale harpooned, and goes eloquently mad. Why has no one rewritten *Moby-Dick* from *his* point of view?

Pop, let's see, "Pop Goes the Weasel." Pop Fligh, the retired ballplayer who becomes the adoptive grandfather of Dondi, in the old comic strip, remember? The rocker Iggy Pop, and, *well*, pop.

Pup, there's Pupdog in *Pogo*, and Officer Pupp in *Krazy Kat*.

Then there's Papagena/Papageno, Papa Hemingway, paper, Joseph Papp, Pappy Yokum, Bo Peep, *Typee: A Peep at Polynesian Life*.

Peeping Tom, "We, the People," Pépé le Moko, Pepé Le Pew, Pepe the Prawn (Muppet), Pepi Katona (the slimy character in *The Shop Around the Corner*), and the Person from Porlock (see *peeve*).

Peter Pan, Wally Pipp, Gladys Knight and the Pips, "Pippa Passes" ("God's in his heaven, all's right with the world"), *Pippi Longstocking*, Louis "Pops" Armstrong, Poe, Pooh, "You can't Pooh-Pooh Paducah, That's Another Name for Paradise," pop art, popcorn, Alexander Pope, Popeye, Popeye Doyle, *Mr. Popper's Penguins*, the W. C. Fields movie *Poppy*, Rupert Pupkin in *The King of Comedy*, and puppets.

You say, oh, the same thing could be claimed for any letter. You're welcome to try.

➤ *pachyderm/pachysandra*

What do an **elephant** and a "small genus of the family Buxaceae comprising procumbent subshrubs and perennial herbs with simple leaves and spikes of insignificant white or pinkish flowers, native to eastern Asia and eastern North America" (OED) have in common? *Pachy* is from the Greek for thick. Thick skin, in the elephant's case. In pachysandra's case, the reference is not to how well this visually benevolent plant (*subshrub?*) covers ground, but to the thickness of the male flower's stamens. Strike you as sexist, to look at pachysandra and focus on its stamens? The *sandra* part derives from no woman's name but from the Greek for male, as in *androcentric*. Now: what makes a flower "insignificant"?

➤ page turning

Now that there are so many e-alternatives to books made of paper, it dawns on me that the physical act of page turning—separating one leaf from the next (some people actually *wet their fingertips* to do this), and the next, and so on, and sometimes one leaf is slightly more or less wide than the next, or leaves may cling to one another, and sometimes you can flip leaves but other times you have to take two of them together between thumb and forefinger and *rub* until they separate, and often a good deal of fumbling is involved—where were we?

The act of proceeding through physical reading material—that is to say, through printed matter—may strike future generations as bizarre. ("Wait— one page is on the *back* of the previous page? What's up with that?" "If you think the so-called **mouse** was clunky, imagine having to separate two razor-

thin sheets of paper, or *leaves*, over and over again, with your fingers.")
Someday, before I punch my last Scroll-ahead button, leafing may strike
even me as bizarre. I wrote eight or nine books on a manual typewriter, and
today I can't conceive how anyone would begin to go about such a thing.
(There was something called a *platen*, I recall, and you cranked paper in
around it and when you struck keys, clickety clack, letters on the end of
metal stalks would swing up and hit the paper—or, rather, would press an
inky ribbon against the paper, a ribbon that would rise up just in time,
unless it got tangled, and sometimes you'd strike more than one key at
once and the metal stalks would get jammed together and your fingers
would get inky trying to separate the keys, and don't get me started on
carbon paper . . . It's a wonder I survived to tell the tale. But by thunder,
me hearties, didn't we bang out some prose?)

If page turning dies out, however, certain pleasures will die with it. I
applaud a magazine article that jumps—from page 24 to page 78, say. That
article has not been cut to fit just one hole, it has been allowed to continue
in the back of the book, where it can loosen its tie and breathe.

And how about the suspense involved in turning a page. Turning it at a
pace that blends your intention and the page's resistance. Or turning several pages in unseemly haste, as I did when I came to this in the lower
right-hand corner of a story in *Vanity Fair*:

> She wore a silky maternity dress under a blue blazer. . . . After a
> while, she took off the jacket, and there were her CONTINUED ON
> PAGE 132

Do you think *Vanity Fair* did that on purpose? Anyway, I leafed and leafed
and came at last to page 132, where I found the following:

> CONTINUED FROM PAGE 74 arms with their hieroglyphic tattoos . . .

Yes, I did feel sheepish, especially since the lady was with child. (See *gillie, girl*.) But in the course of the leafing I was *up*. Maybe after all page turning is a natural pleasure—there is something distinctly engrossing about it.
In the New Orleans zoo I watched a silverback gorilla perusing a flattened
wad of brown paper. He would lift a flap of it, turn it over, study the other
side of it . . .

➤ *pang*

As you say it you can almost feel it, can't you? Ernest **Weekley**, who knew pangs, derived the word from *prong* with the *r* lost, as in *Frances* evolving into *Fanny*. Current dictionaries, doubting that etymology, fall back on "of obscure origin." But I like Weekley's suggestion: "For ground-sense of constriction, cf. *anguish*, *angina*." Those two words, as well as *anger* and Latin *angere* (to strangle), come from a PIE root **angg-*, narrow. Is that what Weekley means by *ground-sense*? Is he suggesting that *ang* is **sonicky**? If he isn't, I am. It tightens the throat, evoking, however distantly, "a sudden sharp spasm of pain which grips the body or a part of it," as OED defines *pang*.

➤ *peeve*

People, including me, love our pet peeves. And I stress *our*. When I sense a peeve about to come boiling up at me from an audience, I pray it isn't one to which I must frankly respond, "No, the truth is, I like *snuck*" or "Well, as far as *gone missing* goes, I can't think of any expression that expresses the meaning meant to be expressed, uh, as well as *gone missing* does, actually." Which will cause the bearer of the peeve in question to look at me as if I had just said, "No, in point of fact, I can't see anything much about your baby that is what I would call cute."

What we can all agree on, I think, is that *peeve* is a word that sounds just right. A cross, we might imagine, between *pique* and *skeeve*.

The adjective, *peevish*, came first. OED says it may derive ultimately from Latin *perversus*, but then again (hold on to your hat):

> An alternative suggestion links the word to classical Latin *expavidus* startled, shy (< *ex-* + *pavidus* PAVID *adj*.) via an unrecorded variant with *-ai-* of Middle French *espave* (of an animal) stray, (of a person) foreign, (as noun) lost property, flotsam (1283 in Old French; French *épave*). The semantic connection is thought to be the behaviour of stray animals.

OED gets like that sometimes. When you click on *pavid*, the first definition is from my seventeenth-century forebear Thomas Blount's *Glos-*

sographia: "fearful, timerous, quaking, starting." The original sense of *peevish*, at any rate, is "perverse, refractory; headstrong, obstinate; capricious, skittish; (also) coy." OED's first example, which I will be so bold as to convert into modern spelling, is from *Piers Plowman*, fifteenth century: "And bade him go piss with his plow, peevish shrew!" That's not Piers calling the disrespecter of his plow a shrew, it's the disrespecter calling Piers one—originally, a shrew could be male or female. A recent translation of that passage renders *shrew* as *bastard*.

Not until 1901 did *peevish* give rise to the verb *peeve*, meaning make peevish, or annoy.

Then in 1909 *The Washington Post* referred to "a fit of peeve." Finally in 1917 we get "little pet peeve." Don't ever call someone's pet peeve a little one. It's like insulting somebody's plow.

One of Samuel Taylor Coleridge's pet peeves was "that vile and barbarous vocable *talented*." We might suspect that Coleridge had been called "talented" by a reviewer, as in "This quite talented writer has produced a book in no wise worthy of this critic's willingness to consider him quite talented." But Coleridge's objection was grammatical: "The formation of a participle passive from a noun is a licence that nothing but a very peculiar felicity can excuse." OED cites this cavil as an example of "groundless objections . . . by writers ignorant of the history of the language." Ooh, snap. You may be a poet, but that don't mean you know whereof the language. (Or even if you are a lexicographer of sorts—the other example of history-of-the-language ignorance that OED cites, under *-ed*, *suffix*^{2}, is Dr. Johnson's disapproval of *cultured*.)

Heck of a poet, Coleridge. Today we may find "five miles meandering in a mazy motion" too blatantly **sonicky**. But do we think we are likely to write anything that will last as long as "a sadder and a wiser man, / He rose the morrow morn"? Or "water, water everywhere, / Nor any drop to drink"? (Granted that everyone misremembers those lines as "but not a drop" and "sadder but wiser man.")

No ray of sunshine was the man Coleridge, though. On hearing Wordsworth's poem about a rainbow, he went home and wrote "Dejection: An Ode." How would you like to wake up feeling chipper and, I don't know, maybe even talented—cultured, too—and you go out walking along, whistling, and here comes Coleridge to inform you that your felicity is "very peculiar." Coleridge sought felicity in laudanum, tincture of opium in alcohol. (Paracelsus, who gets credit for originating laudanum, claimed that his version also included gold leaf and unperforated pearls—ground up, I guess—but come on.)

Talk about pet peeves, if you are a big Coleridge fan you probably say "That *son of a—*" whenever you hear any reference to anybody from the town of Porlock. Coleridge, by his account, awoke one morn from an opiated dream in which he had envisioned a fantastical "pleasure-dome" built in Xanadu by Kubla Khan. With a whole bedazzling poem pulsating in his head, he had managed to write down only a wondrous fragment when, wouldn't you know, "a person on business from Porlock" interrupted. By the time that person was gone, so was the rest of the poem.

Now you and I, if we had something that hot going, would have said "Shove off, Porlock person"—or maybe we wouldn't have. Think about it. It's a burden to have something visionary, or let's say conceivably visionary, or visionary *so far*, to get off your chest and onto paper (or screen), for the ages. Once I e-mailed my friend Kathi Kamen Goldmark the lyrics for what would have been—okay, again, conceivably—the first stanza and chorus of an all-time great country song, "A Sadder Budweiser Man." When she came to put those lyrics to music, she had lost them, and so had I.

It was Coleridge who first came up with the phrase "willing suspension of belief." So let's—no, let's *not* give him the benefit of the doubt. Let's look at Porlock. I'm not saying Coleridge made up the village; it is real enough, to this day, and very near to Nether Stowey, where Coleridge was living at the time. Nether Stowey may suggest something subconsciously tucked away. Another neighboring village, Minehead, may evoke excavation of the brain (or dome). But *Porlock*! A blend of *poor* and *block*. I'm saying Coleridge made up the person, and provenanced him, so to speak, from Porlock.

Look at the last bit of what Coleridge eventually published, titled "Kubla Khan: or, A Vision in a Dream." In the lines that Coleridge was professedly pouring out when the alleged Porlockian came knocking, the poet has quick-cut from his pleasure-dome vision itself to something he has *already* forgotten: a song, played by a damsel on a dulcimer, which, if only the poet could recall it, he would be filled with such "deep delight" that he could build a pleasure-dome of his own:

That sunny dome! Those caves of ice!
And all who heard should see them there,
And all should cry, Beware! Beware!
His flashing eyes, his floating hair!
Weave a circle round him thrice,
And close your eyes with holy dread,
For he on honey-dew hath fed,
And drunk the milk of Paradise.

That's pretty damn good. And if it's not a picture of peculiar felicity, I don't know what is. And it leaves the poet crazed and unfit for human company. Also unfit, quite imaginably, to imagine anything next. The job of the wonder-working writer, wrote Coleridge, is to "trace the *nice* boundaries, beyond which terror and sympathy are deserted by the pleasurable emotions—to reach those limits, yet never to pass them." Oh, some person from somewhere (presumably not the poet's opium connection) may have interposed himself as Coleridge was reeling at the brink, but I'm saying Coleridge wasn't so much interrupted, as stuck. And his visitor got him off the hook.

Snuck, by the way, is "orig. and chiefly U.S.," says OED. WIII says it's "chiefly dialect," which I suppose comes to the same thing. I like it. It sounds quicker and also more underhanded than *sneaked*.

> *pet, peevish*

Recently a mailing from the Massachusetts Society for the Prevention of Cruelty to Animals put this question to me: "Would your pet like to become a blood donor?" In case my pet would, the mailing provided a number in Boston to call.

"Snowpaw, would you like to become a blood donor?"

"*Rrrrr.*"

"*Okay.* I'm just asking, because—"

"*Rrrrr.*"

See *R*.

➤ *ping-pong*

The "sound imitation" origin of this word "is not in doubt," writes Anatoly Liberman in *Word Origins, and How We Know Them*. Well, sure. But *gnip-gnop*, which is what I called it when I was thirteen and played it a lot, is better. And you know the sound of a loose ping-pong ball bouncing on a floor, wild and free and derisively eluding its pursuer—*pingk . . . pingk . . . pingk . . . pink, ping-pingpingpng*—and then rolling, more and more slowly, with the inimitable, unwritable noise made only by a rolling ping-pong ball? Why does it fall to me, a print person, straining every literary fiber, to memorialize that sound? Why hasn't it been used in a movie?

Not to mention the sound of an empty tennis-ball can rolling, wonkily, zephyr-blown, across an asphalt court.

➤ *plank*

This word is believed to derive from the Latin *plancus*, flat. Okay, but *plank* also evokes the sound of a plank planked down onto another long flat board. *Plunk*, as in " 'Quit plunking that damn cello,' I tells him, so he plunks the clunky thing in my lap," is in either sense "probably of imitative origin," says Chambers. You can use *plank* to mean *plunk* in the second sense, but not in the first, perhaps because *plank* sounds off-key. If you *plink* something, it is probably a piano key, at the high end.

The thicker a plank is, the more the sound of a plank planked onto another is like *blonk*.

Pluck, meaning pick, without the resonant *n* of *plunk*, may, or may not, come from Latin *piluccare*, to remove hair from.

Strum is **sonicky** and that's that. And so is *twang*.

Pick comes from various Germanic roots involving pricking and pecking. It occurs to me that *pick* is a term widely applied in sports. In basketball (but not, legally, in football), you set a pick, screening away your teammate's defender. In baseball you pick off a runner (perhaps first catching him in a pickle); and you may "pick something up" in a pitcher's delivery that reveals what he is about to throw; and if you are a **snazzy** infielder, you are said to "really pick it." In football, you pick apart a defense, and to pick off a pass is to intercept it—so interceptions are called picks. In bull-fighting, which some deem a sport, there is the picador, who pokes a lance into the bull's neck muscles so he will keep his head down. In various sports, teams acquire draft picks, and when some players are in a slump, their teammates, ideally, pick them up by perhaps **outdo**ing themselves. In betting on sports, you try to pick winners. I remember Bill Leggett of *Sports Illustrated* (at a time when people displayed less sensitivity in ethnic references) criticizing his own record in the office football pool as follows: "I couldn't pick my father out of a boatload of Chinamen."

➤ *poop-noddy, noddypoop*

Don't confuse 'em. According to OED, *poop-noddy* is a rare seventeenth-century term—still not quite obsolete—for sexual intercourse. It *is* obsolete as a synonym for nincompoop. For that you need *noddypoop*. "Apparently," muses OED, *noddypoop* is formed from *noddy* plus "a second element of uncertain origin. Perhaps compare POOP."

Someday, perhaps, in a last-ditch appeal to younger readers, we will take up *poop*. (According to Anatoly Liberman, every meaning of *poop* is "slangy" except for *poop* as in *poop deck*, and that one probably derives from Latin slang, and furthermore, "The origin of all *poops* but one is unknown; *poop* '[to make] an abrupt sound' is an indelicate onomatopoeia.") For now I am content to report that *noddy* is another word for fool or simpleton.

Another *noddy*, modern-day but perhaps not entirely unrelated to the other *noddy*, is a feature of a filmed or videotaped interview. OED defines that *noddy* (also called *noddy shot*) as "a brief shot of the interviewer (or interviewee) appearing to be listening or nodding in agreement, usually recorded after the main interview and edited to form part of it; the action captured by such a shot."

You love television, don't you? You "trust" television, sort of—no, of course you don't *believe* it, but you let it take you by the eyes. And television pulls shit like that on you. Showing someone nodding at nothing, as if—you know, there is something *significant* about a nod of agreement—as if that person were nodding at something. I'm trying to think whether print pulls anything like that on you. No denying print pulls things on you, I'm just saying I don't think print. . . . Maybe I can't think of whatever it is that print pulls, any more than a tropical fish is aware of the charm of—

whatever its charms are. Personally, I have never been charmed by tropical fish—oh, maybe the print equiv of a noddy is what I'm doing right now,
writing and rewriting these sentences in an attempt to sound like I'm
talking. But here's a difference between TV journalism and print: if there
were such a thing as a noddy in print, print would not have a name for it.
Print has names, which it seldom shares with its audience, for the fatuous
rituals it covers—"grip and grin," for photos of politicians shaking hands
with thereby distinguished constituents, but of course that's a fatuous
photo ritual. Print journalism traffics in clichés, to be sure, but more in-
genuously, for what that may be worth, than TV resorts to noddies.

➤ *portmanteau*

By way of edifying Alice, Lewis Carroll's Humpty Dumpty explains a word
in Carroll's great nonsense poem *Jabberwocky* as follows: "Well, 'slithy'
means 'lithe and slimy.' . . . You see it's like a portmanteau, there are two
meanings packed up into one word." A portmanteau being a piece of lug-
gage that opens into two halves. Portmanteaus not coined by Carroll include *smog, motel, brunch, transistor (transfer/resistor), Brangelina, wholphin*
(cross between a dolphin and a false killer whale, whatever that is—seems
like ocean survival would favor, if anything, a false vegetarian whale), *scratch*
(see **itch**), and *Spanglish*.

Carroll's portmanteaus are not so simply folded. His *chortle*, which has
had legs, is the backside of *snort* replacing the middle of *chuckle*. Here is
how he unpacks another bit of *Jabberwocky*: "Take the two words *fuming*
and *furious*. Make up your mind that you will say both words, but leave it
unsettled which you will say first . . . If you have that rarest of gifts, a perfectly balanced mind, you will say *frumious*." But that is whimsy. The most
firmly packed portmanteaus capture physical acts or phenomena. Seeing
someone give herself a twist and begin to swirl, the language comes up
(pushing aside the existing but inadequate *tirl*) with *twirl*.

Refudiate, the portmanteau issued twice publicly in 2010 by Alaska's
abdicated governor, Sarah Palin, seems unlikely to travel well, for when
her apparent notion that *refudiate* was already a word was refuted, she in
effect repudiated *refudiate* by changing it to *refute* and then to *regret*.

"Shakespeare liked to coin new words too," Palin tweeted. To be sure

Shakespeare is credited with writing a great many words for the first time, but most of these were adoptions and adaptations. For instance *alligator*, spelled *allegater*, first appears in the First Folio edition of *Romeo and Juliet*, but it had been in print as *alligarta* or *alligarto* (from the Spanish *el lagarto*, the lizard) for nearly half a century. He is credited with *dawn*, but *dawning* had been around for centuries; with *bandit*, but he wrote *bandetto*, borrowed from Italian. He was the first to write *leapfrog*, but probably boys were playing it already. He inventively turned *cake* into a verb, as in caked in blood, but the noun had long been established. By and large the words Shakespeare made up from scratch (for instance *directitude*, a servant's apparent attempt, in *Coriolanus*, at a high-flown synonym for *discredit*) were comical characters' blunders. The closest thing to a portmanteau I can find in lists of Shakespeare's coinages is *bubukles*, coined by Fluellen, the staunch but ill-spoken Welshman in *Henry V*. A nineteenth-century scholar traced *bubukles* to the French *bube*, a blotch or sore, and *buccal*, from the Latin for cheek; OED calls it "a confusion of *bubo* and *carbuncle*."

Speaking of packing, here is a definition of *unpack*, from Urbandictionary.com, that might have been composed by a cross between Humpty Dumpty and Alice herself. (Except that "Sunlight," the definition's author, would seem to have paid regrettably less attention to English teachers—note *auther* and *had shook*—than either of those characters):

UNPACK

verb. A tedious activity invented by English teachers. The meaning of every word in a sentence must be explained with an entirely new sentence or paragraph.

The sentence: "Mrs. Goodwater nodded, held up her hands, and there was silence."

Unpacked becomes: "Well, the auther calls her Mrs. Goodwater and not Clara to emphasize her position of authority over the audience. The fact that she nodded implies a positive emotional impact, rather than if she had shook her head or frowned, which would have been negative. This explains that she is on friendly terms with the audience. Since the audience was not living in fear of her authority, they were not quiet immediately. Therefore she also had to hold up her hands, which means she was on the verge of becoming exasperated, and which is also an example of the author's use of alliteration. But when she did that the audience became silent. Since the author used 'silent' instead of 'quiet,' or 'softer,' it shows that he meant every person had stopped talking and they all had their attention on Mrs. Goodwater."

That's why I read books, not English papers.

See **chimera**.

➤ *preemptive*

From the Latin meaning literally to prepurchase. The *empt-* is as in *caveat emptor*. When the Bush administration prepared to make a preemptive attack on Iraq, Colin Powell was quoted as cautioning, "You break it, you bought it."

➤ *prescient*

Odd quote from Frank Rich used as a blurb on *The Next Attack* by Daniel Benjamin and Steven Simon: "*The Next Attack* is prescient to a scary degree."

You can say something *was* prescient. You can say someone's work *has been* prescient. But can you say something *is* prescient? Only if you are being prescient yourself.

See **hunch**.

➤ *prick*

Did you know that *prick* in the sixteenth and seventeenth centuries, according to OED, was "a term of endearment for a man: darling, sweetheart"? From a colloquy by Erasmus as translated in 1671: "Ah, ha! are we not alone, my prick? . . . Let us go together into my inner bed-chamber." (This is not Erasmus speaking to himself, so to speak. It's a likable **strumpet**, Lucretia, addressing a friend and former customer, Sophronius, who, having reformed himself, proceeds to talk her into leaving off her lewd ways. In another translation she calls him "cocky." I always wanted to read me some Erasmus. I'm going to find a good modern translation.)

The sixteenth century was also when *prick* turned up in print meaning, quite frankly, the penis. In 1555, an anonymous author described a prime tactic of highway robbers as follows: "The first precept thereof is to be as secret in working, as he that keeps a man company from London to Maidenhead and makes good cheer along the way, to this end in the thicket: to turn his prick upward, and cast a weavers knot on both his thumbs behind him." (I have modernized the spelling. Don't ask me what dastardly form of apparent bondage is being described. I'm not even entirely sure whose prick is alluded to.)

Not until 1598 did *prick* appear in print as an insult, and then it connoted pert, saucy near sissiness: "A pillicock, a primcock, a prick, a prettie lad, a gull, a noddie." Only by 1927 does OED find *prick* clearly meaning a mean, overbearing male. John O'Hara (who by all accounts could certainly be one): "I'll need you to . . . keep me from getting to be too much of a prick."

See **A**.

> *prior to*

There is no need for this phrase. It reeks of soulless organization. *Before* is what people say.

> proposal, wording of, proper

According to J. B. Morton (Beachcomber), "A man who says, during courtship, 'Will you be mine?' is a potential tyrant. If, however, he says, 'Will I be yours?' he is inviting the girl to be a tyrant. The ideal proposal is, 'Let us be ours.' "

See *fancy*.

> *pshaw*

Some authorities say this is pronounced *shaw*—the *p* would be silent, then, as in swimming. But OED puts a "*(p)*" in there. An option, then, or a wispy *p*. I like the *p* myself, the *idea* of it, but am constrained to admit I never say "pshaw!" one way or the other. Does anyone anymore? OED quotes this from *Vibe* in 1992: "James Brown: the Godfather of Soul? Pshaw! He's the

Godfather of Modern Culture." You never know where James Brown is going to pop up. (I know *pop* is too faint a word.)

OED cites the intransitive verb *pshaw* in a 1991 Michael Dibdin novel: "I pshawed. You don't often get a chance to pshaw these days, and I made the most of it." The transitive form turns up even more recently, in *The Nation*, 2005: "Johnson had always pshawed the notion that his fights were blows against the white empire on behalf of the beleaguered Black man." That would be Jack Johnson. *He* pshawed? I always think of *pshaw* more in connection with, say, George Bernard Pshaw.

➢ *pu-*

From this one PIE root, which is in effect *pooh* or *phew* or *p-yew* or *phooey*, reaction to a foul odor, we get *putrid, pus, purulent, suppurate, foul, filth,* and maybe *puke*. So this entry is a fitting lead-in to the next one.

(And see **well** and **ew**.)

➢ *puffery*

Moody's Investors Service rates the investment-worthiness of government and commercial entities based, supposedly, on rigorous and reliable research. Jonathan Weil on Bloomberg.com pointed out that in its 2005 annual report, Moody's proclaimed: "Independence. Performance. Transparency . . . are the watchwords by which stakeholders judge Moody's." But when Moody's was taken to court for having given its highest ratings to toxic investments, the company asserted that "generalizations regarding integrity, independence and risk management amount to no more than puffery."

Weil, a hardened observer of high (a word that may mean lofty or stoned or stinking) finance, was shocked that Moody's would "characterize the principles it brought to the job of grading investments that wind up in the portfolios of retirement funds and money-market accounts" as puffery. "It would be like the pope revealing that his belief in God was just fluff."

What does Moody's mean by *puffery*? Weil asked a Moody's PR man, Anthony Mirenda. Mirenda replied, "Our legal team's use of that term does not suggest that these statements are in any way false and does not in any way diminish Moody's long-standing commitment to the integrity and independence of our ratings." When Weil asked Mirenda whether the statement Mirenda had just made was puffery, he said, "No, that statement was not puffery."

Piffle. How can people at Moody's hold up their heads?

➤ *pun*

Some people actually hate puns. William Shawn, the near-godlike editor of *The New Yorker*, was one. Dan Menaker, in his book *A Good Talk*, says that even though he was well aware of this aversion, he couldn't resist ending a Talk of the Town item with a pun. Mr. Shawn took it out. Menaker put it back in. Mr. Shawn called Menaker into his office and said, "I think you must not understand that to use this pun would *destroy the magazine*."

Menaker's item was about how people were getting around Manhattan during a transit strike. One man's answer was, "Diesel." Pointing to his feet, he explained: "Diesel get me anywhere."

What I hate is having no occasion to use puns that have come to me out of the blue. For instance:

"Does your husband know his way around a dance floor?"
"Oh, yeah. He's managed to avoid one for thirty-five years."

The Algonquin Round Table, a group of dedicated, highly competitive witticizers who lunched at the Algonquin Hotel in New York in the 1920s, tried to outdo each other in a game of punning on unlikely words. For instance, Dorothy Parker was given the word *horticulture*. She had to use it in a sentence within ten seconds. "You can lead a horticulture," she said, "but you can't make her think." Alexander Woollcott came up with "*Demosthenes* can do is bend, and hold the legs together." I wonder if you'd like to hear my pun on *indefensible*:

He doesn't have much sense, a bull,
And he is mean and immense, a bull,
And jealousy makes him intense, a bull,

And I will tell you all right now,
If he spies you milking his favorite cow,
He'll tear a hole indefensible.

Anyway, here's a pun from a Cole Porter song, "Don't Look at Me That Way," which you may not be familiar with:

"My will is strong, but my won't is weak."

➤ *punctilious*

Meticulous generally connotes commendable particularity (note the *tic* in both words); *punctilious* extends scrupulosity to "extremely or excessively particular or correct" (OED) lengths. I want to say the negative aspect of *punctilious* is reinforced by the echoes of *punk* and *Tillie* (George Kaufman in the Algonquin **pun** game said of sisters Lizzie and Tillie, "Lizzie is okay, but you have no idea how *punctilious*"), but neither of these suggests *fussi*ness over details. According to the Jargon File at catb.org (whatever the hell that means), "Aunt Tillie" is "the archetypal nontechnical user, one's elderly and scatterbrained maiden aunt. Invoked in discussions of usability for people who are not hackers and geeks, one sees references to the 'Aunt Tillie test.'"

Punk has a long interesting history, from prostitute to Billy Idol, but at no point along the way has it been related to *punctilious*, which springs from the PIE root *peuk-* or *peug-*, to **prick**, from which we also get *pugnacious*, *impugn*, *poignant*, *point*, *pounce*, *punctual*, *punctuate*, *puncture*, *pungent*, and *Pygmy*. That last is from the Greek *pugme*, in ancient Greece a unit of measure representing the length from the average man's elbow to his knuckles. It was hard to be punctilious about measurements back then, but the African tribesmen known as Pygmies were probably never *that* short.

At any rate, I applaud when *The New York Times* runs a punctilious correction like this one:

An obituary on Friday about the actor Fess Parker included several errors. Mr. Parker's daughter is Ashley Parker Snider, not Parker-Snyder. Eddy Arnold—not Eddie—was the singer who recorded one of many versions of "The Ballad of Davy Crockett" . . . And a line from that song should have read, "Raised in the woods so's he knew ev'ry tree"—not "Raised in the woods so he knew every tree."

➤ *puppy*

According to Ben Schott in *The New York Times*, a Russian doctor named Marie de Manacéine "discovered," in 1894, "that puppies died when kept awake for 4–6 days, or 96–144 hours."

What kind of person—? And I'll bet this so-called doctor complained: "One had constantly to keep poking the puppies, and poking the puppies, and addressing the puppies more and more sharply, and then when one needed a break, one's assistant might be expected to take over—but Igor was not to be trusted. When my back was turned Igor would indulge the puppies in little catnaps (oops); and as I beat him for this, oh, the excuses [here she adopts a sarcastic version of a hunchback's whine]: 'The puppies whimper and yip! The puppies whimper and yip! And they blink those sleepy puppy eyes!' This from a person with a *penchant* for suspending human subjects head-down over hot coals—but give him puppies to keep awake, and 'Oh, oh, it's tearing me up inside!'"

To be fair, the Russian word for puppy, as best I can determine, is pronounced something like *sh'chenok*. No excuse for Dr. de Menacing, but a puppy regarded as a *sh'chenok* may smell less sweet. And we cannot assume, even given Dr. de Maniac's French name, that she was familiar with the evolution of Middle French *poupée*, doll, into English *puppy*, meaning toy dog for a while before it extended to young dogs. (French for puppy is *chiot*, more endearing than *sh'chenok* but far more chichi than *puppy*. The very sound of *puppy* is enough to make a normal person—one who is aware of how intensely puppies value sleep—want to go *oo-wooby-wooby-wooby*.)

The Old English word for a young dog was the drastically less *awwww*-inspiring *hwelp*, which became *whelp* and lurked around for centuries. In 1682, Sir Thomas Browne wrote, "I kept an Eagle two years, which fed upon Kats, Kittlings, Whelps and Ratts." As late as 1894 (while over in Russia Dr. Demoniac was jostling puppies to death), Rudyard Kipling employed the simile "mean as a collier's whelp." (Colliers, who made and sold charcoal, were "notorious for cheating," according to Etymonline.com, so no wonder their puppies turned mean.) You wouldn't say "cute as a collier's whelp."

Whelp sounds like a backhanded slap. *Puppy* cropped up in the late sixteenth century. It has superseded *whelp*, and that is a good thing.

From the same Old French stock (and farther back from Latin *pupa* meaning girl or doll), we get *pupil*, in the ocular sense, because of the tiny image of oneself one sees reflected in that dark spot in the middle of another person's eye. The other *pupil*, student, is from back in that etymology somewhere; originally it meant orphan child or ward. Etymonline.com quotes Plato: "Self-knowledge can be obtained only by looking into the mind and virtue of the soul, which is the diviner part of a man, as we see our own image in another's eye." Now that I look at that, it's not so clear. Is Plato saying we do have the power, in this limited sense, to see ourselves as others see us? Or that two people seeing eye to eye are each just seeing an image of himself or herself? (See **each other**.)

I don't know whether we can see ourselves in puppies' pupils, or vice versa. The next time I get hold of a puppy that will hold still long enough with its eyes open, I will look.

➢ *purl*

A purling stream swirls, murmurs, and gurgles. Maybe an "imitative formation," says OED grudgingly.

The other *purl*, to knit with inverted stitches, may be seen to bear a faint family resemblance—Chambers connects that *purl* to Middle English *pirlying*, revolving or twisting. But no bloodlines have been found.

q · Q · q

During World War I, the British and U.S. navies lured German submarines to their destruction by setting out "mystery ships," which were camouflaged to look like half-sunk merchant vessels but in fact were seaworthy and armed. A submarine would close in for what looked like an easy kill and be surprised. These mystery ships were also called Q-boats. Why? OED says "probably arbitrary" or "perhaps" from "the initial letter of *query*," or "probably after slightly earlier use of *P-boat* for a patrol boat." Two probablies and a perhaps, and yet no hint of the explanation that strikes me as most likely. What were German submarines called? In German, *Unterseeboots*; in English, U-boats. Call me alphabet-obsessed, but don't you think somebody said, "Troll with a Q, and a U is bound to follow"?

➤ *Q-tip*

Did you think this would be in OED? I didn't either. But it is. The *Q*, according to OED, is for *quality*. "The product was apparently invented in 1923 by Leo Gerstenzang, a Polish-born American, who initially named them *Baby Gays*." Not that there was anything wrong, or particularly Polish, about that. "In 1926 the name was changed to *Q-tips Baby Gays*, and later shortened to *Q-tips*."

➤ questions not to ask an author, with answers

Q. How is your book coming?

A. Don't know. Let's hope.

Q. How is your book doing?

A. Don't know. Let's hope.

Q. Are you working on anything right now?

A. No, I'm being fed by whatever those birds are in the Bible that fed whoever that was.

Q. You can work anywhere, right?

A. Not here, for instance.

Q. What do you want people to take away from your book?

A. If I told people that, why would they buy it? My focus is on what *I* want to take away from my book: enough revenue to help keep me afloat while I'm figuring out some way to write another one.

Q. Do you write on a computer?

A. I hope in time to catch up with that technology. So far, I'm using a bloody finger on bathroom mirrors.

Q. What is your book about?

A. That must seem a reasonable question. It probably is a reasonable question. It makes me want to sob brokenly. I *conceived* the son of a bitch. I *proposed* the son of a bitch. My agent and I found a *publisher* for the son of a bitch. I *wrote* the son of a bitch. And *rewrote* the son of a bitch. And rewrote the son of a bitch *again*. And *again*. And *read* the son of a bitch printed out. And *fiddled* some more with the son of a bitch. And read the son of a bitch in *galleys*. And *haggled with the copy editor*—with pleasure, but still—over the son of a bitch. And read the son of a bitch *again* in *corrected* galleys. And survived the *reviews* of the son of a bitch. And *presented* the son of a bitch to forty-eight insanely various *audiences*. And now I have to *sum up* the son of a bitch? Let's just say, you'll love it.

Q. Don't you love it?

A. William Faulkner handed the typescript of *The Sound and the Fury* to his editor and said, "It's a real son of a bitch."

See *upaya*.

➤ *quip*

OED borders on acknowledging that this word, whose origin is unknown, has a **sonicky** element by saying "perhaps influenced by words of similiar ending," like *clip*, *nip*, and *whip*, "which contain the idea of something sharp or cutting." Sharp, cutting, and quick, I would say. A *zinger*, or particularly telling quip against someone, is certainly "echoic," as OED says of *zing*.

I would urge journalists to eschew *quipped* as a verb meaning "observed, humorously," as in (from *The Wall Street Journal MarketWatch*), "This next year, history may not repeat itself, but as Mark Twain quipped, it could rhyme." Setting up a statement with *quipped* renders it less humorous, less clever; not more.

r · **R** · r

Nick Benson is a third-generation stone carver and calligrapher, who has designed letters and inscribed them in stone at the John F. Kennedy Memorial, the Franklin Delano Roosevelt Memorial, the National World War II Memorial, and the National Gallery of Art. Asked whether he had a favorite letter, he replied:

"R is one of my favorite letters because it incorporates all the strokes of the alphabet. You have the vertical, the horizontal, the curved form, and the diagonal. That's what we use often as a sample, test letter. It's a good letter."

R's are *yare*. The verb *are*, by the way, became standard English in the sixteenth century, replacing the third-person-plural *be*, which survives in expressions like "the powers that be" and "Here be dragons."

➤ *racism*

When it came out that Supreme Court then nominee (now Justice) Sonia Sotomayor had once said, *publicly*, that "a wise Latina woman" would know more about certain matters than a white man would, Newt Gingrich—a white man—posted this Twitter message:

"White man racist nominee would be forced to withdraw. Latina woman racist should also withdraw."

Ugh. Sound like white man tweet with thumbs of movie Injun. If there is evidence that wise white men are discriminated against, it is that we see so few of them in positions of authority. Meanwhile foolish white men, in such positions, seem to be taking every opportunity to make statements even more foolish than might have been expected. Maybe foolish white men are determined to embarrass themselves, so they will be put out of power, so they can take offense at being made fun of. Except that voters who like foolish white men seem to love it when a foolish white man exceeds expectations.

➤ *rank*

Over centuries, this word's meaning has evolved from "strong, upright" to "offensively strong" or worse. Is it the influence of *rancor* and the first syllable of *rancid*, or is it just the sound? Rhymes with unpleasant words: *stank*, *dank*, *crank*, *yank*, *spank*, *clank*, *sank*, *wank*, *lank*, *blank*, *prank*, *tank*, *skank*, *shank* as in hitting a golf ball wrong, *hank* as in "hank of hair." Of course so does *thank*, but the *th-* softens it?

➤ recursion, excessive

This is the first sentence from a March 2010, newspaper item: "A federal appeals court has ruled that Anna Nicole Smith's estate will get none of the more than $300 million the late *Playboy* model claimed a Texas billionaire to whom she was briefly married meant to leave her after he died."

And this, from *The Berkshire Eagle*, is recursion gone astray: "The recognition that a simple blow to the head can lead to lifelong debilitating injury is spreading is good news." Should begin "That the recognition"; then it would be just excessive.

And this, from *The New York Times*, is recursion run amok: "Nevertheless, it would be a mistake to let the disappointment of the second half of Mr. Salinger's career—consisting of a long short story called 'Hapworth 16, 1924' that reads as though he allowed the pain of hostile criticism to blunt the edge of self-criticism that every good writer must possess, followed by 45 years of living like a hermit in the New Hampshire woods—to overshadow the achievements of the first half." We are not going to win contemporary readers with sentences such as that. Sentences such as that don't even justify our thinking it's contemporary readers' fault.

➤ *redundancy*

From the Latin to reflood, to overflow (the *und* part plays a happier role in **undulation**). As Noah must have said to the Deluge after a week or so: enough already! Cut, cut, cut! To the quick, to the chase, to the bone! Maybe, these days, you do have to tell people what you're going to tell them; tell them; and tell them what you told them. But those are three different things. "I'll tell you what I mean by 'Get on with it': *Get on with it*; 'G-E-T O-N W-I-T-H I-T.' "

Okay, sometimes redundancy works. After Ernestine Jamison of Houston, Texas, found a frozen snake's head in a bag of frozen green beans she was about to thaw out for her family, she was quoted in news accounts as follows:

"When I saw it was a snake's head I just threw it down and called my kids and said I got a snake head in the green beans, everybody said 'oh Lord, you got a snake head in the green beans.' "

But that's a rare case. Even great oratory can do with tightening, and sometimes popular history will oblige. When Winston Churchill told the House of Commons "I have nothing to offer but blood, toil, tears and sweat," one word was redundant. It's almost an SAT question: Which word in this series doesn't fit? Hint: three of them are bodily fluids. You don't need the other one anyway, it's covered by *sweat*. And by the way, doesn't *sweat*, the word, kind of lie there? Don't get me wrong, it's a good word, but is it a good word to place right there? Wouldn't we get more—how shall I put it?—more *loft*, if we ended on *tears*?

➤ rhythm

In Austin, Texas, Town Lake was renamed Lady Bird Lake, but nobody calls it that, even though Lady Bird Johnson is generally well regarded in Austin. The problem, I would submit, is that *Lady Bird Lake*, rhythmically, piles in on itself. *Lake Lady Bird* would have caught on.

➤ *robinhood*

What the familiar red-breasted bird achieves fully upon leaving the nest. Compare *eliotness*, the quality that is *so* T. S., the essence of "The Waste Land." And *siouxcity*, roughly the opposite of insouciance. Or how about this one: *oklahomacity*, the state of belonging to a land that is grand.

> *rumpsprung*

WIII and AHD inexplicably ignore this thumping good word for something saggy. OAD's definition is fine as far as it goes—"*informal* (of furniture), baggy and worn in the seat: *a rumpsprung armchair.*" But how called for is that "informal"? I daresay you wouldn't use *rumpsprung* in announcing a Supreme Court decision, but what would you use instead? And *rumpsprung* may apply not just to furniture but also to trousers, a dress, or even a person (OED example: " 'In my opinion,' Mrs. Neuberger told the reporters, 'Vancouver women are rump-sprung.' ")

The only attempt to define *rump-sprung* (the hyphen is optional but unnecessary so should be dropped, except in an attempt to fake a line of Gerard Manley Hopkins, see Introduction, above) on Urbandictionary .com is disappointing. If you were taking the time to contribute to a dictionary, for millions of people to read, wouldn't you take care to avoid writing *pertaing* for *pertaining* and *uphostry* for *upholstery*? And by way of illustration, surely you would do better than this: "I can't sit on the near end of the sofa, its rump-sprng to aunt Ethel's ass"? What kind of lexicographer fails to notice that he has misspelled the very word he is defining? And that *its* should be *it's*. And ending with just "to Aunt Ethel" would avoid **redundancy**. How much time would it take for people who write on the hyper-lickety-split Internet to stop and look at what they have written before they commit it to eternity?

s · S · s

I kept thinking that I had read somewhere that an enormous S had appeared somewhere—in the sky, in a cornfield as seen *from* the sky . . . ? At length I Googled "enormous s." Presented with "about 18,100 items," I had time for only thirty, which did not include whatever it was that I was trying to remember, but did include the following:

At myfamilydigest.net/holidays/news (cached), "Fourty [*sic*] Eight Ways to Hold Enormous s Time." Beneath a photograph of an attractive and smiling young family, tips on making a special day even more special:

> A Mother's amorousness is one of the most effectual forces in this world. Here are 48 ways to celebrate her delight this Mother's Day. Pick 1, 2 or besides ways to cause this Mother's interval additional special.
>
> 1. Construct a Recall Basket. Fill the hamper with slips of paper, everyone detailing a recognition you, your siblings, and your Giant carry shared. Bestow her the basket and annex all of the family members sitting approximately her as she reads each mind slip . . .
>
> 3. I enjoy been called a "Guy's Guy," on the contrary I thirst for you to ante up Mom a tea party. Invite family as great as friends who are rapid to your Mom. Prepare some super-sweetened iced tea or flavoured broiling tea and serve my world-famous, not to be missed, will-make-you-toes-curl-they-are-so-good tea sandwiches (see my method below) and cookies. By the way, I don't presume in those in fact little tea sandwiches. You'll beam my trimming directions below . . .

4. Create Mom famous. Dossier you and the rest of the family and friends saying what they enjoy approximately Mom . . .

5. Booty Mom outside to the mall for some shopping.

And so on.

At vido4viet.com, a video, "Miss Diva Bbw With Enormous S," which had been "removed by the user."

At ncbi.nim.nih.gov: "Although, in both the stool and sputum direct smears of the patient, enormous *S. stercoralis* larvae were present, and no eosinophilia was found. . . ."

At Stanfordalumni.org/news/magazine, a story about advances made possible by the Global Positioning System. Stanford professor Brad Parkinson is "a guiding force" among researchers who "are perfecting a way to find anything, anytime, anywhere on the planet."

> So it happened that anyone flying over a patch of farmland in central California two summers ago could have seen a perfectly formed, enormous S carved into the field. A team of Parkinson's graduate students had demonstrated that a driverless John Deere tractor, equipped with a GPS receiver linked to an automatic control system, could plow a field even in darkness or fog and achieve accuracy to within a few centimeters. In just 40 minutes, the tractor steadily plowed through John Deere's half-mile-square experimental field, executing perfect turns and reverses guided by a computer program.

At *The New York Times*'s web archive, "Topics of the Times," September 3, 1913:

> Precisely what was done on Monday by the French aviator PEGOUD is not made unquestionable by the dispatches now at hand. By some of them, and the more detailed, he is said to have traversed from above downward the course of an enormous "S," while others say that he made a complete vertical loop, more like the letter "O."
>
> The former feat, since it involves two perpendicular descents instead of one, would seemingly be the more difficult and perilous, but that, in the case of men like these, does not, perhaps, render it

certain, or even highly probable, that the simpler exploit is the one
that was performed. In either case there would be involved the
amazing achievement of flying for a time with the aeroplane
overturned and the occupant hanging from instead of resting on it.

And so on. Will wonders never cease?

➤ -sh, sh-

Would people relish saying "when push comes to shove" so much if *push*
and *shove* didn't mesh so well? It's a juicy, in fact mouthwatering sound,
sh, however spelled: *delicious, lush, luscious, sensuous.* A long soft comforting *shhhh* is something a mother says to soothe an unhappy baby. It's
also a sound that can suggest pushing too far: *lubricious, licentious, salacious,
mush.* Does the use of *lush* to mean a drunk derive in part from the con-
vention that people in their cups say *shay* instead of *say*? It's not a sound
one wants to hear too much of. *Sh'boom* is good, and so is *whoosh*, but recently some friends and I listened to a jazz trio whose drummer brushed
his high-hat cymbals so insistently he overshadowed the piano and the
sax. Our table was tempted to try shushing him, but that would have compounded the problem.
See *juice*.

➤ shrapnel

For Henry Shrapnel, who invented the "case-shot shell," which exploded on
impact and scattered deadly bits of metal through the air. *Shr-* as in *shreds,
shriek*. The man's name was rippingly appropriate for what he wrought. If he
had been named Witticomb or Perkins ("torn apart by perkins"?), or had
invented the birdbath instead, he'd not be remembered today.

As to contemporary shrapnel, see *The Good Soldiers* by David Finkel,
who was embedded with U.S. soldiers in Iraq. One morning as Captain Al
Walsh slept, a mortar shell landed outside his door:

> In came a piece of shrapnel, moving so swiftly that before he
> could wake up and take cover, it had sliced through his wooden
> door, sliced through the metal frame of his bed, sliced through a

280-page book called *Learning to Eat Soup with a Knife*, sliced through a 272-page book called *Buddhism Is Not What You Think*, sliced through a 128-page book called *On Guerrilla Warfare*, sliced through a 360-page book called *Tactics of the Crescent Moon*, sliced through a 176-page *Calvin and Hobbes* collection, sliced through the rear of a metal cabinet holding those books, and finally was stopped by a concrete wall. And the only reason that Walsh wasn't sliced was that he happened in that moment to be sleeping on his side rather than on his stomach or back, as he usually did, which meant that the shrapnel passed cleanly through the spot where his head usually rested, missing him by an inch. Dazed, ears ringing, unsure of what had just happened, and spotted with a little blood from being nicked by the exploding metal fragments of the ruined bed frame, he stumbled out to the smoking courtyard and said to another soldier, "Is anything sticking out of my head?" And the answer, thank whatever, was no.

See **smithereens**.

➤ *sic*

Here's a good reason to use words right: you don't want a [*sic*] put on you. According to an item published in 2010 in the *New York Post*, a prison inmate in Florida sued a girlie magazine for failing to respond when he wrote to ask how he could go about ordering a copy of the April 2007 issue, featuring a nude pictorial of burlesque star Dita Von Teese. The people who put out the magazine, he alleged, had violated his constitutional rights by denying him "access to the media." The bottom line, he claimed, was this: the staffers "are being prejudice [*sic*]" against him as a prisoner. The [*sic*] was the newspaper's. It's bad enough to be locked up, but when the *New York Post* can tell you've used a word wrong, it's the [*sic*] of death.

➤ *sigh*

Isn't this a funny-looking word? I suppose advocates of simplified spelling would change it to, what, *si*, *sie*, *sye*? OED says it's a back-formation

from *sihte*, the past tense of *siche*, "through the guttural having more phonetic appropriateness than the palatal sound." A dialect form was *siff*.
Siche meant to sigh, but it was pronounced, I take it, more or less to rhyme
with *hitch*, the palatal *ch* sound formed by the tongue pressed against the
hard palate. *Sike*, a variant of *siche*, was even less sigh-sounding. *Sithe* was
a little better (and the dialect *siff* much better), but not quite right. So the
word moved to the glottis, the back of the throat, where the *gh* resonated
as something like the *ch* in German *ach*. That soft *ch* does have a sighing-
ness about it, but modern English pronunciation took out the *c* and retained a breath of *h*, and there you had *sigh*.

A similar evolution produced modern-day *high*, which Dr. Johnson
defined as "long upwards." You don't want such a significant signifier to
end up caught in the back of your throat, as in the Old Frisian *hâch* or *hâg*;
so people in the fourteenth century (if I may speak for them) started pulling its pronunciation up out of the guttural and spelling it more or less
phonetically: *he*, *hee*, *hey*, *hi*, *hii*, *hie*, and *hye*. None of which looked quite
rootsy enough, I guess, so the *-gh* survived.

And a good thing, too. That ghostly postguttural *-gh* in both *sigh* and *high*
contributes depth. In college I wrote a paper about the sighs in Shakespeare.
The research got so fraught in the middle of the night (you'll notice there's
a *gh* in *fraught*, and another one just past the middle of *night*, along about,
say, three thirty a.m.) that I would have switched to another topic if the paper had not been due in the morning. Lady Macbeth sighs a sigh that causes
her doctor to exclaim, "What a sigh is there! The heart is sorely charged."
Ross tells Macduff that things have got so bad in Scotland that "sighs, and
groans, and shrieks that rent the air" go unremarked upon. Ophelia tells
her father that Hamlet came out with "a sigh so piteous and profound / As it
did seem to shatter all his bulk / And end his being." The king for his part
hears reports of Hamlet's raving and reflects, "There's matter in these
sighs, these profound heaves." Therefore, he explains to Laertes, putting
something off (something like, say, killing Hamlet) is a bad idea:

> That we would do,
> We should do when we would; for this "would" changes
> And hath abatements and delays as many
> As there are tongues, are hands, are accidents;

And then this "should" is like a spendthrift sigh,

That hurts by easing.

Spendthrift sigh alludes to the common belief in Shakespeare's day that every sigh shortens life by depriving the heart of a drop of blood. After the king goes on in that woulda-shoulda-coulda vein for a bit longer, he prods Laertes directly. What would Laertes be up to, if he could get at his father's killer? Laertes' one-line response is no sigh: "To cut his throat i' the church."

See *gikl*.

> *since*

After this, I hope we will all avoid the logical fallacy known as *post hoc ergo propter hoc*, which is Latin for "after this, therefore because of this." As in, "I told you and told you not to go outdoors without your galoshes, but you didn't listen, and now look, you've got hypoglycemia."

But it's a seductive fallacy. We want a sequence to be consequential. The early forms of the adverb *since—sithenes, syns, synnes*—meant only "afterward, later," as in "He went out to get some mustard sardines and hasn't been heard from since." And the conjunction in the same forms meant only "after the time that," as in "since my baby left me." But after all, is it merely after your baby left you, or because your baby left you, that you've been living down on the corner of Lonely Street? Around 1450, according to Chambers, *synnes* came to mean not only after but also because.

The second episode of *The West Wing* was titled "*Post Hoc Ergo Propter Hoc*." President Bartlet confides in his trusted father-figure doctor his doubts that he is willing enough, as president, to visit violence on anyone, even the nation's enemies. Another matter comes up, and he gives his aides a little lecture about not falling into the fallacy of the title. Then he learns that the doctor has been killed in a plane blown up by terrorists, and he vows to wreak vengeance. *Post* Doc, or *propter* Doc?

> *slave*

One night in a noisy sing-along Oxford, England, pub, many years ago when I was even stupider, it struck me as odd that "Rule, Britannia" includes the line "Britons never, never, never shall be slaves." Struck me, more specifically, as, I don't know, kind of imperiopathetic. And I started singing things like "Britons never, never, never shall be tiedupandforcedtospeak-Frenchwiththeirpantsaroundtheirankles," until my American friends, fortunately, told me to for God's sake shut up.

Now I come to find out that around 850, when Danish settlers were moving into British territory and dominating the resident Celts and Anglo-Saxons, the Old English word *Wealh*, which was Germanic speakers' term for a Briton (and whose traces survive in *Wales*, *Wallace*, and *Cornwall*), began to be used to mean serf or slave. So what "Rule, Britannia" is driving at is that our friends the Brits never never never shall be slaves again. Certainly they were not going to embrace, permanently, a word that meant both slaves and them. Around 1300, English borrowed *sclave*, meaning servant or slave, from Old French *esclave*, from Medieval Latin *Sclavus*, slave, from *Slav*.

Slav was Slavic-speaking people's word for one of themselves. It was related to their words for "glory," "fame," and "word" or "talk"; in effect they were calling themselves, honorifically, "people who understand each other," as opposed to foreigners, *nemci*, "mumbling, murmuring people." Then the mumblers conquered the Slavs and turned so many of them into wholly owned workers that *Slav* came to mean *slave*. The Latin and the French versions derived from that. The English version evolved back toward the original.

As you may imagine, words for slave in Slavic languages do not sound anything like *Slav*. The Russian word, for example, is pronounced roughly *rahb*. It comes from the Old Slavic *rabu*, slave. The Czech *robota*, drudgery, and *robotnik*, slave, gave us our *robot*, which was popularized by Karel Čapek's 1920 play, *R.U.R.* (the initials, at least in translation, stand for Rossum's Universal Robots). The ultimate root is the PIE *orbh-*, whence English derives *orphan*.

It is insensitive to call an individual who lived in slavery, a slave. A more **granular** as well as a politically more correct way to refer to Sally Hemings, for instance, is as "an enslaved person."

On the other hand, people who say *ciao* on parting are using a short form of the Italian *sono vostro schiavo*, which means, literally, "I am your slave."

➤ slaver/slobber

You might think that *slaver* (the one that means drool and rhymes with *cadaver*, as opposed to the one that means a person or ship involved in **slave** traffic and rhymes with *graver*) is simply a lah-di-dah form of *slobber*, or that it somehow derives from *saliva*.

But according to etymologists, the two words grew up more or less independently. *Slaver* is deemed akin to Norwegian *slabbe*, to slop, eat noisily; English dialect *slabba*, to roll in mud; Old Norse *slafast*, to droop or slacken; Lithuanian *slōbti*, to grow weak. *Slobber*'s relatives include Low German *slubbern*, to sip, lap, and *sluf*, loose, slack, tired; Old Norse *lüfa*, thick hair (no relation to *loofah*); Middle Dutch *lobbe*, thick underlip; Lithuanian *slubnas*, slack, tired, drooping; Frisian *slobberje*, to slurp; and, my favorite, Middle Dutch *overslubberen*, to wade through a ditch.

Saliva is from Latin. Before that, nobody knows, nor gives a spit. *Saliva* has no family; it isn't **sonicky**.

➤ slip

"Of doubtful form and obscure origin," humphs OED. Perhaps that *humph* is unfair, but I don't know why OED uses *doubtful* in this way. It's as if the word has no real claim to itself. "Mysterious form" would be more scientific.

OED suggests comparison to the Norwegian *slip*, *slipa*, meaning the slime on a fish, or German dialect *schlipper*, curdled milk. Does either of those references do justice to "Excuse me while I slip into something more comfortable"? Actually, in *Hell's Angels*, Jean Harlow said, "Would you be shocked if I put on something more comfortable?," which is pretty perky itself, but *slip*—thanks to movie lovers' faulty, enhancing collective memory—adds a lot. Not to mention "slip *into*."

"Put on" could be a sweater, over what she's wearing. "Slip into" is a kinephonic (see **sonicky**) picture. If you're wearing outerwear, a tweed skirt, say, you're not going to be slipping into something without taking the skirt off and getting down to a silken level.

"Slipping around." "Slip-sliding away." "Slip the surly bonds of earth."

➤ *slush*

A good **sonicky** term for melting ice or snow, liquid mud, or soggy non-sense. But why *slush fund?* The OED quotes an 1839 source: "The sailors in the navy are allowed salt beef . . . From this provision, when cooked . . . nearly all the fat boils off; this is carefully skimmed . . . and put into empty beef or pork barrels." Some of this slush was used to *slush* or *slush down* the masts, to keep them from drying out and snapping, and unsquea-mish tars used some for flavoring, but the bulk was sold for use in oil lamps, "and the money so received is called the slush fund." These pro-ceeds went to buy treats or performance rewards for the crew. All above-board. But the sound of *slush* is—aptly—unpleasantly slippery. By 1884, *slush fund* was used to mean off-the-books money for the lining of pockets and the greasing—again, aptly—of palms.

Not until 2006 did OED recognize *slush pile*, "the unsolicited manu-scripts submitted for consideration at a publishing house, magazine, etc., considered collectively," originally an Americanism (going back at least as far as 1952) that had sloshed up in the *Times Literary Supplement* in 2004. As of November 2009, WIII still hadn't got round to *slush pile*, al-though there were websites called SlushPile.net and Slushpilemag.com. **Wikipedia** (where the concept "slush pile" doesn't apply) had posted a brief but adequate entry explaining the term. And Salon.com had published Patricia Chui's account of her years as a publisher's slush-pile reader. "I wish I could say," Chui wrote, "that serving as a conduit between the pub-lishing elite and the uncorrupted masses taught me valuable lessons in compassion and grace. Instead, it convinced me that the world is full of lunatics." One submission she fielded was a collection of love poems whose author signed herself "Mrs. Jesus Christ." On the other hand, one of the thousands of submissions that came in did get published by her firm. You are not a lunatic, probably. But if you are coming from out of the blue with a book proposal or manuscript, you're better off sending it to agents. Libraries have agents' addresses.

➤ smithereens

Awfully satisfying to utter, this word, and let's face it: so is the phrase "blown to bits." Yet we may deplore moviemakers' tendency to fall back on explosions.

Wouldn't you think there would be an interesting story in this word? Wouldn't you think this word would spread out in all directions? But it's just from the Gaelic *smidirín*, a diminutive of another word that means small fragment. (Or else, cautions OED, *smidirín* is from *smithereens*.) No connection to any part of a smithy, or of anyone named Smith. No one, except me (hello?), seems to want to link *smithereen* to *smidgen*, which is perhaps from the unrelated Scottish *smitch*, a tiny amount. I would love to link *smithereen* to *smith*, as in *blacksmith*, and both of them to *smite*. But no.

➤ snazzy

It's a good word, eh? OED quotes a 1935 book titled *Underworld & Prison Slang*: "That's a snazzy dressup you've got." Chambers says "sometimes thought of as a blend of *snappy* and *jazzy*." I don't see why not. OED first picks *jazzy* up in the *Chicago Sunday Tribune* in 1915: "'Blue' Marion sat down and jazzed the jazziest streak of jazz ever." *Snappy* meaning "neat and elegant; smart, 'natty,'" popped up in *Punch* in 1881, in reference to a little boat.

See **yare**.

➤ sneeze

According to Gary Clothier, Mr. Know-It-All columnist for the Newspaper Enterprise Assn., "The scientific name for sneezing is sternutation." I don't deny this; I just find it irritating. *Sternutation* is from the Latin, of course. Does science gain anything by calling sneezing sternutation? Does science think everyone will start giggling and blushing if it indulges in kinephonically evocative words of Germanic rather than Latin derivation?

"Some people sneeze when looking at a bright light, such as the sun, which is known as photic sneeze reflex," Mr. Know-It-All goes on, "and some sneeze after eating a large meal. This oddity is called snatiation. Do you know that a person can't sneeze while asleep?"

Interesting. According to a **Wikipedia** entry, *snatiation* is a ***portmanteau***, as one might expect, of *sneeze* and *satiation*, coined by Dr. Judith G. Hall, a pediatrician (also a "dysmorphologist," which would appear to be someone who studies birth defects). The same entry also calls *snatiation* a "backronym" standing for "**S**neezing **N**on-controllably **A**t a **T**ime of **I**ndulgence of the **A**ppetite—a **T**rait **I**nherited and **O**rdained to be **N**amed," which is just silly. But the word *backronym* (another portmanteau) is worth a look. According to the Wikipedia entry for *backronym*, "Its earliest known citation in print is 'bacronym' in the November 1983 edition of *The Washington Post* monthly neologism contest (1983–2004): journalist Bob Levey quoted winning reader 'Meredith G. Williams of Potomac' defining it as the 'same as an acronym, except that the words were chosen to fit the letters.' Actual use of the word is found in texts since at least 1994." The Wikipedia example of an acronym is quite right: *radar*, from "**Ra**dio **De**tection **A**nd **R**anging." Its example of a backronym is the U.S. Justice Department's giving "their Amber Alert program the meaning '**A**merica's **M**issing: **B**roadcast **E**mergency **R**esponse,' although the term originally referred to Amber Hagerman, a 9-year old abducted and murdered in Texas in 1996."

Thanks to Mr. Know-It-All I have learned some things that are not to be sneezed at. But calling yourself Mr. Know-It-All doesn't entitle you to indulge in syntactical short circuits like ". . . the sun, which is known as photic sneeze reflex." Earlier in the same column, while answering a question about Francis Gary Powers, the U-2 pilot who was captured by the Soviet Union, Mr. Know-It-All gives us this blatant **dangling modifier**: "After completing several successful flights, a surface-to-air missile brought him down in May 1960."

Bill Watterson in his late, lamented *Calvin and Hobbes* comic strip once rendered a sneeze as "*Kbthchh!*"

➤ *so*

It may seem unfair that in order to become globalized, Chinese people must learn English. How would you like to master from scratch all the uses of, say, the word *so*?

"So!"

"So what?"

"That is so you: 'So what.'"

"No, no—so far as that goes . . ."

"It hasn't gone so far, so far."

"So? So far, so good."

"So you say."

"All the more so!"

"No. Just so-so."

"You want everything to be just so."

"So do you—just so *you're* happy."

"Not so."

"Yeah, yeah, and so on, and so on . . ."

"So that's it, then?"

"So long."

"So soon?"

"In a minute or so."

"Say it ain't so."

"You so-and-so."

"So's yer old man. So to speak."

"I am *so* out of here."

"So much for my hopes and dreams."

"So . . . ?"

"'So . . .' what?"

"You are *so* . . . So *say* so!"

"I'll miss you so!"

"Ah, so."

"So help me!"

And so to bed.

Let those of us who were born into English be glad we are not required (so far) to master Chinese. My friend Marianne Swan lived for a year in China. To mean *so-so*, as in "not so hot," the Chinese say "*mama hoho*," which means, literally, "horsehorse tigertiger." A Chinese person, knowing that Marianne had been fighting *flulike* symptoms, asked her how she felt. "*Mama hoho*," said Marianne. Now you would think that a willingness to express one's feelings in such outlandish terms would be meeting Chinese at least halfway. But she didn't get the tone just right. So the Chinese person thought she was saying—who knows? At any rate, the Chinese person looked at her in stark bewilderment as she said *"mama hoho"* in every combination of tones she could muster. Eventually she gave up. By then she was feeling much worse than *mama hoho* anyhow.

It's a good tipoff, by the way, that people are *so* goddamn backward that they actually *do* plan to shoot it out with the Antichrist, if in their scripturesque website utterances they put *so* ahead of *God*. So spake the so-called Hutaree, an extremist militia organization busted in Michigan for plotting to murder policemen, blow up their funeral, and start an anti-Antichrist revolution: "Hutaree will one day see its enemy and meet him on the battlefield if so God wills it." You can hear Jahweh rumbling, "NO, NO, IT'S LIKE, 'GOD SO LOVED THE WORLD THAT . . .' NOT 'SO GOD LOVED THE WORLD THAT.' TIME TO FORSAKE THESE BUTTHEADS."

See *such*.

➤ *sonicky*

I won't say I *coined* this word until it circulates more widely. As of August 18, 2010, it could boast 27,200 Google hits, but they are a mixed bag. Some of them refer to Dwight D. Eisenhower's son, Icky. (What a nickname. Sort of like Little Ike, I guess, but it can't have given the poor kid much of a swagger. Icky died of scarlet fever before he was four years old. Ike's son John once told me, on short acquaintance, that his father was "a son of a bitch," but surely Ike didn't call his first son Icky because he was sickly.)

I did make *sonicky* up, for *Alphabet Juice*. I needed a word that combined *sonic* and *kinesthetic*. Maybe *kinesonic* or, to keep it Greek, *kinephonic*, would have sounded more nearly scientific, but I didn't want to put on airs, and I thought *sonicky* had more kick to it. I needed a better word than *onomatopoeic*, *echoic*, or *imitative* to describe an intrinsic significant value that isn't clearly onomatopoeic, as in *snap*, *crackle*, and *pop*, but does evoke meaning by a combination of its sound and its movement.

The value of a word, or even just a syllable. Consider *ob-*.

I forget in which city *ob-* came up. Sun Valley, Key West, Chapel Hill? At any rate, the audience was receptive as I held forth, as an author must, about *Alphabet Juice*. I told the Wilt Chamberlain story and the *hoo-hoo* story, and touched upon the issue of pig-noise verbalization. I emphasized my opposition to a tin-eared principle of theoretical linguistics: that the relation between words and their meaning is **"arbitrary."**

That means *skimpy* might as well switch meanings with *voluminous*? *Fuzzy* with *sleek*? *Gobble* with *spew*? Any huckster, any animal caller, any lover, any poet, anybody knows better than that. The sounds of letters and the words they constitute, and the kinetics involved in their oral utterance, and the rhythms of their combinations, have inherent significant value. And words have roots, and words evolve, and some words substantiate their meanings better than others. To study language without considering these aspects of it is like studying forestry without considering trees. Or, okay, bark and leaves.

I was not talking about just quaint flamboyant words like *flabbergasted* or *lickety-split*. I was talking about common words whose physicality we take for granted.

Mouth the word *through*, I urged the audience. Note how it flows through your mouth. Then mouth the word *thwart*. And *throttle*. For that matter, mouth the word *mouth*. These words have what I call *sonicky* value. It was time to throw open the floor (interesting expression—you can't throw the floor open, you can just throw open the floor) for questions.

Well, said someone, if words aren't arbitrary, why can't everyone understand every language? You can't just look at, *or* mouth, the vast majority of words and tell what they mean. So surely most words are in fact arbitrary.

Arbitrary as in random? In that case how would they get attached to meaning? Arbitrary as in laid down by decree? What red-blooded language user would stand for that? Calling any word arbitrary is using the word *arbitrary* arbitrarily, to mean something like "less than self-evident."

"But obviously," I said, and here I quote myself directly, "a lot of words are without much in the way of sonicky value. For instance, *obviously*."

That's when *ob-* hit me. *Obdurate. Obfuscate. Object. Oblate. Obliterate. Obnoxious. Obscure. Obsequious. Obstacle. Obstinate. Obstreperous. Obstruct. Obtrude. Obtuse. Gob.* **Blob.** *Cob. Snob. Stob. Bobble. Hobgoblin. Thingamabob. Plumb bob. Bobbing for apples.* Don't tell me there's nothing sonicky about *ob-*; *ob-* is as obvious as the nose on your face. It sticks out like a knob.

I'm not saying some caveperson started to say *ahhh* and blocked it off (bobbed it, in fact) by pressing his blunt lips together and thought, "Hmm, that has value—might be used to evoke a kind of dull-thud-but-with-possibility-of-bounce element, as in 'Well, it's a job.' " We know that *ob-* is from the Latin preposition *ob*, meaning against, toward, before. I'm just saying *ob-* works in some physical way.

OED defines eighteen different *bob*'s, including an old verb meaning to strike with the fist or anything rounded or knobbed, "perhaps onomatopoeic, expressing the effect of a smart, but not very heavy blow"; and the current verb meaning "to move up and down like a buoyant body," which OED says is "apparently onomatopoeic, expressing short jerking or rebounding motion." Does either of those verbs actually make the sound of *bob*? The second one makes no sound at all. And yet we do—even austere OED does—pick up a sensuous connection: kinesthetic but somehow mixed with sound. The way the body forms the sound *bob* has a familiar ring.

And *high* is a higher word than *low*, and *back* moves from the front of the mouth to the back, whereas *forth* pushes forward. And *life* sounds livelier than *death*, and *up* peppier than *down*, and *grudge* runs deeper than *pique*, and a *nod* is shorter than a *bow*, and a *bounce* is springier than a *bump*, and *be* is more solid than *seem* . . . And see, as a handy example, **splotch**.

➤ spelling

People who spell, on the Web, like drunken sailors—how do they use Word search? If you don't spell what you're looking for exactly right, Word throws up its hands. "The search item was not found," you are stiffly informed. On Google, on the other hand, you don't have to spell, because as soon as you enter a couple of letters, Google is nudging you like a dog with a ball in its mouth. Or, rather, like a parent hovering over an Easter-egg hunt: "Not that way, Sweetie, you don't want to go there do you? How about over *this* way? That's right, you're getting warmer, no, now you're cooling off, maybe you'd like to, uh-huhhhh, that's better, that's better, warmer, oh now you're red hot—*don't step on it*. Oh for God's sake." On my iPad I enter *Xa* and here come the "Google Suggestions": *Xanax, xanga, xavi, xampp, xabi alonso* . . . Or say I'm trying to spell *Xanadu* by ear. By the time I get to *Zanad*, Google is urging the correct spelling on me, and if I persist all the way to *Zanadu*, Google gives it to me but with the heading, "Did you mean:

xanadu." And mixes a couple of *Xanadu* sites in with the *Zanadu*'s (there are quite a few, for instance Zanadu Sportswear on Staten Island), like real blueberries among the Froot Loops. It's helpful, all right, maybe even loosely educational, but it doesn't foster independence.

See *E*.

➤ *splotch*

OED says, "Of obscure origin; perh. merely imitative." As in the case of **bubble**, I have to ask: Why *merely*? Is *splotch* not a stroke of genius? Does it not capture, with panache, "a large irregular spot or patch of light, colour, or the like; a blot, smear, or stain"?

To be sure, the original meaning of *merely* was "magnificently, excellently, splendidly, wonderfully," but that is way obsolete. And you know why? Because *mere* doesn't sound splendid or wonderful. It sounds more like *meager*. It's a tight little word in your mouth. Now *mere* pops up, or peeps up, in "a mere bagatelle," "a mere two dollars an hour," "merely a flesh wound," "the merest whisper."

There's nothing *mere* about *splotch*. It explodes from the mouth and makes an unmissable mess of itself. Etymonline.com says "possibly a blend of *spot*, *blot*, and *botch*." I'd lob a smitch of *splash* in there too.

➤ *sports talk*

Ballplayers operate in a physical world. Denard Span of the Minnesota Twins hit a foul ball that struck his mother, sitting in the stands, in the chest, understandably making her cry and causing him great concern. "It tore him up pretty good," said one of the Twins' coaches, who relieved Span somewhat by determining that "It hit her in the meat." Didn't hit a bone, in other words, so nothing broken.

Sometimes that physicality gives rise to an instinct for metaphor. Reggie Jackson, asked what would make him decide to retire, said, "I don't want to go on wringing out the rag of ability." By way of pointing out the truism that anyone playing first or third base had to be not only a good fielder but also productive with the bat, Reggie said, "To hang out on the corner, you got to lean on the pole."

Chipper Jones of the Braves said that Jamie Moyer, the wily forty-seven-year-old pitcher for the Phillies, was still effective because "He stays off the barrel." That may sound like something from an old navy joke, but what it means is that Moyer adjusts the speed and location of his pitches in such a way that a hitter can't get the fat part, the barrel, of his bat on the ball.

On the other hand, Alex Rodriguez, after fessing up that he had taken a performance-enhancing substance, said, "I laid my bed, I'm going to have to sit on it." Come to think of it, maybe that was an intentional hedge.

Bill Virdon, who was fellow Pirate Bill Mazeroski's roommate for years, said he couldn't remember Mazeroski having ever said anything other than "Time to get up" and "I got it."

Billy Martin was more voluble. When he was managing the Yankees, in intense competition with Earl Weaver's Orioles, he said, "I don't like to talk strategy and the different ways guys handle their clubs, but let me say I could win with the Baltimore team under any condition: a salami and a pizza in my mouth, two big cheeses in my ears, blindfolded and not knowing the situation."

➤ *sportswriting*

Too often violates the literal physicality of metaphors. There is no excuse for writing that someone has undergone "a handful of surgeries." Or has "shut the door on a milestone."

And here is a pet *peeve* of mine among standard sportswriting constructions. From ESPN.com: "Tony La Russa reached the 2,500-win mark on Sunday, joining Connie Mack and John McGraw as the only managers in MLB history to accomplish the feat." No. Should be "Tony La Russa won his 2,500th game as a manager on Sunday. The only others to accomplish this feat were Connie Mack and John McGraw."

➤ *squelch*

This word is "imitative," OED admits. But "imitative of the sound made" by "a heavy, crushing blow or fall on a soft body," as Chambers puts it? Let's all go get a grape (I can wait) and step on it.

Okay. Let's try it with a tangerine. One that's about to go bad, so as not to waste a good one.

I stepped on a hamster once. Accidentally. Her name was Ann. It was kind of a pop. *Plpp*, only more explosive. It haunts me still. Squelching something doesn't make the sound *squelch*.

Yet *squelch* is **sonicky**, for sure.

Let's look at other *squ-* words. All the ones in Chambers:

Squab, squabble, squad, squalid, squall, squalor, squamous, squander, square, squash, squat, squawk, squeak, squeal, squeamish, squeeze, squib, squid, squiggle, squint, squire, squirm, squirrel, squirt, squish.

One thing these words have in common, except for *squab, squad, squamous, square, squire*, and *squirrel*, is that they are all said by Chambers to be of either imitative, unknown, or uncertain origin (or to derive from other words with such origin). Chambers, irritably, on *squirm*: "sometimes said to be of imitative origin, but imitating what and by what association is not stated."

Another thing these words have in common, except for *squab, squander, squid, squire*, and *squirrel*, is that their meanings involve tightness, narrowness, compression, being forced down (maybe not in the case of *squamous*, scaly, but scales are thin and flat).

How do you make the *squ-* sound? You set it up with a hiss and then you press the tongue forcefully against the roof of the mouth, as if you were squashing, say, a grape. There you have the kinesthetic element of sonicky.

➤ *sting*

According to Richard Conniff in *The New York Times*, the entomologist Justin O. Schmidt has established the Justin O. Schmidt Sting Pain Index, regarding insect stings. Schmidt has been stung by a hundred and fifty different species on six continents. He rates sting intensity on a scale of 1.0 (sweat bee) to 4.0 (bullet ant), but what interests me are his verbal assessments.

Sweat bee sting: "Light, ephemeral, almost fruity. A tiny spark has singed a single hair on your arm."

Bald-faced hornet: "Rich, hearty, slightly crunchy. Similar to getting your hand mashed in a revolving door."

Harvester ant: "felt like somebody was putting a knife in and twisting it."
And people of a certain other gender sometimes complain that men are
no good at expressing feelings!

It is good to put words to sensations, so that they stay put. I was stung by
an army ant in the Amazon rain forest. Like getting hit with a ball-peen
hammer.

➤ strumpet

A synonym for *whore* that rhymes with *trumpet*! If that ain't brassy, what
is? But etymologists don't have much fun with it. "For conjectures, see
Skeat," says OED. Walter W. Skeat's conjectures, in this case, aren't very
interesting. Etymonline.com finally gets us somewhere, reporting that in
the eighteenth and early nineteenth centuries the word was "often abbre-
viated as *strum* and also used as a verb, which led to some odd dictionary
entries," to wit, in Captain Francis Grose's *A Classical Dictionary of the
Vulgar Tongue*, 1796: "TO STRUM: to have carnal knowledge of a woman,
also to play badly on the harpsichord or any other stringed instrument."

(OED acknowledges both *strum* and *thrum* to be "echoic.")

These days *strumpet*—as in "cream-splattered beach strumpet Pamela
Anderson"—tends to connote style rather than profession. Bette Midler is
said to have "created the whole archetype of the brassy, size-accepting
strumpet-as-entertainer." On nytimes.com, in choosing her favorite recordings, Marisa Meltzer, coauthor of *How Sassy Changed My Life*, writes:
"I will never get tired of the simple confidence of 'Strumpet.' When Lois
Maffeo sings 'They said I'm walking around like I own the whole place,
well I do / Anybody can have it all, too,' she captures the riot grrrl ethos
perfectly."

Meltzer describes her first impression of that ethos as follows: "The
photos of girls in halter tops, torn fishnets and smeared red lipstick, with
words like 'slut' written across their stomachs, freaked out and excited
my 14-year-old self. I think I've always aspired to be a little more of a bad
girl than I really am, so riot grrrl—with the word 'girl' transfigured into a
ferocious growl—became my chosen outlet."

I must say that "Anybody can have it all, too" strikes me as insincere. But it's better, from a male point of view, than swooning over vampires who don't bite.

See **gillie, girl**.

➤ subjunctive

It is in my interest, at least presumably, to encourage reading. So for the Big Read project of the National Endowment for the Arts, I produced a testament:

> I read because I like it. I get kicks from reading. If reading were bad for me, I would read. If reading were illegal, I would read. If the only way to get at any reading material were to lift one end of a big concrete slab up off it and hold the slab there with my hip while I was reading, I would read. And reading isn't bad for me, it isn't illegal, and it doesn't require heavy lifting. What a deal!

Then I thought to myself (as opposed to out loud), Maybe I should change all those *were*'s to *was*'s. "If reading was bad for me," and so on. That might make the statement sound more natural, and therefore more appealing to someone who is teetering on the brink of deciding whether to give reading a shot.

But no. If I'm going to make a flat-out statement that what I have just said is contrary to fact, how can I, in good conscience, eschew the subjunctive?

Well, Noël Coward—*Noël Coward*!—evidently committed such solecisms without turning a hair. According to *The New York Times*, Coward once remarked of his play *Blithe Spirit*, "There's no heart in the play. If there was a heart, it would be a sad story."

And then there are people who—because they *will* use *if* where a **punctilious** person would use *whether*—fall into the quasi subjunctive. Here, from an article in *The American Scholar*—*The American Scholar*!—is a rare example of a spurious subjunctive and a true subjunctive, in that order, in the same sentence: "All this had occurred by the time Dickinson asked him if he were too busy to read her poems, as if it were the most reasonable request in the world."

Walking in Savannah a while back, I came upon a car that must have been parked there for months, because it was covered with a thick coat of grimy dust. On the windshield, someone had written with his (or her) finger, "I wish my girlfriend was as dirty as this." My first impulse was to cross out *was* and insert *were*, but then I thought, Nah. Descriptivists have more fun.

➤ *succinct*

I wish some reputable etymology connected this word to *succulent*, juicy. *Succulent* derives from Latin *succus*, **juice**, which OED says is related, by "parallel root," to the verb *suck*, which OED defines as follows: "To draw (liquid, *esp.* milk from the breast) into the mouth by contracting the muscles of the lips, cheeks, and tongue so as to produce a partial vacuum."

That is a definition that **so** does not suck. Let us pause for a moment to appreciate the gritty radicality, the **granular**ity, of a definition that strictly refrains from assuming that the reader has the slightest inkling of what, in this instance, *suck* means. A definition that assumes, on the contrary, that the reader may very well be from someplace where sucking has not, to this date, been tried. A definition that therefore renews our awareness of the strange intimate physicality of human concepts.

But: *succinct*. You can tell me that *succus* has no place in *succinct*, and I can quote no authority to refute you. To be sure, *-cinct* is the defining syllable. It derives etymologically from Latin *cingere*, meaning to gird (as in to cinch up a saddle). And pronouncing *-cinct* aptly tightens up the mouth like a mosquito's tweeter. The *suc-* in *succinct* is not from *succus* but from *sub-*, which we think of as meaning under, as in *submarine*, but which in Latin also means close to, up to, toward.

But a succinct (brief, lean, terse) statement worthy of its adjective is one that compresses a lot of juice. A person donning a girdle (Latin *cinctura*) first sucks in to tighten. Suck . . . cinct.

But don't let me go on and on and on about *succinct*. You want a good example of succinctness? Annette Gordon-Reed is the author of *Thomas Jefferson and Sally Hemings: An American Controversy*, which made a solid case, even before DNA evidence came in, that Jefferson and Hemings, who was legally his slave, had an enduring intimate relationship. In 2009 Gordon-Reed was asked by a Public Broadcasting Service interviewer what would have happened if Jefferson had acknowledged Hemings as his wife. It would have ended his political career, said Gordon-Reed. "That was such a taboo at the time."

The interviewer, who would seem to have confused American history with that of some other, gentler, planet, persisted:

> Some people have suggested that he had an opportunity. America was still a fledgling nation, and that if he had been forthcoming about this, he may have helped us get past a difficult racial impasse that we subsequently had to deal with in history. If Jefferson had taken a position like this, might it have helped America?

Gordon-Reed:

No.

> ## *such*

From the same PIE root, *swo-*, as *so*. The Old English version of *such* was *swylc*, a contraction of primitive words translatable as *so like*. The age-long jam session that gave rise to *such* and *so* also involved *which* and *sic* and German *sich*.

> ## *supercalifragilisticexpialidocious*

OED is funny on this. The makers of the movie *Mary Poppins*, which came out in 1964, were sued by the writers and publisher of "Supercalafajalistick-espeealadojus; or, The super song," written in 1951. The plaintiffs lost, reports OED, "in view of earlier oral uses of the word sworn to in affidavits and dissimilarity between the songs." OED quotes from the decision: "The complaint alleges copyright infringement of plaintiff's song '*Supercalafajalis-tickespeealadojus*' by defendants' song '*Supercalifragilisticexpialidocious*.' (All variants of this tongue twister will hereinafter be referred to collectively as 'the word.')" Understandable if a bit high-handed, since there were two words involved. According to "The Straight Dope" column, the affadavits about the word's having been used before 1949 came from "two New Yorkers, Stanley Eichenbaum and Clara Colclaster." What their linguistic expertise was, I don't know. Neither of them turns up in an online search of *The New York Times* since 1851.

The blog *Shroud of Thoughts*, by taking the word's syllables one by one, rather neatly though not scientifically construes that it could mean not just something to say when you can't think of anything to say, as Mary Poppins says, but "atoning for instruction by fragile warmth." The same blogpost says that in the 1942 werewolf movie *The Undying Monster*, "a male character says of a female character, 'She has an over active super-califragilis.' He defines . . . *supercalifragilis* as 'female intuition.'" Nothing about that on imdb.com.

As monster-haunted-manse movies go, *The Undying Monster* is not bad—crisply shot by Lucien Ballard, who would go on to a distinguished cinematographical career entailing Sam Peckinpah's *The Wild Bunch*, Stanley Kubrick's *The Killing*, and Henry Hathaway's *True Grit*.

Heather Thatcher, an English actress of considerable experience—she was "Anna Dora, an Actress as Actresses Go," in *The Private Life of Don Juan*, and, later, "Lady Dalroy" in *Gaslight* and a countess in *Anna Karenina*—plays Miss Christopher, or Christy, a detective's assistant. Christy is a bit Poppinsesque, in fact, with the notable exception that "she gets restless," as the detective puts it, "unless there's something happening that makes her blood run cold." Having arrived in the manse, Christy says, "You can laugh if you want to, but there's something here. Something strange. Very strange. I can feel it."

"I should have warned you," says the detective, "Miss Christopher suffers from an overdeveloped supercalafagalus." (No *r* sound after the *f*. Hard *g*.)

"A supercala-*what?*" asks another female character.

"Feminine instinct," says the detective, and a cozy pre-feminist chuckle is had by all. I don't think *supercalafagalus* is close enough to *supercalifra-gilisticexpialidocious* to establish anything. The movie was adapted from a much crazier and better 1922 novel of the same name by Jessie Douglas Kerruish. Nothing like *supercala*-anything appears in the book, which is a far richer verbal pudding than the movie. Here is the final word of the spell under which man turns into beast:

"Heysa-aa-a-a—"

The word began as a human shout, broke halfway, turned to the unspeakable droning snarl of the hidden room, and swelled into a crackling, roaring, screaming, demonic howl. It was like the hoarded lust and hunger and hate of all the ages, expressed in a voice that passed the bestial in its perversion of the human.

In the book, the intuitive woman is the hero—a vigorous psychic named Luna, who finds herself caught up in the glorious yet horrifying perception that the man who, unbeknown to himself, is the werewolf is also the man of her dreams. Well (spoiler alert), she saves him, but it isn't easy, it isn't pretty, and it exhausts, permanently, her special powers. Also leaves the fellow rather gobsmacked.

"You've known all the time I'm no better than a mad cannibal? . . . That I mauled and half-ate a woman . . . ?" he asks rhetorically. "I begin to understand. I'll realise by and by."

See *fancy*.

➤ *syllabus*

When students are handed a summary of what is to be covered in a class, they are holding a living ghost. The word *syllabus* was created by a misprint.

In a fifteenth-century edition of Cicero's *Letters to Atticus*, the Greek *sittybas*, meaning parchment labels on a manuscript, was rendered as *syllabos* and translated to mean a table or index. It looked like a Greek word (a lot more like one than *sittybas*), it had a *nice* dignified ring to it, it served a purpose in English as *syllabus*, and etymologists were able to connect it to the verb *sullambanein*, to take together. We do get *syllable* from that Greek verb, but *syllabus* has no more to do with it, as Ernest **Weekley** wrote in *The Atlantic Monthly* in 1924, than with *syllabub* (a drink of wine and milk, bleh, of unknown origin).

So *syllabus* is what is called a "ghost word." In most cases, such words are preserved only in dictionaries, and in subsequent copycat dictionaries. These are words, as Walter W. Skeat wrote, that never had "any real existence, being mere coinages due to the blunders of printers or scribes, or to the perfervid imagination of ignorant or blundering editors." For instance, *dord*, defined to mean density, appeared in the 1934 edition of *Webster's New International Dictionary*, because someone had misread a consultant's three-by-five card suggesting that "D" or "d" be included as an abbreviation for *density*. In 1939, an editor discovered the error, and the next edition had no *dord*.

But by the time my seventeenth-century forebear Thomas Blount included *syllabus* (he was the first) in his *Glossographia*, he was right to do so, because it had passed into educated usage.

➤ synesthesia

In *Alphabet Juice*, you may recall, I spoke of people who strongly associate letters with colors—Rimbaud, for instance, regarded *o* as blue. A rarer phenomenon, according to *The New York Times*, is people who "involuntarily 'taste' words when they hear them." Julia Simner, a cognitive neuropsychologist at the University of Edinburgh, told the *Times* that she had found ten such people in Europe and the United States. One of them "hates driving because road signs flood his mouth with the flavors of things like pistachio ice cream and earwax . . . Another subject tastes only proper names: John is his corn bread, William his potatoes . . . 'Stephanie' linked to sage stuffing, 'civil' to gravy, 'London' to potato, 'perform' to peas, 'union' to onions, 'microscope' to carrots, 'city' to mince pie and 'confess' to coffee."

t · T · t

If you ever forget how to pronounce *T*, you could go to OED, under *T*, and be reminded that

> contact of the tip of the tongue with the teeth gives the true dental *t*, which is common in continental European languages, very distinct in Anglo-Irish, and heard in north-western English dialects before *r*, where it is often represented in dialect specimens by spelling *thrue* or *t'hrue* for *true*, and the like . . . The Indian languages, Aryan as well as Dravidian, distinguish two kinds of *t*, the dental, and the retracted or "cerebral" . . . , of which the latter is formed by contact of the retracted tip of the tongue with the roof of the palate. The English *t* is formed between these two extreme positions, the contact being with the back of the gum or the front margin of the palate; its sound is much closer to the cerebral than to the dental.

That sounds about right. As I sit here thinking, and chewing on a Stim-U-Dent plaque remover, mint flavor, which over the years has become my titty-while-writing (couple of packs a day), replacing all forms of tobacco, I wonder whether life in general doesn't fall somewhere between the cerebral and the dental.

➤ *ta*

Not an abbreviation of *thanks*, but a "natural infantile [and adult British] sound of gratitude," says Ernest **Weekley**. I'm thinking of taking it up. Despite my firm belief in casual good manners, I get tired of saying "Thank you" so much, and hearing other people saying "Thank you so much," so much.

I'm thinking in terms of business travel. Cabdriver, ticket-counter person, news-and-notions cash-register person, coffee cash-register person, three or four security persons, airline person who takes my ticket, flight attendant, another flight attendant, the first flight attendant again, person in the seat next to me, flight attendant again, the other flight attendant again, the pilot, and on and on and on:

"Thanks."

"No, thank *you*."

"Thanks a lot."

"Thanks very much."

"Thankyouthankyou."

"Tha-anks."

"Ta" is sufficient, I think. Or "Tak," Danish, **nice** and crisp. According to OED, Old Frisian (q.v.—this may elucidate the frog reference) was *thonk*. AHD says *thank* and *think* are both from the PIE root **tong-*. Maybe I'll start saying "Tong." No, too resonant.

Here are some exotic alternatives from Omniglot.com:

Abenaki, *wiliwni*; Afrikaans, *dankie*; Ainu, *hioy'oy*; Albanian, *faleminderit*; Aleut, *qagaasakug*; Arapaho, *hohóu*; Aromanian, *hristo*; Basque, *eskerrik asko*; Bislama, *tangkiu*; Bulgarian, *blagodarya*; Cimbrian, *Vorbàis Gott!*; Corsican, *à ringraziè vi*; Czech, *dík*; North Frisian (again, q.v.), *foole tunk*; West Frisian, *tige tank*; Georgian, either *gmadlobth* or *didi madloba*; Okinawan, *nifee deebiru*; Zulu, *ngiyabonga*.

Other people sure talk funny, don't they? Except the Bislamans.

➤ *T and A*

If your doctor says, "I recommend we remove your T and A," he or she is behind the times but not a maniac. *T and A* used to refer, in medical circles, to tonsils and adenoids.

➤ *tare*

From the Arabic for "that which is thrown away," *tare* means the container as distinct from the contents. If you want to know how much the monkeys in a barrel of monkeys weigh, you weigh the whole thing and then subtract from that the weight of an identical empty barrel, the tare. We might compliment a writer's style by saying its tare is slight, it is nearly all cargo.

Next we might speak of metonymy, one example of which is the container for the thing contained ("If you ask Aunt Neecy, the theory of relativity is a crock"). But if you ask me, any term for a rhetorical device, as opposed to that device in use, is tare.

The signifier for the signified? Back when I majored in English, you didn't get into all that crap. Instead you read, like, Yeats, and your eyes bugged out of your head.

➤ tenrec

According to the first edition of AHD, tenrecs are "any of various insectivorous, often hedgehoglike mammals of Madagascar." A lovely flow of words, even including the sudden, unlikely *hedgehoglike*. But *often* hedgehoglike? That raises (no, it does not beg) the question, what is a tenrec like when it's not hedgehoglike? Does it get to drinking and loom more wolverinish?

Fourth edition AHD's version is more specific, if less musical: "Any of various insectivorous mammals of the family Tenrecidae, of Madagascar and adjacent islands, similar to the hedgehog but having a long pointed snout and often no tail." We are left to wonder, now, how it manages to have a tail just some of the time.

See *ukulelelike*.

➤ *their, them, they,* the singular

Lani Guinier: "It is easy to understand the idea of viewing an individual on the content of their character rather than the color of their skin." (Would we say "It is easy to understand the idea of viewing an individual on the content of their character rather than the gender of their self"?)

Would we go up to an infant or dog and say to the person with the infant or dog, "How old is they?" No, we would say, "How old is . . . he . . . or . . . she?" Or vice versa. Nothing wrong with that honest tentativeness.

But we can avoid the singular *they*, *them*, *their* without letting gender raise its (*its?*) troublesome head. Consider this horrible sentence: "If someone who is an authority says, 'This is what I want to see done,' those who see them as an authority will pursue that goal or at least support it, not because they feel threatened or powerless, but because that's what they want to do."

Feh, on several grounds. But let's focus on who is *them*, who are *they*. Let's rewrite that sentence into something humanly tolerable: "If someone in a position of authority says, 'This is what I want to see done,' then those who have reason to recognize that authority will try to get the thing done, not out of feeling threatened or powerless, but because they want to." Which you might think would go without saying in a democratic society. But at least in this version the working *they* aren't being sucked up into the boss's *them*.

How about this story in *The New York Times*. Headline, fine: A VIDEO POSTED ONLINE POSES A RIDDLE FOR POLICE. Let's go to the story:

> The amateur video lasts for just a few minutes. It shows a group
> of young people standing over a man seated in a New York
> subway car, taunting him, waving a plastic bottle in his face and
> eventually striking him with their hands as he cowers under their
> blows.

The question (the despicability of these young people's behavior, one way or the other, aside) is whether this video was real or staged. Okay, so far. But here's what a New York Police Department spokesman said: "We are attempting to see if it was a real event, and if so, did a victim identify themselves."

Themselves? It is stupid, stupid to refer to a victim as *themselves*, when we know that he is one individual male. Not only stupid, stupid, but depersonalizing. The singular *them* is not just dumb, it's potentially wicked.

Sometimes, however, the person in question is an abstraction, a generality. We don't know the person's gender. In that case, what is fussy and awkward about *he or she*? Here is a sane sentence from Elizabeth Kolbert in *The New Yorker*: "If, instead of sweetened beverages, the average American drank water, Finkelstein calculates, he or she would weigh fifteen pounds less." Does something about that offend your sensibilities? Would you rather allude to "the average American" as "they"? The average American isn't that fat, or that vague, yet.

➤ *there*

I can see why we say *so there*, defiantly, as in "I am going to run away with Emil, and get my pet name for him—which happens to be Mr. Goosey—tattooed all up and down both of my arms, and devote my life to his career of inspirational sayings, so there!" We surely don't know what we are *doing* when we say that, but we do know what we are saying: "There it is, that's the deal, get used to it."

That *there* is an example, says OED, of *there* "used interjectionally, usually to point (in a tone of vexation, dismay, derision, satisfaction, encouragement, etc.) to some fact, condition, or consummation, presented to the sight or mind."

Okay. It's a little bit like "Now see here!"

But why do we say "There, there," to comfort someone? Maybe we are saying, "Just step back for a moment, away from the *here* and now, and look with some detachment at this thing that you are taking so hard. So some weirdo named Emil drove off and left you at a Laundromat in Tegucigalpa. You're young, you'll meet somebody else you can call Mr. Goofy."

"*Goosey!*"

"Oh . . . Looks more like an *f*. I see the *e*, but I just thought you'd misspelled *Goofy*."

"*Aaaaarrrr.*"

In other words, "There, there" means "Why not be as objective about your heartbreak as I am?" Not very comforting. But there you are.

➤ *thigh*

Where the leg gets really serious. Yeats's apocalypic beast approaches "moving his slow thighs." Samson attacking Philistines "smote them hip and thigh." Mercutio tries to call Romeo away from the Capulets' orchard by invoking the lady Romeo was smitten with, pre-Juliet. Sounds pretty good to me:

> I conjure thee by Rosaline's bright eyes,
> By her high forehead and her scarlet lip,
> By her fine foot, straight leg, and quivering thigh,
> And the demesnes that there adjacent lie.

That's one thing about thighs: what they're close to. "Don't you feel my leg, don't you feel my leg, cause when you feel my leg, you're gonna feel my thigh, and if you feel my thigh, you're gonna go up high," sang Blue Lu Barker and, after her, Maria Muldaur.

But thighs can be impressive in themselves. Larry Brown, the great professional running back, had thighs so robust, each one looked like two thighs bound together.

OED traces the word back to the Lithuanian *tukti*, to become fat. Which is the context in which I have often heard women discuss this juicy part of the body. "In college they called me 'thunder thighs.'"

"Yeah, heh-heh—I mean, hey, sounds good to me."

"*Noooo*."

Under *thigh-slapper*, "an exceptionally funny joke, description, or the like," OED cites, from *The Wall Street Journal*, 1965: "The thigh-slapper . . . the President got off to reporters when Lynda Bird showed up in a billowy muu-muu dress." I'm betting Lynda Bird Johnson's reaction was less than full of mirth. (From the same root as *merry*.)

See **elephant**.

➤ *thong*

"Etymologically, according to John Ayto's *Dictionary of Word Origins*, "a *thong* is something that 'binds' up. The word comes from a prehistoric Germanic *twangg-, which also produced German *zwang*, 'constraint.' In the Old English period it was *thwong*; it began to lose its *w* in the 13th century."

Back then a thong was just a leather strip, a shoelace, for instance. Now it is underwear. I'd like to see it regain not only its *w* but also its second *g*, given the resonance of Monica Lewinsky's thong, or, as I would prefer, her *thwongg*, in political history.

I wouldn't want to wear one, though. Talk about binding up.

➤ *though,* the lazy

I keep seeing lazy *though*'s in the press. Here's a random example from *The New York Times*: "The president has repeatedly challenged [the Washington political and media culture's] focus on short-term results, though it remains unclear whether he will succeed." Why *though*? When *though* or *although* introduces a subordinate clause, it means "in spite of the fact that."

You could make it ". . . focus on short-term results, but it remains unclear whether he will succeed." Or, simply, ". . . focus on short-term results. It remains unclear whether he will succeed." But either of those makes the reader want to respond, "Well, duh."

You could be assertive: "So far, he is not succeeding." Or you could risk a bit of wordplay: ". . . short-term results. The results of that challenge have not been short term."

How about this *though*, from an Associated Press story about "monkey carcasses, smoked anteater, even preserved porcupine" being smuggled into Europe from Africa as "bushmeat": "Some animals were identifiable, though scientists boiled the remains of others and reassembled the skeletons to determine the species." I don't know who is in charge of conjunctions at the AP, but he or she should be advised that that *though* is neither fish nor fowl.

See **but**.

➤ tight like that

Ian McEwan, quoted in *The New Yorker*: "You spend the morning, and suddenly there are seven or eight words in a row. They've got that twist, a little trip, that delights you. And you hope they will delight someone else. And you could not have foreseen it, that little row. They often come when you're fiddling around with something that's already there. You see that by reversing a word order or taking something out, suddenly it tightens into what it was always meant to be."

➤ *tit*

This is the original spelling. It captures the ticking noise that a nursing baby makes. The unphonetic *teat* replaced *tit*, as more polite. Still pronounced *tit*. Why are people embarrassed by **sonicky** spelling?

(For breast the French have *sein* and *mamelle*, both from the Latin, but they also have *tette*, meaning tit, and *téter*, to breast-feed. An infant's feeding time is *l'heure de la tétée*.)

➤ *toadless*

If I asked you whether you thought OED had *toadless* in it, your answer would be, "Is the *Oxford English Dictionary* toadless? No toads in it? Of course there *must* be, reflecting the influence—"

And I would interrupt: "No, I didn't ask whether you thought OED was toadless, I asked whether you thought OED had *toadless* in it."

"*Toadless*? How do you mean?"

"I mean the word *toadless*. A separate entry for that word."

"Shouldn't think so. Silly sort of word."

But OED does have *toadless*. It doesn't have *frogless*, *lizardless*, *crabless*, *duckless*, *goatless*, *rabbitless*, *gooseless*, *chickenless*, *snailless*, *hareless*, *squirrellless*, *ferretless*, *moleless*, *otterless*, *mouseless*, *ratless*, *badgerless*, or *weaselless*. It does have *toadless*. And it doesn't even call *toadless* a nonce word (one coined for a specific occasion), as it does *cowless*.

Toadless. The elements are *toad*, whose derivation is obscure ("The etymological jungle stretching around the designations of the toad is almost impassable," writes Anatoly Liberman, who does draw a tentative connection to *toddle*), and -*less*. The meaning is "devoid of toads." A 1921 example: "No dog can be thoroughly happy in a toadless garden."

The OED also has *toadess*, "a female toad," with only one example: "The toad's highest idea of beauty is his toadess." And *toadery*, "a place where toads are kept or abound." And *toadlet* and *toadling*, each meaning "a young or little toad." And *toadality*, "the personality of a toad."

"Bless my soul," you will say. "But we both must know," you will add, "whose influence this reflects."

Mr. Toad, of Toad Hall.

➤ *touchy*

I continue to assume, as I have always assumed, that a touchy person is an oversensitive one—who is too readily, and irritably, provoked. (Similarly, a *spooky* horse is one that is easily spooked.) But *-y* as an adjectival suffix most often means "inclined to." A picky person is not one who is inclined to *be* picked, but one who is inclined to pick. A pushy or needy or jumpy person is inclined to push or need or jump. A touchy-feely person is inclined to touch and feel. The other day in an airport I heard one young woman say to another, "He's too touchy. And his hands are all *sweat*. Uighlk." Here's an Urbandictionary.com definition: "Touchy McToucherson: Refers to someone who cannot keep **their** hands to themselves," seven thumbs up, none down. If the meaning of *touchy* is shifting toward "touching too much," then its long-standing meaning is beginning to reverse, and misunderstanding will ensue:

"Don't be so touchy!"

"What? *Me* touchy? I'm not leaning far enough away from you? You're the one with the big paws!"

➤ translation, of Mark Twain, into English

The English author Bram Stoker, in *Dracula*, had Van Helsing, the vampire hunter, refer to "an American" who defined faith as "that faculty which enables us to believe things which we know to be untrue."

Stoker had met, near worshipfully, Mark Twain, who had observed that "faith is believing what you know ain't so."

➤ *tsk-tsk*

Not only animal sounds but also human ones are hard to spell. This time-honored orthographical venture is an attempt to spell the sound, closer perhaps to *tsch-tsch* or *tch-tch* (almost has a *j* in it, but not quite—see, it's hard), made by the tongue against the hard palate to express commiseration or disapproval. *Tsk-tsk* (or *tsk, tsk*, which is slower and a touch more reproachful) has come to be pronounced sometimes as if it were a word, *tisk, tisk*.

OED offers no pronunciation of *tsk* but helpfully calls it "alveolar click formed by suction" and records Lawrence Durrell's alternate version: "Balthazar . . . walked slowly . . . making the little clucking noise he always made with his tongue . . . Tsck, tsck." That's pretty good, better than Kipling's attempt (see OED's *tck* entry), "Tck! Tck! And thou art in charge."

OED suggests we compare *tsk* to *tchick*, which it defines as "a representation of the click made by pressing some part of the tongue against the palate and withdrawing it with suction. Properly, the unilateral palatal click, used to urge on a horse." *Withdrawing* it with suction—*nice*ly put. But wouldn't withdrawing it *from* suction be better?

Here is an anecdote recorded by Zora Neale Hurston. A man sends his daughter off to school for seven years, and when she returns he sits her down and dictates a letter to his brother:

"Our mule is dead but Ah got another mule and when Ah say (clucking sound of tongue and teeth) he moved from de word."

He asks his daughter whether she's got that. She says no, sir. He waits awhile and asks again. She says no, sir.

How come?

"Cause Ah can't spell (clucking sound)."

"You mean to tell me you been off to school seben year and can't spell (clucking sound)? Why Ah could spell dat myself and Ah ain't been to school a day in mah life. Well jes' say (clucking sound) he'll know what yo' mean and go on wid de letter."

Notice "clucking sound of tongue and *teeth*." But OED is right, the tongue is close to the teeth, but not quite there—unilateral palatal, on one side of the palate (I prefer the left side). You know what, though? There's no *t* in there at all. See *T*.

Nadine Gordimer in *Nature* captures the sound of a sprinkler: "Tsk-tsk-tsk-tsk-tsk: the long, wavering squirts jerk round, changing direction under their own pressure," and Francine du Plessex Gray in *World Without End*, that of castanets: "tsk tsk tsk tsk tsk tsk tsk."

OED's first citation of *tsk* is 1947. This is oddly late since the quotation is as follows: "Do you get . . . a sound resembling the noise of commiseration which is sometimes written in literature as 'tsk-tsk' or 'tut-tut' "? I've just searched *tsk tsk* through thirty-seven pages of Google Books, and the earliest appearance I find is 1930 in *Life* magazine. It's also in *Our*

Town, 1938. A fairly recent coinage, at any rate, compared to **tut-tut**. (Shakespeare *tut*'s quite often, but never *tsk*'s.)

According to *The New Joys of Yiddish*, "The man who habitually clicks, 'Tsk, tsk!' is . . . called a *tsitser.*"

See **ch**.

> ### *tut-tut*

OED traces *tut* back to 1529, and *tut, tut, tut* to 1536. "A natural utterance," says OED, "expressing impatience or dissatisfaction with a statement, notion, or proceeding, or contemptuously dismissing it." Don't you love a good definition? Pronunciation t ʌ t, which is to say, *tut*, but "the spelling *tut* sometimes represents the palatal click."

I have to say, in all respect to this venerable form, **tsk-tsk** is an improvement.

> ### *tutu*'s, the two

Two words to be confused at your peril: *tutu* and *tutu*.

If someone says to you, "I believe you've eaten your tutu," you may feel complimented—*if you're in New Zealand*. In that country there grows a poisonous shrub, the tutu. (Originally, a Maori word.) According to a nineteenth-century account cited by OED, the leaves of the tutu "may be eaten with safety by cattle gradually accustomed to its use, but are often fatal to newly-landed animals." Which makes you wonder how many times the tutu has to kill you before you get accustomed to it. At any rate, if a person is said to have eaten his or her tutu *in*, as I say, *New Zealand*, it means he or she has become a real New Zealander.

If someone tells you that you appear to have eaten your tutu anywhere else, you will be justifiably nonplussed. In the great majority of English-speaking countries, not to mention France, a tutu is a ballet skirt with stiff frills sticking out all around. The romantic tutu is ankle length, the classic tutu much shorter. This *tutu* is from French baby talk, an alteration of *cucu*, a diminutive of *cul*, which means, not to put too fine a point on it, buttocks.

We may suppose that a very young French child was taken to a ballet, and what did the child take note of? *Les jetés? Les pirouettes? La musique? Non.* The bottoms. (Frill framed, to be sure.) When my friend Madeline Jaynes's small step-granddaughter visited her in New York City for the first time, Madeline took her to the zoo, to the Imax, to the Statue of Liberty, to lunch in Chinatown, and on and on. When the child returned home to rural Georgia and was asked what she had seen, she replied: "We walked Willie on a leash and Willie pooped and Mammy picked it up."

We may see from *tutu* that the French language is very different from yours and mine. *Hiney-hiney* would never do for a ballet costume. *Culottes* and *cul-de-sac* are also from *cul*. Much **nice**r than *buttottes* or *rump-of-the-bag*. The ribald seventies review *Oh! Calcutta!* was a **pun** on "*O quel cul t'as!*" Even if there were a city that sounds anything like "Oh, what a fanny you have!" (I can't think of one, and I have tried), it wouldn't have the right, how shall I say this, *ton*.

See **bum**.

➤ Twain, Mark, little bits he never used

From his notebooks:

> "Like sweetheart of mine whose breath was so sweet it decayed her teeth."

> "Boy dipped the worm in the hot tea,—said, 'By G— you won't tickle *me* any more, I don't reckon.'"

> "In that Russian town of Yalta I danced an astonishing sort of dance an hour long, and one I had never heard of before, with the most beautiful girl that ever lived, and we talked incessantly, and laughed exhaustingly, and neither one ever knew what the other was driving at."

> "The water begins to taste of the casks."

> "Political parties who accuse the one in power of gobbling the spoils &c, are like the wolf who looked in at the door & saw the shepherds eating mutton & said—

'Oh certainly—it's all right as long as it's *you*—but there'd be hell to pay if I was to do that!' "

". . . like the fellow's sow—had to haul her ears off to git her up to the trough, & then had to pull her tail out to get her away again."

"It's as easy as killing your father **whom** you take for a burglar. It is as hard to hit as a burglar—*any*body can hit a relative, but a Gatling gun won't get a burglar."

➤ typos, going with them

From *The Berkshire Eagle*, June 24, 2009: "The solution was to create a parking area in a former gavel pit on Rockwell Road." A gavel pit! Where presiding officers bury their worn-out little hammers? If this old pit could pound!

Or maybe it's a place where presiding officers compete, trying to out-gavel one another, like pit bulls—gavel pitted against gavel. The very next day, a headline in *The New York Times*: ONE STATE SENATE BUT TWO GAVELS AS A POWER STRUGGLE CONTINUES IN ALBANY.

The *Times* reports that the state senate, regrettably comprising thirty-one Democrats and thirty-one Republicans, "like feuding junior high schoolers refusing to acknowledge each other, began holding separate legislative sessions at the same time. Side by side, the two parties . . . talked and sometimes shouted over one another, gaveling through votes that are certain to be disputed. There were two Senate presidents, two gavels, two sets of bills being voted on."

Republicans passed more bills, eighty-five of them compared to the Democrats' fourteen, but Democrats seized "the official Senate gavel, which is large and made of black walnut, its whack echoing through the chamber with authority." The Republican president "was left to peck at a table in front of him with a small, ten-inch gavel used by Republicans for their private conferences."

The origin of *gavel*, by the way, is unknown. Etymonline.com says "perhaps connected with Ger. dial. *gaffel*, 'brotherhood, friendly society.' "

See **garden path phenomenon.**

u · **U** · u

It would break my heart to see the Weblish *u* replace good old English *you* in . . .

I was going to say, in print. Can it be that the very word *print* is beginning to look quaint, even to me?

It would break my heart to see *u* replace *you* any more generally than it already has online. Sure, **you** can be withering, but it's a stand-up, up-front, embraceable word. That *u* is ugly, dismissive, depersonalizingly personal. It looks more like a grunt (this little piggy went *u*, *u*, *u*, all the way home) than a form of address. "You're not as hot as u think u are" is an example, according to *The New York Times*, of anonymous messages appearing on a nasty "social networking site" that is said to be drawing mean teenagers like *flies*. Note that whoever deposited that message lacked the imagination to form a contraction of *u* and *are*. Or maybe the opening *You're*—can anyone resist a message beginning in *You're?*—was designed to draw someone into the range of those belittling *u*'s.

In the Old English *éow*, the Northumbrian *íuih*, and the Old Frisian *iuwe*, you can hear the centuries of effort (yearning, *we*, and *wow*) that went into *you*, that gave it the tensile strength to absorb *ye* and *thee* and *thou*. Better not throw two-thirds of that energy away, **yo**.

➢ *ukulelelike*

Who would have expected any instrument to warrant such an adjective? (You wouldn't call a balalaika ukulelelike at all.) But I was pleased to see it used by the music critic Jon Pareles, writing about Brazilian samba music, in *The New York Times*: "the syncopated strumming of the ukulelelike cavaquinho." It made me start singing, from *Meet Me in St. Louis*, "if you like-a me like I like-a you and we like-a both the same . . ." And it made me wonder about *ukulele*'s provenance.

The ukulele may have been named for Edward Purvis, a British army officer of the late 1800s. *Ukulele* is Hawaiian, not as you might imagine, for Purvis, but for "leaping flea" (*uku*, flea, *lele*, to leap.) Purvis, a member of King Kalakaua's court, was himself so nimble and diminutive, especially compared to the locals, that the Hawaiians nicknamed him Ukulele. And he was so adept at playing the ukulele that the instrument took his name. Or vice versa: the instrument's name may have been inspired by the way the fingers of adept players of ukulele licks leapt on the strings. (The notion that "My dog has fleas" refers to the *uku* root is doubtful, given that as far as I know I just now made that notion up.)

The cavaquinho is ukulelelike, all right—a ukelele is more or less a smaller cavaquinho. Portuguese colonizers introduced the cavaquinho to Brazil, and a shipload of Portuguese workers brought it, in 1879, to Hawaii. According to WIII, *cavaquinho* is Portuguese for a hollowed-out piece of wood. Brazilians have sometimes called it *machete*, conceivably (but don't quote me) for something like the same reason jazz musicians call a saxophone or a bass guitar an ax.

A great Brazilian composer of samba became known as Nelson Cavaquinho for his distinctive two-finger expertise on the instrument, which, however, he soon gave up for the guitar.

On YouTube you can watch a performance on the cavaquinho that has elicited this comment (in Portuguese, I'm guessing): "XAROOOOOOOP!!!"

The sound track of *The Third Man* is nothing but zither music. Has there ever been a movie whose sound track was nothing but ukulele music? That was the question I e-mailed blind to the Oak Park Ukulele Meetup Group (Harrison St. Ukulele Players!) (exclamation point theirs), whose website I Googled up. The gracious response:

Aloha Roy ~

Honestly, I can't think of any off the top of my head. Possibly "Hula Girls" which was composed by Jake Shimabukuro, but I can't remember the entire sound track. That's a really good question. If you find the answer, please let us know . . . we might be interested in taking on the challenge of playing the entire sound track . . . maybe.

Take care ~
GiGi

Jake Shimabukuro, it turns out, is an Okinawan-American ukulele virtuoso. He plays everything from "Thriller" to Bach's Two-Part Invention No. 4 in D Minor on the ukulele. In November 2009, he performed his arrangement of the Beatles' "In My Life" with Bette Midler for the queen of England. I have to say, though, that what he gets out of a ukulele is not—and this is a tribute—what most people would think of as ukulelelike. To my ear, on "While My Guitar Gently Weeps," at least (you'll note it's not "While My Ukulele Gently Weeps"), Jake sounds more balalaikalike. His ukulele did in fact supply *part* of the sound track of *Hula Girls*, which was named best film at the 2007 Japanese Academy Awards. (Sound track album Hitchhike Records.)

But only one track is just Jake soloing. On other tracks is music that might be called balalaikalike, boom-chockalockalike, funiculi-funiculalike, and not particularly like any other music than itself. Mostly quite lovely. None of it—if when we think of ukulele we think of Tiny Tim, Arthur Godfrey—even slightly ukulelelike.

See **plank**.

➤ undertaker yarns, lost

"Put in the undertaker yarns," Mark Twain wrote in a notebook as he was planning *A Tramp Abroad*. Here are his notes for some that he never got around to sharing with us:

" 'Do her good? Why she's down in the cabin on ice.' "

"Sent husband home in box with turnips as vegetable freight—corpses being costly."

"His farmer who came & priced a coffin for his wife who was only *sick*."

➤ *undulation*

From Latin *undula*, wavelet. "Would you," Walt Whitman requested of the sea, "the undulation of one wave, its trick to me transfer."

Beautiful word. But **wavelet** ain't bad.

➤ *upaya*

This is a Sanskrit word for an element of Buddhist enlightenment that may seem mundane. *Upaya* means "means." Skillful means to an end—the end being to express what you mean, in ways that other people can take on board. In a *Dilbert* strip, an employee wearing a pained expression and a beret says he's really an artist, he's working there only to support himself. "You must not be much of an artist," says Dilbert, "if you have to work here."

And Wally, who is always carrying a coffee cup and ingeniously avoiding doing anything like work, adds the clincher: "It's not art if nobody likes it."

We know this to be the opinion of a Philistine. Much great art has been disliked by nearly everyone until later. But Wally has a way of getting to the bottom of things. Once he said he was going to start playing golf. Would he take lessons? "You get to hit the ball more," he said, "if you don't."

Allen Ginsberg used *upaya* in a *New York Times* interview in February 1972. He said *upaya* was something his mother lacked. "She used to say, 'I'm a truly beautiful woman, a great soul and that's why they're after me.' On one level that was true—on the level that the nature of the modern mechanical, scientific robot government was inimical to any manifestation of human individuality and non-mechanical organic charm." But instead of translating her visions into practical, communicable terms, she insisted that President Roosevelt was spying on her and there was a man on the corner with poison germs for her. So people concluded she was crazy.

From that, Ginsberg "realized that if I ever got to the point where I was insisting on an idea or facts that everyone around me said were wrong I'd better pay attention. That inhibited me from going all out in any apocalyptic direction." He didn't give up and become an optometrist—nothing *that* useful. But he did learn to write, and to chant, and to set himself up as a credible figure of his time.

At that time many mediagenic young people were doing drugs, letting their hair get very long, going mystical, and advocating revolution. Ginsberg was on their side. But many young revolutionaries, he told the *Times*, were blaming everything that was wrong in their lives on the government. "They say, 'The reason I am having trouble is that they are after me.' A lot of madness begins with a grand universal insight, the insight that there is more in the world than subways and offices. When the young revolutionary tries to explain this, or to explain why automobiles are wrong, he meets so much resistance that he takes to insistency on his point. If he develops *up-aya* he leads people on a long slow walk into the mountains above the smog where they can breathe the clean air and look down and then he can say to them, 'Don't you realize now what all those cars are doing down there?' "

Let me stress that it isn't marketing, exactly, that we are talking about here.

Which is not to suggest I have any reservations about the marketing of this book.

So let me clarify: *upaya*, as I see it, is not the sort of marketing exemplified by the character in *Dilbert* who says, "I need someone who can make our product sound competitive without vomiting on his own copy."

See **questions not to ask an author, with answers**.

➤ *urge*

What a **sonicky** word, and yet etymology presumes to tell us no more about it than that it comes from the Latin. That's such a letdown, it's like French etymology. French thought is deductive, Cartesian (so they were right about invading Iraq), as opposed to inductive messy English, because everything in French is from Latin.

Okay, there's *zut*. According to my copy of *Larousse grand dictionnaire étymologique et historique du Français*, which I read with some difficulty, *zut* is an onomatopoeic cross between *zest* (not the English word *zest*, but part of the onomatopoeic expression *entre le zist et le zest*, neither one thing or another, which suggests to me a French pronunciation of "this and that") and *flûte*, which means flute but serves also (perhaps—just my suggestion, again—because it derives from the German) as an interjection meaning, more or less, damn!

And, okay, *oui* is interesting: a combination of ancient French *o*, meaning that, and *il*, meaning it, so *oui* is a kind of **portmanteau** of "that's it"—but the *o* comes from Latin *hoc* and the *il* comes from Latin *ille*.

French food, wine, films, countryside, Paris: *exquise*. French etymology: eh.

v · V · v

Linguists have concluded that ancient Romans did not have the *v* sound. They had a letter, not to mention a numeral, that looked like a *V*, but they pronounced it *w*. So when Julius Caesar said, *"Veni, vidi, vici,"* "I came, I saw, I conquered," he pronounced it *Waynee, weedee, weekee*. If you think that's disappointing, how about *Venus*, which Romans pronounced *Waynus*. It seems so wrong. If Julius Caesar came back today, he would be no commanding figure at, say, art openings. He'd be saying "Weeweean, I lo-wed your weedayo—werry weeweed." Except that video artists aren't generally named Vivian—that might save him.

We might excuse the Romans by pointing out that they had no internal combustion engines, so they never heard anything go *voom*, and no phonograph needles, so they couldn't see that a letter that came to a point should create groovy vibes. The Anglo-Saxons had managed to come up with a *vee* sound, but they spelled it with an *f*: Old English for *love* was *lufu*, pronounced *luh-vuh*. When the Normans conquered, they brought in *v* or alternatively *u* to spell the *vee* sound. Not until the seventeenth century did *v* take sole control of that sound, and not until the mid-nineteenth was *v* accorded its own place in the alphabet. Try taking it out now, though.

> *vim*

"Commonly," says OED, *vim* is regarded as the accusative singular of Latin *vis*, strength or energy. The OED's "commonly," there, must refer to the high-school Latin teacher (if any still exist) in the street. That estimable but perhaps predictable manner of person would presumably expect OED to plump for what looks like slam-dunk Latinism.

But no. OED flashes an openness to the **sonicky** by noting an 1850 adverbial usage of *vim* ("He thought of his spurs, . . . an' drove them *vim* into the hoss's flanx"), which "suggests a purely imitative or interjectional origin."

Aha. And how is the pronunciation of *vim* imitative of spurring a horse? It's a quick word, *vim*, but more forceful than, say, the word *quick*. *Vim* generates force by starting, *v*, with both labial and vocal-cord vibration, simultaneously in the front and the back of the oral appartus. Then *ih* thrusts that force forward from down deep, and the *m*, up front but still with laryngeal backup, slams it home.

➤ vowel

OED: "A sound produced by the vibrations of the vocal cords; a letter or character representing such a sound (as *a*, *e*, *i*, etc.)." So why does the word start with a consonant? Because *v* revs up those vibrations (as in *va va voom*). So why isn't *v* a vowel? Because it is produced by vibrations of the lips, with vocal-cord backup.

Speaking of backup, OED follows its definition with this quote, in smaller type, from "Sweet *Primer of Phonetics*," which is not where Tennessee Williams got the idea for *Sweet Bird of Youth*: "A vowel may be defined as voice (voiced breath) modified by some definite configuration of the super-glottal passages, but without audible friction (which would make it into a consonant)." For a view, indeed a tour, of the superglottal passages, see *E*.

The word said to have the most consecutive vowels in it is Hawaiian: *hooiaioia*. It means "certified." Looks to me more like something someone would say after sitting on something drastically unexpected. In a certain tone of voice I guess it could sound like a stamp of approval, but how can anyone sustain a certain tone of voice through that many vowels? In English, the record holder for consecutive vowels is said to be *queueing*. Records are made to be broken. How about *queueiary*? The English are a *queueiary* race. Or *queueial*. A sporting event in which people lined up competitively might be called a *queueo*, but that would only tie *queueing*, not exceed it, vowelly—which is how OED spells the word for "having many vowels; characterized by vowels," though its most recent example, from a Chicago newspaper of 1883, drops a consonant: "In their soft, vowely tongue."

Vowel is from the Old French *vouel*, from Latin *vocalis*, voiced. Seems fitting that English dispensed with the hard *c*. Too consonantal, like a crack in a record, a catch in the throat.

One of the pleasures of reading baseball box scores in an especially narrow-columned newspaper is seeing players transformed into alien beings when their vowels are squeezed out. C. Guzman becomes *CGzmn*; Zimmerman, *Zmmn*; Willingham, *Wlngh*; Alb. Gonzalez, *AlGnzlz*; DavMurphy, *DvMrp*. In each of these cases there is room for a couple more letters, so if by chance some human hand was involved in setting the box score in type, the setter must have been trying to see how short he or she could make a name without blowing people's minds.

w · **W** · w

The mustache of Kaiser Wilhelm II was his monogram. In the early 1890s, as the dashing young emperor of Germany and king of Prussia, he "was constantly photographed," according to Miranda Carter's *George, Nicholas and Wilhelm*. "Even his moustache—teased into the shape of a wide up-thrusting *w*—was so famous it acquired a name: '*Er ist erreicht!*' 'It is achieved!' " The achievement was made possible by "the miracle of pomade—its key ingredient the remarkable new product, petroleum jelly." Later, caricaturists exaggerated Wilhelm's trademark to make him look foolish and sinister.

Once when I turned on a hotel room TV, it was tuned to a religious channel. The show's host, signing off, was giving out the URL that people should go to for further spiritual counsel: "www—or as I call it, 'wubbly wubbly wubbleyoo' . . ."

I swear to God.

➢ *wasp*

Not a bad word for the insect in question, but *vespa*, the Latin and Italian (and also the modern Icelandic), has more buzz, more sting (and works for pesty motor scooters). The Lithuanian, *szirszu*, is better still.

French for wasp is *guêpe*. I don't think so. For Wasp, maybe.

➢ *wavelet*

Want to read a masterly definition? OED's of *wave*:

> A movement in the sea or other collection of water, by which a
> portion of the water rises above the normal level and then subsides,

at the same time travelling a greater or smaller distance over the surface; a moving ridge or swell of water between two depressions or "troughs"; one of the long ridges or rollers which, in the shallower parts of the sea, follow each other at regular intervals, assuming an arched form, and successively break on the shore. Sometimes the word is applied to the ridge and the accompanying trough taken together, and occasionally to the concave curve of the surface between the crest of one ridge and that of the next.

But the word *wave*, in this sense, falls short, kinephonically. Originally, the noun *wave* was *waw*, which gets at the swelling and the looming aspect. Here comes another one: *waaawwww*. A sixteenth-century example in print: "The water of the river . . . was so troublous of wawe, that the brydge therwith was all to shaken." *Wave* replaced *waw* owing to the popularity of the verb *wave* meaning "move to and fro or up and down."

Wavelet, on the other hand—pretty little word, isn't it?—sounds better than *wawlet* would. Run *wavelet* through your mouth and it gravely washes or laps back on itself.

I always thought *eddy* (from the Scots *ydy*), from the sound of it, meant a wavelet, but I come to find out it's a whirlpool! So let's gear down to *ripple*. Rhymes with *nipple* and *stipple*, and is unrelated to *rip* as in *riptide*, according to OED, which confesses that it does not know where this *ripple* comes from, this *ripple* defined as "a light ruffling of the surface of water, such as is caused by a slight breeze; a wavelet."

"As the train pulled out I jumped up and down and hollered 'Good-bye, you fine, sweet thing! And do you love me?' and she peeked out the window and gave me this little, aw, man, this little wavelet."

➤ Weekley, Ernest

We may not think of etymologists as flesh and blood. But they are. Ernest Weekley, 1865–1954, author of *The Romance of Words* and *An Etymological Dictionary of Modern English*, was a big, robust fellow, an athlete in youth, in maturity described by a colleague as "a man of distinguished presence and natural dignity of bearing." But when, in 1912, his wife ran away with D. H. Lawrence, Weekley wrote to his mother-in-law: "Please Mama, make her understand what a state I'm in: I cannot see her handwriting without trembling like a cripple."

He had fallen *head* over heels for Frieda von Richthofen, a distant relative of the Red Baron, when he ran into her while hiking in Germany. They married when she was twenty and he thirty-four. She was full figured and had long, untamable wheat-colored hair. "I only wish, for her sake," Weekley wrote in another letter, "that I could offer her a more brilliant future than that of being the wife of a plain English professor: she ought to be an empress."

Over the years Frieda set down several accounts of their wedding night. "In spite of his age and strong passions," goes one of them, "he had never let himself go. His love had been of the ideal, pure adoration kind, sex he had not let enter consciously. How he suffered now!," as they rode by train to their honeymoon hotel.

In their room, he told her, "I must tell you we aren't married yet," as if she didn't know. When she sat on his knee, she could feel his legs trembling. "Go to bed, my child," he said. "I'll go and drink something, then I will come and say good-night to you."

That wasn't what this child had in mind. Eager to lose her virginity, she undressed and climbed up on a big oak armoire, "beautifully carved with a stiff Eve and an ape-like Adam." By one of her accounts, when Ernest returned she sat there with her legs dangling. By another of her accounts, she jumped on him, naked, from the armoire. It should be said that on the spectrum of irresistible women, Frieda was well toward the fleshy end. Still, by all of Frieda's accounts, Weekley responded far less readily than we would wish him to have done to her hearty availability. "He was horrified." Two hours later Frieda herself "was in an unspeakable torment of soul. It had been horrible, more than horrible."

But it got better. Frieda was soon pregnant with the first of their three children. Judging from the character based on Weekley in Lawrence's autobiographical novel *Mr. Noon*, Weekley became a passionate, and for some time a satisfying, lover of his wife. He tended, though, to be sarcastic. And in Nottingham, where Weekley taught, there was nothing going on to match the aristocratic life Frieda had lived in Germany. In 1912, when the Weekleys had been married for thirteen years, and Ernest's first etymological book, *The Romance of Words*, was just out and attracting excellent reviews, he happened to take D. H. Lawrence on as a part-time French student. At twenty-seven Lawrence was six years younger than Frieda and four inches taller but looked smaller. He was working class and had not yet become an important writer. He was obsessed with sex. He and Frieda eloped to Germany.

In letters, Weekley threatened to kill him, her, and the children. Then he settled on demanding that she give him a righteous divorce—"We are not rabbits"—and forsake all access to their children. Over the years Frieda tried surreptitiously to see her children but managed only a few moments with them until they were grown.

Lawrence had guilty visions of Weekley as Christ. Frieda didn't. "I rather like Christ," she told Lawrence. Lawrence wrote to Weekley, "Mrs. Weekley is afraid of being stunted and not allowed to grow, and so she must live her own life. All women in their natures are like giantesses." To someone else, later, Lawrence wrote, "What is interesting in the laugh of the woman is the same as the binding of the molecules of steel or their action in heat; it is the inhuman will . . . that fascinates me."

If only somewhat of Lady Chatterley, Frieda was distinctly the model of Ursula in *The Rainbow*. Under her influence Lawrence wrote more rhapsodically, blurred his characters' boundaries. She had affairs with other men but was still married to Lawrence when he died. In a letter defending his first great novel, *Sons and Lovers*, she wrote, "I have heard so much about 'form' with Ernst [*sic*], why are you English so keen on it . . . I hate art, it seems like **grammar**, wants to make a language all grammar, language was first and then they abstracted grammar."

Weekley never married again. In 1921 his etymological dictionary was published. The first thing it says about *horn* is that it is "connected with betrayed husband in most Europ. langs., perh. from the practice of grafting spurs of capon on the bird's comb, where they become horns." He cites the Byzantine Greek *keparthopos*, cuckold, literally horn bearer. And he quotes from Chaucer's *Troilus and Cressida*:

"He was tho glad his hornes in to shrinke."

Here's what is up at that juncture in Chaucer's long poem: the heretofore cooling-it Troilus has realized how deeply in love he is with Cressida—just as she begins to look at him slightly askance. Before, he had let his eyes drift to other women—the horns in question allude to a snail's eyes on their stalks—but now they are shrunken and fixed on her, so that he hardly knows how to look or wink. And now she is not so into him. Before, he had scorned those who spoke of the pains of love. Now Cressida has given him a look that makes him realize how she loved him before, and how she doesn't anymore. Her look kills the spirit in his heart. And she dumps him for the Greek warrior Diomede.

At *cuckold*, Weekley quotes Chaucer again: "Who hath no wyf he is no cokewold."

At *husband*, Weekley quotes the Wycliffe Bible: "Gif the housbonde man wiste in what houre the theef were to cumme."

Weekley defines *wittol* as "husband conniving at wife's infidelity." Apparently "from *witewal* or *woodwale*, the green woodpecker, from a belief that it hatched the cuckoo's eggs and reared the cuckoo's young as its own. No doubt the application of the nickname was partly determined by a punning allusion to *wit*, knowledge."

Weekley's next entry is *wivern*, which he calls a heraldic term for "dragon." OED doesn't recognize *wivern*.

Weekley had written to Frieda, "Are you not worse than a prostitute?" At *whore*, Weekley cites the Anglo-Saxon *hor*, adultery, cognate with Latin *carus*, dear. This is slightly out of keeping with other etymologies. John Ayto is so brash as to begin, "A *whore* is etymologically a 'lover,'" going back to the link with *carus* ("source of English *caress* and *charity*"), but he doesn't connect the word to adultery at all. OED notes *whore*'s PIE root in common with *carus*, but while it gets around eventually to the Old Norse *hór*, adultery, it cites no such Anglo-Saxon word. Only Weekley puts adultery and dearness together and leaves the roots of *whore* at that.

Frieda's roots were in Saxony. At *Saxon*, Weekley quotes an Irish bishop: "The filthy compound of burglary and murder, and sodomy, bigamy and infidelity, child-murder, divorce and sexual promiscuity that covers the standing pool of Saxon life."

OED cites Lawrence 1,653 times, of which thirteen are for various combinations with *sex*, from *sex-anger* to *sex-compulsion* to *sex-thrill*. Weekley rates forty-five citations. The closest to spicy is his suggestion that *boloney* was "influenced perhaps by the contemptuous sense associated with the German *wurst*."

When Weekley died, after a long, distinguished academic career, his children found in his desk a photograph, which had been cut to fit a pocket watch, of Frieda, in her first pregnancy, and him together.

See **ling, lit, don't invite 'em**.

> *well*

Headline in *The New York Times*: THREE MEN DIE IN SEWAGE WELL, OVERCOME BY TOXIC FUMES. How can there be such a thing as a sewage well? According to Robert D. McFadden's report, a man and his son and an employee "apparently [fell] one after another into the Stygian gloom of a putrid, manhole-size, 18-foot-deep well they were trying to vacuum."

The accident occurred in an industrial neighborhood of Queens that is "crowded with waste collection companies and adrift in noxious odors that suggest rotting food and oil. The avenue is littered with oil stains, broken glass and dirty piles of something resembling eggplant."

First the son went down into this well and passed out into its depths. Then the father, a native of Israel, went down to save him. Then the employee, a native of El Salvador, went down to save them both. They were all found floating in "four feet of murky water." They had succumbed one after another to lethal levels of hydrogen sulfide, "a common byproduct of the decomposition of organic matter."

Well. Let's take off our hats to (multicultural, incidentally) altruism. You would go down into such a hole after your son, your heart in your throat, but the worker who went down there after his boss and the son of his boss went above and beyond. Otherwise, what a horrible story. A malevolent well—it's bad enough to think of drowning in a well, or drinking out of a poisoned well, but a well *of* poison is like an evil mom. Next to air, water is the primary thing we need to live, and we need to count on a well (as millions of people in the world, to be sure, cannot) as a source of clean water. We wish into a well. In *The Faerie Queene*, Edmund Spenser refers to Geoffrey Chaucer's work as "the well of English undefiled."

Between *well* as in a source of water and *well* meaning healthy or in a good manner, etymology has found no connection. Both *well*'s (one as *wel*, one as *wall*) date back to earliest written records, but they come from two different roots spelled *wel-*. The water *well* comes from a *wel-* (the connection to bubbling, the boiling up, of spring), which also produced various words involving turning and rolling: *waltz*, *wallow*, *revolve*, and *vulva*. The healthy *well* comes from a *wel-* whose offspring involve wishing and willing: *wealth*, *will*, *voluntary*, *gallant*, *gallop*, and *well*, the verb, as in "tears may—may *well*—well up in our eyes as we read that story in the *Times*."

Yet surely at some level of the mind the two *well*'s are well acquainted. (As are *ear* and *hear*, which also lack a common root.) As far back as Old English, *well* was an interjection, an expression of surprise or of turning something over in one's mind:

Ah, well. Well, I don't know. Well, well, well. Well, then. *Well!*

Which *wel-* do those *well*'s bubble up from? The health-related one, says OED: "Employed without construction to introduce a remark or statement, sometimes implying that the speaker or writer accepts a situation, etc., already expressed or indicated, or desires to qualify this in some way, but frequently used merely as a preliminary or resumptive word." Sounds a bit like the bubble-up well at work, doesn't it? At any rate, *well* is a comfort sound, relaxing to pronounce.

If I had any influence over the waste business, I would urge it to call a repository of sewage a pit, not a well. A well isn't a dump; it's a source: an oil well, of oil; an inkwell, of ink; a wheelwell, of wheels. The well in your boat where you keep fish you've caught has freshwater coming into it, so the fish won't spoil.

Behind the sewage pit in question, reports the *Times*, are bays "where the trucks pull up with materials to be sorted for recycling. Signs indicate the types: 'Putrescible' and 'Non-putrescible,' separating solid wastes from those that are likely to become rotten."

There's an ugly word, *putrescible*. From *putrid*, from Latin *putretre*, "to rot." From the PIE **pu-**, "to rot, stink." Quite natural, but *p-u*.

Edward G. Robinson to his corrupt employer in *Five Star Final* (1931): "I want you to wake up in the night and see your own squashy, putrid soul."

➤ , *well*,

As in, say, "If you ask me, that godforsaken dog of yours has been, well, forsaken by God." This device, if you ask me, has grown threadbare.

➤ *well-intentioned*

Why do we say this instead of *well-intended*? I suppose a person isn't intended, unless by his or her creator: Adam was well-intended, just not so well designed. But *well-intentioned* is clunky. "Has good intentions" serves perfectly well and doesn't clog up a sentence. Coleridge actually used *well-intentionedness*. Try saying that out loud a few times.

➤ *wheatear*

If you're new at bird-watching? And you go out with a veteran birder? And both of you spot a small bird with a bluish-grey back, black wings, and white belly and rump? And you say, "What's that one?" And your friend says, "Wheatear"?

Do not embarrass yourself by responding (in a tone implying rather heavily, first of all, that you weren't born yesterday and, second of all, that your friend must not be quite the hotshot authority he makes himself out to be), "No, I don't think so. You'll notice that this bird has no ears at all." First of all, all birds have ears, generally holes covered by feathers. Second of all, *wheatear* is a corruption, dating back to the seventeenth century, of "white arse."

➤ *whistle*

"Of imitative origin," as the dictionaries say—imitative of (AHD) "a clear, sharp, musical sound." In Middle English, according to Etymonline.com, *whistle* was also used to convey "the hissing of serpents." Sonically, that works for me. It might even evoke the way snakes proceed, slick (or rather, slithery) as a whistle. (Here's a question: can a snake back up?)

But where is any music in *whistle*? When I was a boy, a younger neighbor (Neal Elliott, whose father, Sambo, was one of the first three people inducted into the Softball Hall of Fame) couldn't whistle. He would call his dog Lady by crying, "Whurt Lady whurt!" Neal knew instinctively that there should be an *r* in *whistle*. You don't make an *r* sound in whistling, but your tongue is up against the roof of your mouth as if you were just about to make an *r*. If you didn't have the term "wolf whistle," how would you try to capture that sound in letters? Maybe *fweeeet-fwyew(r)*. *Whistle* ought to be *whir*, in fact, and *whir* (vibration, buzzing, bustle) should be *whistle*.

Whistle is Middle English from Old English *hwistlian*. *Whir* is Middle English probably from Norse *hvirfla*. You'd think *whir* could have had dibs on the musical sound. But the buzzy *whir* got in ahead of it somehow. Might there have been a compromise? *Whirstle* has too many consonants in a row—if it looked pronounceable at all, it might be taken to rhyme with *firstly*.

There are *r*'s in the animal-music words *twitter* (God help us) and, more to the point, *chirp*, *chirr*, and *chirrup*. How is *chirrup* pronounced? To rhyme with *syrup*, one way or another. AHD and WIII prefer *chur-up*, which doesn't fit the spelling (OAD prefers the pronunciation *chir-up*) but does follow suit with *chirp* and *chir*. As to *syrup*, AHD and OAD prefer the pronunciation *sir-up* over *sur-up*. WIII prefers *sur-up*, as do I: *sir-up* is too far from *slurp*. *Slurp* is an exquisitely **sonicky** word. The German *schlürfen* may be even more refined—in an imitative, if not a mannerly, sense. When you make a slurpy sound, by the way, your tongue does the aforementioned *r*-move. See **slaver/slobber**.

➤ *whiz*

OED: "An act, or the action, of whizzing; a sibilant sound somewhat less shrill than a hiss, and having a trace of musical tone like a buzz; a swift movement producing such a sound."

That's some exquisite defining by ear. Except . . . there's just a touch missing. The pronunciation, OED makes clear, is *hwiz*. In the definition, is the *h* taken sufficiently into account? A hiss (not the word *hiss*) is pretty much all *s*'s. I would add to the mix elements of the OED's broader-brush definition of the verb *whiz*, "To make a sound as of a body rushing through the air; . . . (of trees) to rustle." Now I hear the breathiness. As in *whoosh*.

Then there's "take a whiz," meaning urinate. I've never cared for that expression. Perhaps it's gender bias. Women have sometimes complained that my kinephonic analysis of *piss* (see *Alphabet Juice*) fails to accord with their perspective. From my standpoint, I want a *p* in there. Once I broke up with a woman I was still in love with (which is to say, she broke up with me), whose last words to me, as she emerged with surprising dispatch from an airport ladies' room (I had been fretting, at least ostensibly, that I would miss my plane), were "I'm a good whizzer."

➤ *who, whom*, tsk, tsk

The American Scholar: "Vote for whomever you please, but . . ." Wrong. It's not whom you please that you'd be voting for (although that person might be pleased to hear that you did), it's who pleases you.

The New York Times: "Some of the residents have a sense of whom Dalkowski was, or might have been." Doesn't that *sound* wrong, on the face of it?

The New Yorker: ". . . her own desires, in particular, for the happy-go-lucky blond cousin, Rodolpho . . . , whom Eddie thinks is 'a weird.'" *The New Yorker*!

➤ Wikipedia

One problem with citing Wikipedia in permanent (so to speak) ink is that scrupulosity would require "according to Wikipedia (as of 11:43 a.m. October 28, 2010)." And of course Wikipedia, unlike academia, can be wrong.

In the *Dilbert* comic strip, one office worker says to another, "My first baby weighed 12 pounds. I gave birth in the cab of a stolen backhoe."

A third worker, the guy who always has to top everything, butts in:

"That's nothing! I once passed a gallstone so big that it became secretary of labor in the Clinton Administration."

First worker: "I find that hard to believe."

Topper guy: "Give me ten minutes and then check Wikipedia."

However, Wikipedia grows more and more nearly reliable. Footnotes and all. And it sure is handy as a first resort. Last time I looked, though, it was still calling me an actor and a musician. And you can't fix information about yourself. If some gentle reader could change "also a reporter, actor, and musician with the Rock Bottom Remainders . . ." to something like "also a reporter, speaker, and versifier who can't act but did appear as himself in a cameo in *Treme* and is heartbrokenly unable to make music in any form yet performs in an ill-defined capacity with the Rock Bottom Remainders . . . ," Wikipedia would be that little bit more nearly golden.

➤ wisdom

From a review (by James Longenbach in *The New York Times Book Review*) of poetry by Mary Jo Salter: "Rather than dispensing wisdom, Salter asks eviscerating questions." Now, Salter is a fine poet, but doesn't anyone who is literary approve of wisdom anymore? Or disapprove of evisceration?

By wisdom I mean, for instance, this from Warren Buffett: "Never ask a barber whether you need a haircut." Or a lesson Chico Marx taught Harpo when they were boys: "Never shoot dice on a blanket." Or something Edgar says to Gloucester in *King Lear*: "Ripeness is all. Come on."

➤ *wise, -wise*

These come from two branches of the same PIE root meaning to see, to know. From one branch we get *vision*, *idea*, and *wit* as well as *wise*. The branch that gave rise to *-wise*, as in the sociable *likewise*, the clotted *under-developmentalwise*, and Dylan Thomas's spooky "Altarwise by Owl-light," took the vision aspect of the root off into various Germanic-language words meaning appearance, shape, manner. In English, we have *way* and also *wise*, as "in no wise," which survives today pretty much only as a suffix.

Ever since 1973, when it appeared, I have saved a United Press International story about two tornadoes hitting Burnet, Texas, at once. "My home is all over everywhere," said one local man; and another, "It just tore the trailer house all to pieces and we were on the ground when it was over—125 feet from where we started out." But no one was killed: "the good Lord was good to us fatality-wise."

> Oh what the weather's done to us
> Exceeds our wild surmise,
> But the good Lord has been good to us
> Fatality-wise.

➤ *wobble*

Is this not a great word? From the PIE root **webh-*, whence also (according to AHD) *web*, *weevil*, *waffle*, *wag*, *walleyed*. Well, *walleyed* more precisely "from Old Norse *vagl*, chicken roost, perch, beam, eye disease, from Germanic **waglaz*."

But don't you think the sound fits the action, somehow? (See **sonicky**.)

A spinning top wobbles. A thrown or punted football wobbles somewhat, however tight the spiral. In the eighteenth century, a boiling pot was said to wobble. To wobble can be, says OED, "To shake or quiver like a jelly or fleshy body." The word has also been spelled *wabble*, as when certain heavy birds "go to fly up they wabble a great way before they can raise themselves upon the wind."

Earth wobbles. This phenomenon is called the Chandler wobble, sounds a little like a dance step:

> You do your hips this way,
> A little like a sway
> And a little bit like a hobble.
> Then proceed sort of hoppy,
> Just a little sorta sloppy—
> You're doing the Chandler wobble.

As so often happens, in 1891 a Jr. managed to get something named after himself. American astronomer Seth Carlo Chandler Jr. calculated that the earth's spin deviated from perfect rotation by twenty feet at the North Pole, and that it went through a full wobble every 433 days. But why didn't the wobble correct itself? In 2000, NASA's Jet Propulsion Laboratory announced that "the century-old mystery"—what causes and sustains the earth's wobble—had been solved. Richard Gross, a geophysicist at the lab, had determined that "the principal cause of the Chandler wobble is fluctuating pressure on the bottom of the ocean."

Had to have something to do with a bottom.

➢ *woe*

A natural exclamation of lament, various forms of which (the *vey* in Yiddish *oy vey*, for instance, and Welsh *gwoe*) go way, way back to Indo-European roots. In Middle English, *woe* was *wa*. OED says *wail* is an offshoot. Comicbook children (I'm thinking of *Little Lulu*, now, which, okay, dates me, but that was a damn good comic book) cry like this: *WAAAAAAAH*.

Today we see *woe* primarily in headlines, CHILEAN BUDGET WOES PER-SIST; in jocular expressions, "a tale of woe"; and in *woebegone*, "beset by woes," geogrified in *A Prairie Home Companion*'s Lake Wobegon.

In Mandarin Chinese, *wo* is *me*.

See *so*.

➤ *woomph*

I love how OED is all over *woomph*:

> *slang.* Also woomf. [Imitative.] (Expressing) a sound similar to a "whoof" (WHOOF *int.* (*n.*) 2) but with a deeper or more resonant component. Cf. the synonymous WHOOMPF *int.* (*n.*).

And if (I say *if*—as though anyone, in that magnificent dictionary's history, has resisted the impulse) you proceed to click on *whoof*, you learn that *whoof* goes back to around 1766, that it has been spelled alternatively *whuph*, *whoogh*, and *woof*, and that it was employed perhaps most **granular**ly by John Updike in *The Coup*: "He took up a hand mike . . . , *whoofed* into it experimentally."

➤ writer's block

On the day after I was born, Tennessee Williams, in New Orleans, which is my favorite city, wrote this in a journal:

> It is never as bad as you think.
> It is never as good as you think . . .
> But it is much more likely to be good if you *think* it is *wonderful* while you are writing the first draft.

Do all great writers feel that manic about their first drafts? I'm afraid to ask. If they said yes, it would make me feel even more depressive about my first drafts. Writer's block, in my experience, is the fear that you will write something really bad. It comes to me in midsentence. I have to keep shaking it off, like a broken-field runner shaking off tackles. (See *gillie, girl*.)

But broken-field runners don't keep doubling back. Look at the first sentence of this entry. I must have changed it seven or eight times, already.

"On the day after I was born, in New Orleans . . ." would mean that I was born in New Orleans. "Tennessee Williams, in New Orleans, which is my favorite city, wrote this (quite unaware that I had been born one day before) . . ."? Too choppy. For one thing.

Maybe I don't start the workday right. Maybe I should do something like what Olivia de Havilland told the actor who played her son in *Lady in a Cage*: "When they call 'Places,' think of the camera as your lover and you're breathing in and out together. In and out. In and out."

But when you're writing, no one calls "Places." You have to call "Place" for yourself. After you do that, you'd feel silly breathing in and out with your blank page. I mean screen. It's not as though your blank page, okay, okay, screen, has nowhere else to be. And your blank screen gives you such a blank look.

What if I ask a great writer how he or she gets under way and the rather startled response is, "Well, you must mean after I motate."

"Motate?"

"You don't *motate*?"

"Oh, sure, *motate*. I thought you said *mutate*."

"You don't *mutate*?"

"I *do* of course mutate, I just thought you were saying you mutate *first*."

"Uh-huh."

And word gets out, and I never get invited to a writers' conference again. I just made up *motate* and *mutate*, as terms of the writer's craft (I think), but my point is, I have a hard time getting under way. Then sometimes I feel like I'm really cooking, but meanwhile I'm thinking, Yeah, yeah, we'll see. This is one of several reasons why, even if Tennessee Williams had not beat me to it, I would never have written *A Streetcar Named Desire*.

A writer, like everybody else, probably does need this sustaining virtue: the inclination to assume that when you do something wrong it doesn't necessarily mean anything, much, and when you do something right it does. So even as I'm dreading the mess I'm about to make, I tell myself to lighten up. I deal in leavened dread.

The older, or let's say the more distinguished, I get, the more disheveled my first stabs at sentences get, for some reason. So I have to be more lapidary. Sound technicians have a term for such a process: "polishing the turd." You just have to hope it will develop along the lines described in *The New Yorker* by Matthew Carter, the great designer of typefaces:

> The heavy lifting begins when the alphabet is finished. I begin then to see how the letters go together to make words, how they line up next to each other, how they sit on the page or the screen, how they work with the punctuation and the symbols. I print up forty or so pages, and when I first see them I feel suicidal. Nothing is working. If it isn't working, I don't necessarily know immediately why it isn't. It simply looks bad. Then starts the long process of going back and making changes here and there. You change something one day, and the next day you change it back, because you realize that it wasn't the problem. Nothing gets better, you despair, until one day you're looking—you've changed something small—and you realize suddenly you're looking at a typeface.

A footnote: According to Leo Tolstoy's daughter Alexandra, she and her sisters were reading *War and Peace* aloud, "and father came into the room, and he stood there with his hands inside the belt of his blouse, and he said, 'Who wrote that? It isn't badly written.'"

See **tight like that** and *upaya*.

$$x \cdot \mathbf{X} \cdot x$$

Are you an x-er or a *checker*? According to a study by the American Graphological Institute, people who fill out forms by placing an ✕ in the box of their choice differ psychologically from those who use the ✓ (known in Britain as the tick). Since the ✕ is associated with wrong answers in early schooling, and the ✓ with correct ones, and since ✕'s tend to huddle within the box whereas ✓'s swing up and out, it is not surprising that checkers tend to be more cheerful and adventurous than x-ers, who often suffer from low self-esteem. Of the more than two hundred successful television stars studied by the institute, 81 percent were checkers. Of the same number of violent criminals, almost the same percentage were x-ers.

No, I made all that up. But if there is an American Graphological Institute, it might want to look into this.

➤ Xanadu

Anglicization (X more exotic looking, let us suppose) of Kublai Khan's summer capital, Shang-tu, in what is now Inner Mongolia. First appeared in English as *Xandu*. Extra a scanned better for Coleridge.

In the late thirteenth century, according to Marco Polo, Shang-tu had two palaces, one made of marble and the other of varnished cane. The walls inside the marble one were all decorated with gilt and astonishing pictures of animals and men. The cane one, held together by bonds of silk, was taken down at summer's end. The khan would ride in the environs with a leopard perched on the back of his saddle. When he saw an animal that caught his fancy, he would sic the leopard on it, then have the prey taken away and fed to his falcons. Nothing is left but rubble and traces of wall.

As Xanadu did Orson Welles a stately pleasure-dome decree, in Florida, for Charles Foster Kane, in *Citizen Kane*—"world's largest private pleasure ground . . . twenty thousand tons of marble . . . Xanadu's landlord leaves many stones to mark his grave."

See **peeve**.

➤ *Xit*

A man or boy by this name is said to have been the royal dwarf of Edward VI, who became king of England from 1547, when he was nine years old, until he died six years later. Xit was a boy's dwarf, then. To what extent was he jester or playmate or laughingstock? All we know of Xit is *X* for unknown and *it* for whatever—not even how he got his name or how it was pronounced. Jennifer Loach's biography of Edward VI provides a rich description of the boy king's court. To wear, presumably on special occasions, Edward had a sable skin "with a head of gold, containing in it a clock, with a collar of gold, enamelled black, set with four diamonds, and four rubies, and two pearls hanging at the ears, and two rubies in the ears, the same skin having feet of gold, the claws thereof being sapphires." He "took over his father's **fool, Will Somers**," and was also attended by harp players, lute players, flautists, singing men, a bagpipe player, minstrels, a virginals player, a rebec player, viol and sackbut players, a thirty-member choir, a troop of yeomen "all blond and of the same height," and John Heywood, England's first publisher of proverbs ("Haste maketh waste," "Look ere ye leap," and "She looketh as butter would not melt in her mouth"—all his). Not a word about any dwarf.

We do know a few things about Jeffery Hudson, 1619–1682, "the first English dwarf of whom there is anything like an authentic history," according to the eleventh edition of the *Encyclopaedia Britannica*, published 1911. The son of a normal-sized butcher who kept and baited bulls for a duke, Hudson stood eighteen inches high and perfectly proportioned at the age of nine. He did not grow further until he was thirty (to three foot nine). "At a dinner given by the duke to Charles I and his queen," according to this century-old *Britannica*, Jeffery "was brought in to table in a pie out of which he stepped, and was at once adopted" by the queen. He is said to have served in the Civil War as a captain of horse, earning the nickname "Strenuous Jeffery," and to have "fought two duels—one with a turkey-cock, a battle recorded by Davenant, and a second with Mr. Crofts, who came to the meeting with a squirt, but who in the more serious encounter which ensued was shot dead by little Hudson, who fired from horseback, the saddle putting him on a level with his antagonist."

I guess you could mess with Jeffery just so much. (OED defines a *squirt* in this seventeenth-century sense as "a small tubular instrument by which water may be squirted.") But standing eighteen inches, he was pitted against an adult male turkey? Those are big birds. And I come to find out that Davenant's poem "Jeffereidos" was published in 1630, when Jeffery was eleven years old. A Lilliputian *child*. That's the kind of sporting proposition the court of Charles I and Queen Henrietta Maria enjoyed? I wanted to know more about this. Not only because of my concern for Jeffery Hudson, and the paucity of *X* words and information about Xit, but also because one of the few things I remember, word for word, from graduate school is this note I took while trying to master the whole of English and American literature for a comprehensive exam: "Syphilis cost Davenant his nose." How did *that* look?

First of all, the bird. Originally in England *turkey-cock* referred to the male guinea fowl, which was brought into Europe from Guinea, in Africa, and which would have been for Jeffery a smaller, but loud and elusive, opponent. By Jeffery's time, however, a turkey-cock meant a turkey—the American bird of which Benjamin Franklin would eventually say, "He is . . . a Bird of Courage [unlike the national-symbol eagle], and would not hesitate to attack a Grenadier of the British Guards who should presume to invade his Farm Yard with a red Coat on."

The name *turkey* made some sense when applied to guinea fowl, because they were brought to Europe by way of Turkey. But turkeys were brought in from Mexico. So European imperialists came to the Americas, found an American bird, brought it to Europe, called it after a country it had never even seen, and then, when they came to colonize the Americas, called that bird, in its own home continent, what they had been mistakenly calling it back where they came from. (However, my 1975 edition of *The New Columbia Encyclopedia*—which maybe you think I should throw away, but it's sitting in my lap right now and you'd have to pry it out of my cold, dead fingers—says the turkey's name "derives from its 'turk-turk' call.") The turkey we know today, at any rate, had arrived in England by the time wee Jeffery Hudson supposedly fought a duel with one, so we are probably talking about a big damn gallinaceous bird.

Okay, *gallinaceous*. That's the turkey's species—no, I mean order. From the Latin for hen. And yet, OED tells us, the word has been used "humorously" to mean "resembling that of a cock; 'cocky.'" It sounds cocky, doesn't it? Why? Maybe *gall* and *bodacious*.

"Rotted away" is how one literary historian describes Davenant's nose, though an engraving of the period confers him with (besides laurel leaves) a nubbin. Have you ever noticed the nose of Jack Palance? Davenant's is portrayed as like Jack Palance's but even smaller. Eventually he married the widow of the doctor who treated his syphilis with mercury, and after she died he married again, to a rich woman, so he couldn't have been too bad-looking. But he killed a man who mocked his appearance, so he had that in common with Jeffery.

And he won the queen's lasting favor by sending her "Jeffereidos," in two cantos. It is a satire on Jeffery Hudson's entire public career to that point. Recall that he's eleven. He hasn't served the royal cause in the Civil War or slain Mr. Crofts yet, but he has already been sent to France as part of a delegation to pick up a midwife for the queen. And on the way back to England he has been captured by Turkish pirates.

Davenant depicts Jeffery as hiding from the pirates in, presumably, the ship's privy, "where they sooner might / Discover him, with smelling than with sight." The pirate captain declares, "This that appears to you, a walking Thumbe, / May prove, the gen'ral Spie of Christendome." On the assumption that Jeffery is indeed a master of international intrigue, the pirates take him ashore and interrogate him (enabling Davenant to rhyme *beseech you* with *Richelieu*), but conclude he is after all just a dwarf. So they turn him loose, astride their fastest poodle. After a progress of seven inches, his mount throws him. At this point, the turkey-cock attacks. Jeffery draws his tiny sword.

Some feathers float in the air. Witnesses cannot say for sure, the poet tells us, whether these feathers were knocked off the turkey-cock by Jeffery's tiny sword, but

> This they affirme; the Turkey in his look
> Express'd how much, he it unkindly took

That wanting food; our Jeffery would not let him,
Enjoy the priviledge to eat him . . .

At that the midwife shows up and Jeffery pleads:

Thou that delivered'st hast so many, be
So kinde of nature, to deliver me!

Davenant goes on to say that no one knows how Jeffery got back home, but it seems likely that the pirates had had enough sport of him and sent him back to be a figure of old English fun, not a jester but a jestee. I venture to say that the turkey-cock duel (maybe some kind of oblique reference to the Turkish pirates?) was Davenant's invention, and that in the war, Jeffery was a mascot. But on the Web you can find moldy historical fiction, supposedly based on tradition, in which Jeffery overhears a porter reading "Jeffereidos" aloud and inveigles the porter, who happens to be seven feet tall, into a duel inside the palace bakery oven, where the porter can't swing his sword and the dwarf is able to jab him several times in the legs with a knife before the fight is broken up. And by all accounts I can find, Jeffery did shoot this Mr. Crofts. Let's hope Xit got some satisfaction too.

➤ *X-ray*

My friend Dave Barry has written that this ray was discovered by scientists trying to determine whether "anything came after W-rays." Perhaps. We know what came after Fay Wray.

➤ *xylophone*

This instrument is related, through *phone* (Greek for voice, sound) to *fame*—being talked about. But I wouldn't count on it. The *xylo-* is from the Greek for wood. Compare *xylem*, which you may have encountered in high-school biology class, and *xylene*, which, aside from being the name of the girl who sat behind you, is a hydrocarbon obtained in part from wood and used in rubber cement.

The vibraphone, or the vibes, has metal keys, but has anybody ever been famous on the vibes, even, besides Lionel Hampton? Then too, fame is tinsel, whereas percussion may be golden—on, say, the bouncily named marimba, whose provenance is African, or on the glockenspiel, from the German *spiel*, to play, and *glocken*, bells. From the sound of *glock* you'd think a glockenspiel's keys were made of wood, or of horse hooves, but no, a glockenspiel's keys are metallic—*glock* is the Old High German stab at capturing *ding-dong*.

y · Y · y

In Massachusetts we have Big Y supermarkets. I asked a checkout lady where the name came from. She blanched. She stammered. She cast her gaze furtively around. I thought to myself (but then, to whom other?):

Aha! I may have stumbled upon something here. Perhaps the Big Y is Yahweh Himself. Or the *Y* in question is the *Y* that (for some reason, perhaps because *H* was taken) is the symbol for *hypercharge*, which according to AHD is "a quantum number equal to twice the average electric charge of a particle multiplet or, equivalently, to the sum of the strangeness and the baryon number." Or perhaps it relates to some secret ritual involving the *yataghan*—"a Turkish sword or scimitar having a double-curved blade and an eared pommel, but lacking a handle guard." Or, even more mystically, *ylem*, "a form of matter hypothesized by proponents of the big bang theory to have existed before the formation of the chemical elements." Or *yottahertz* (septillion cycles per second), or *yippee* (whee!), or *Yggdrasil*, "the great ash tree that holds together earth, heaven, and hell by its roots and branches in Norse mythology." Or all of the above at once!

The checkout lady's voice trembled. "We learned it in orientation," she said. "But I forgot."

She must have taken me for someone from headquarters come down to take her job away for insufficient grounding in company lore. I swore to her that I was nothing more than a guy with an interest in letters. Then I came home and Googled.

According to *Wikipedia*, the chain began with the Y Cash Market in Chicopee, Massachusetts, "at the intersection where two roads converge to form a Y."

At least that's what Big Y tells the public.

➤ *y'all*

I trust that my remarks in *Alphabet Juice* and elsewhere have put to rest the tin-eared notion that *y'all* is singular and *all y'all* is plural. If you want a further guide to using this vernacular second-person plural, all you have to do is watch *The Wire*, whose grasp of idiom is impeccable. Does Omar ever address one person as *y'all motherfucker*? No, he addresses more than one as *y'all motherfuckers*. Or, just *y'all*. If Omar does not represent authority to you, then you should give Baltimore a wide berth.

And to review: the difference between *y'all* and *all y'all* is the one-would-have-thought-rather-readily-graspable difference between *you guys* and *all you guys*.

Okay. But I want to pass on to you what the late musicologist and folklorist Dr. Willis James, in a Smithsonian Folkways archival recording, calls "the super plural." In his childhood Dr. James knew a fishmonger in Jacksonville, Florida, whose marketing cry to passersby went like this:

> I got shrimpsies,
> I got crabsies,
> I got fishies,
> I got all these
> For y'allsies.

See **you-all**.

➤ *yare, yar*

"My, she was yare," Katharine Hepburn as Tracy Lord says in *The Philadelphia Story*. She follows up with a definition: "It means, uh, easy to handle, quick to the helm, fast, bright, everything a boat should be . . . until she develops dry rot."

She's speaking of the sailboat, the *True Love*, that she and the Cary Grant character, C. K. Dexter Haven, shared when they were married. By implication she is also talking about their marriage, and about herself. In the end (caution: SPOILER), when C. K. proposes to her again, she says, "Oh Dexter, I'll be yare now, I promise to be yare."

For centuries *yare* has been applied to both people and boats. Seamen are exhorted to be yare in *The Tempest*: "fall to 't, yarely, or we run ourselves aground . . . Heigh, my hearts! cheerly, cheerly, my hearts! yare, yare!" And in *Antony and Cleopatra*, someone says, "Their ships are yare, yours heavy." The Old English was *gearu*, meaning ready, prepared. Good to go.

Kate pronounces it to rhyme with *are*. OAD and WIII accept that pronunciation, but prefer to rhyme it with *care*, which is the only pronunciation AHD and OED acknowledge. "My, she was *yehr*"? I don't think so. But *yehr* in sailboat-owning British English wouldn't really have an *r* sound in it. "My, she was *yeah*"?

WIII, alone, says the word can also be spelled *yar*—as in fact it usually is spelled online—and then pronounced as Kate did. I don't know how it's spelled in the original script, but *yar* is trimmer, makes sense phonetically—*yar* is more yare than *yare* is.

➤ *ylid*

A chemical compound of some kind, who cares, but here's what's interesting, and to me, annoying: this adjective is compounded of two suffixes: *-yl* and *-ide*. What's up with that? "After you, Mr. -Yl." "No, after *you*, Mr. -Ide."

Granted, you wouldn't want to make it *idyl*. But isn't there something creepy about two tails with no head? The noun form by the way is given as *ylide* ("silylated ylides of phosphorus, arsenic and sulphur . . ."), the adjective form, *ylidic*. So where does that leave *ylid*?

The craziness doesn't stop there. The next entry in OED is *-ylidene*. A suffix. Now we're up to a three-tail tail. Furthermore, *-ylidene* (rhymes with "vanilla bean") is to be "used" (watch this carefully) "in place of *-idine* when the name of the parent compound does not end in *-yl*."

So what if the parent compound is an *ylide*? You see what I'm getting at? We're up to *ylidylidene*. And *it's all suffixes*.

Nice rhythm to it, though. Rhymes with "silly Willadean."

➢ *yo*

My wife has long maintained that English has no equivalent expression to *nicht wahr* or *n'est ce pas*. I thought of one once, but it didn't satisfy her, and now I've forgotten what it was. One that comes close, only with scant interrogatory tinge, is the sort of recessive *yo*, defined by OED, in September 2009, as follows: "*slang* (orig. in African-American usage). In weakened use, following or punctuating an utterance for emphasis or as a general conversational filler." OED cites David Simon's *Homicide*: "Somebody 'round here been doin' some talking, yo."

The more exclamatory *yo*, as in Rocky Balboa's "Yo, Adrian," is a different matter. In 1993, Ernest Paolino, a Philadelphia native, wrote a letter to the editor of *The New York Times* claiming *yo* as a product of south Philadelphia, many of whose residents in the 1930s were immigrants from southern Italy. In the Neapolitan dialect, wrote Paolino, "*guaglione* (pronounced guahl-YO-nay) signified a young man. The chiefly unlettered immigrants shortened that to guahl-YO, which they pronounced wahl-YO. That was inevitably shortened to *yo*. The common greeting among young Italian-American males was 'Hey, whal-YO!' and then simply 'Yo!'"

The possessive *yo'*, as in "Yo' mama," is a contraction of *your* (as pronounced *yore*). Not of **you**.

➢ *you*

"You!" she said.

There are few more withering remarks than "You!" spoken in a certain way. Jeanne spoke it in just that way.

—P. G. Wodehouse, "Rough-Hew Them How We Will"

See **U**.

➢ *you-all*

I have discovered dismaying things in dictionaries before—for instance, that judging from her photograph in AHD, the Wild West outlaw queen

Belle Starr, played in movies by Jane Russell and Elsa Martinelli, actually looked like Harry Dean Stanton. But that shock was nothing compared to finding that the *Oxford English Dictionary*, which Ernest **Weekley** justly called "the noblest monument ever reared to any language," is all wet on *you-all*.

"Used in place of *you* pers. pron. Used, with no clear pattern, both as *sing.* and as *pl.*" That's what OED says. For examples of *you-all*'s use as singular, it quotes the following people:

A. Singleton: "Children learn from the slaves some odd phrases; . . . as . . . will you *all* do this? for, will *one* of you do this?" A. Singleton turns out to be Arthur Singleton, pen name of Henry C. Knight, author of *Letters from the South and West*, 1824. Knight was a New Englander. He visited Virginia. The fineness of his observation may be gauged by his reference to enslaved women's breasts as "dark globose hanging fountains" and his casual remark, "I know not whether the slaves, in general, are not happy as their masters." He says that in Virginia, the husk of corn is called the shuck. That's right. Then he says, "What we call cob, they call husk." I have never heard of such a thing in my life.

Edna Ferber, in *Show Boat*, a question addressed to one person (Magnolia Ravenal): "You-all one of them Suhveys?" Edna Ferber was born in Kalamazoo, grew up in the Midwest, and was living in New York City when she heard, in Connecticut, about showboats. Her first venture south, to catch a showboat, was in 1925, to Bath, North Carolina, where during a two-day stay she could hardly bear to touch the bedsheets or the food. She had a wonderful lore-gathering trip north on the showboat. To write the book, she went to the Côte Basque, in France. So she had not steeped herself in *you-all* culture. Furthermore, you notice that her fictional questioner (a black man in Chicago, who would have grown up in the South) does not say, "You-all one of them suhvey-*takers*"? His *you-all* seems to refer to her organization, as in, "So you work for BP. You-all sufficiently ashamed of yourselves?" His next question to Magnolia is not "Wha' you-all want?" but "Wha' you want?"

Gerald Durrell. In a travel book, he writes of being asked, in South Africa, "Is youall to catch the Parika train?" Durrell is traveling in a party of three. I can't speak for South Africans, but in the United States, a singular verb might well be used with *you-all*, but that is irregular grammar, not a sign that the *you-all* in question is itself singular. People from the Southern United States who wax adamant about the plurality of *you-all* are not trying to deny that Southerners use incorrect grammar. We are denying that *you-all* is an unfunctional affectation.

Two contributors to *American Speech*. One claims to have often heard *you-all* "used in speaking to one person" as a plural in the Ozarks, the other to have heard it used "again and again . . . in speaking to one person." As we have seen in our BP example, the use of *you-all* in speaking to one person does not mean that it refers to only one person. Also you will note that all these authorities on *you-all* have *heard* it used. Everyone I have ever discussed this with, who *used* you-all, has confirmed that they meant it, and that other people who use *you-all* understood it, to be plural. Sometimes not obviously plural, as in our BP example, but *you-all* is not singular.

You say to me that OED is a higher authority than I am. I say to you goodness gracious yes; but not in every, particularly American, particular. For instance:

OED says the verb *bloop* means, in baseball, "To score (a run or runs) by hitting the ball just beyond the reach of the infield." I guess that gets the trajectory of a bloop right, if by "beyond" is meant over, but I'm bothered by the implication that anyone is likely to bloop on purpose; and the part about runs is dead wrong—also wrong under the noun *bloop*, where OED takes a *bloop single* (the noun used attributively) to mean a single run scored by a bloop. A bloop single is just a one-base hit. In cricket, a single is a hit that scores a run, but in baseball (as OED says correctly under *single*) it just gets the batter on base.

OED defines *triple play* correctly, but *double play* inadequately, as a play "in which two runners are put out successively by throws of the basemen." A double play may involve other fielders than basemen—or just one fielder, unassisted, with no throws.

By way of defining *hit and run*, in baseball, OED quotes from *D.A.*, which turns out to be short for *Dictionary of Americanisms*, published in 1951, whose definition of *hit and run* was way out of date then and by a century or so now: "A play wherein a base runner starts with the pitcher's throw as the batter attempts a hit, a sacrifice hit." No sacrifice is involved in a post-1910-or-so hit and run—ideally, the runner draws the shortstop or second baseman over to the base and the batter places a hit through the resultant hole.

According to OED, a *field goal* in American football is "a goal scored from the field of play." Where else would you score a goal from? A field goal is a three-point goal made by kicking. OED's definitions of *safety* and *touchdown*, in American football, and *sacrifice fly*, in baseball, are not right either.

And to all of you who insist to me that you have personally heard someone in the South use *y'all* as a singular, I say that is like telling me that the South has mice that are over five feet tall, because you saw one at Disney World.

See **y'all**.

z · Z · z

"In southern Ontario," according to the linguist J. K. Chambers, "the pronunciation of *Z* as *zee* is stigmatized, as might be expected. American immigrants to the region . . . routinely report that their name for *Z* is one of the first things they change after arriving there, because calling it *zee* unfailingly draws comments from the people they are talking to." Canadians have expressed resentment that *Sesame Street*'s rhyming *zee* is poisoning the *zed*'s of our neighbor to the north's innocent children.

It is true that *zed* is standard in every English-speaking country besides the United States, and that it has an old-world pedigree: from the French *zède*, from the Greek *zeta*. But the French don't say *bède* nor the English *bed* for *b*, which derives from *beta*. I can't see anything particularly to be cherished about *zed*, except that it brings the alphabet to a halt better than open-ended *zee*. In support of *zee*, we can point out that it rhymes with *b*, *c*, *d*, *e*, *g*, *p*, *t*, and *v*.

OED cites Edward Augustus Freeman, the English author of *Some Impressions of the United States*, as having reported, in 1893, that "the name . . . given to the last letter of the alphabet . . . in New England is always *zee*; in the South it is *zed*." I was not around in 1893, but I have never heard tell of *zed*'s ever having had any currency in the American South. (As in ZedZed Top? E-Zed Rollers?) Maybe Freeman heard an Anglophile in Charleston, South Carolina, say *zed*, or he heard someone call someone Zed, short for Zedekiah, a biblical name. (Yes, the creep in *Pulp Fiction* who rapes the Ving Rhames character, who in turn shotguns him fatally in the groin thanks to the intervention of the Bruce Willis character, is named Zed.) Beware of English people's impressions of American English (see **you-all** and, in *Alphabet Juice*, **y'all**). But Freeman goes on genially to suggest a third way: that *z* be pronounced neither *zed* nor *zee*, but rather *ez*, by analogy with *l*, *m*, *n*, and *s*.

I did a Google Book Search for "zed in America" and found a volume printed in London in 1860, *Notes and Queries: A Medium of Inter-Communication for Literary Men, Artists, Antiquaries, Genealogists, etc.* I take it to be a semiannual compilation from a weekly magazine of academic correspondence—the Victorian equivalent of an Internet chat site. John Camden Hotter, of Picadilly, writes: "We pronounce the last letter of our alphabet *zed*; in America it is universally termed *ze*." That seems right, if a bit skimpy on *e*'s. Hotter, who says he has returned from teaching school in the United States, adds: "A million spelling-books in America has it *ze*, whilst perhaps another million here has it *zed*."

From Hotter's *has*'s, we might conclude that for literate nineteenth-century Picadillians, *spelling-books* was singular. (Compare **you-all**.) Perhaps the subject is construed as "a million of spelling-books." Would Hotter have written "a thousand [of] years has passed" or "a dozen [of] eggs has been laid"? Too late, now, to write in and find out.

➤ *zeroth*

"Coming next in a series before the one conventionally regarded as the first," says OED.

So if your first and present wife finds out you were married before, that would be known thereafter as your zeroth marriage, you hope.

If there are two strikes against you and no balls, and the pitcher is throwing ninety-nine miles an hour, home plate may feel like zeroth base.

Or say a long-suppressed amendment to the U.S. Constitution is in danger of being discovered. That amendment was in fact the first one approved by the Congress. That amendment stated, "By the expression *the people* hereinthroughout is meant *white men of property*." But then Jefferson, who had written it, got up and said, "No, seriously, gentlemen, it goes without saying. Let's start with freedom of speech and so on," and everybody laughed and acknowledged it a goodly jest. Then that (and the Dan Brown novel about it) would be known as the Zeroth Amendment.

> *zest, zester*

The other evening my wife showed me an instrument she had just acquired: "I've got a *zester*," she said. "I didn't know there *were* zesters, and now I have one."

She spoke zestfully. It was a **nice** moment, and it's a nice device, especially designed for the scraping of zest from citrus rinds.

Zest was defined in 1674 by Thomas Blount in his *Glossographia*: "the pill [peel] of an Orange, or such like, squeesed into a glass of wine, to give it a relish." *Squeeze*, to use the modern spelling of the same sound, is an aptly **sonicky** word. One test of sonickiness is, can the word be pronounced exaggeratedly to evoke its meaning more thoroughly—perhaps as the voice-over accompanying a more literal, that is to say more bodily, expression: "Come here you sweet thing and let me give you the biggest *ssqwweeeeezzze*!"

"Enough! I can't breathe!"

The original, now obsolete, word was *quease*. (Not related etymologically to *queasy*, apparently, though one wonders.) The initial *s* intensifies, sets up, prolongs the squeeze.

Zest is a quicker word for a brisker action. OED's second citation, after Blount, is from a 1712 history of drugs: "Citron Oil . . . is made . . . by the Zest or the rasping or grating of the Citron Peel."

Origin is obscure, says OED. Hendrickson says French *zeste* may come from Latin *scistus*, meaning cut. The *z* sound suggests friction, as in the sound of an electric shaver hitting whiskers, and *-est* is superlative. At any rate *zest* is firmly rooted in physicality and orality, having referred first to citrus essence, then to general spicing up of food and drink, then generally to "keen relish or enjoyment displayed in speech or action" (OED).

See **vim**.

> *zizz*

A rare case of a one-syllable contradiction in terms: OED says *zizz* can mean "gaiety, liveliness, 'sparkle'" or, on the other hand, a nap. The first meaning uses the *z* sound as *pizazz*, *sizzle*, and *whiz* do. The second uses it to evoke sawing logs. On Z as an only indirect representation of snoring, see *Alphabet Juice.* Come to think of it, *Z* evokes sawing visually, not just because of its cartoon associations, but in its shape.

➤ *zolotnik*

An old Russian unit of weight. Ninety-six of them made up a *funt*, which was 14.4 ounces, so a zolotnik was roughly a sixth of an ounce. Crazy Russians! But *zolotnik* is cognate with the Polish monetary unit *zloty*, each coming from the respective language's word for gold.

And *funt* is related to German *Pfund* and English *pound.* Here's how that went down: Germanic people, in trading with Latin speakers, took the *pondo* in Latin *libra pondo* to be the monetary unit, when it fact the *pondo* meant "by weight," the *libra* being the unit. It's as if you were to take the *weight* in "thirty-weight oil" to be the measurement, so that when someone at the gas station asked you what weight oil you wanted, you said, "Yes."

"What do you mean, 'Yes'? What *weight?*"

"*Weight* weight."

Or it's sort of as if that. (Maybe it would be clearer if we use as an example a ten-penny nail. Or would have been clearer if we had; I don't think either one of us wants to go back through that.) OED says *libra pondo* meant "pound by weight," but wait. It meant "*libra* by weight." Since *libra* is from the Latin for scales, you can see why the Goths, or whoever they were, were confused.

Perhaps it was when some Roman slave, or some Latin scholar, said, "No, wait, excuse me—you've got this wrong-end-to."

"What do you mean, 'No weight?' "

"What? Oh, no, I meant 'No, wait as in *w-a-i-t* wait.' "

The Goth is losing interest.

"Forget that. My point is, *pondo* is not the unit; *libra* is the unit"—perhaps that's when *lb* was adopted as the abbreviation for pound, and a cursive *L* with a little line through it for the monetary pound (originally, a poundweight of silver). So British authorities could say, "The *libra* is there, it's just silent. It's understood." The little line was added after people got confused, thought they were just looking at an *L.*

So let's not be so quick to say, "Crazy Russians!"

Scale, by the way, is related to *shell* and *skoal.* Originally meaning cup, it was extended to the little pans of the early balancing mechanism used to weigh things.

➤ *zwischenzug*

An interim or temporizing move, in chess. And in this book, while I'm trying to come up with just the right word to go out on.

➤ *Zydeco*

Danceable Creole-Cajun hybrid music, from *les haricots*, the beans, from the song, "Les Haricots Sont Pas Salés," which means the beans aren't dirty. Nick Spitzer, who knows, spells it *zodico*, presumably pronounced *zoddico*, which would fit the *a* involved in a Creole or Cajun (or anybody else's) pronunciation of *les haricots* better, but *Zydeco*, for some reason always capitalized, is established.

➤ *zythum*

A beer. Why not end our session here with a beer? Zythum, we are told, was an ancient Egyptian beer brewed from malt and wheat, no hops.

OED: "Much of the word's continuing use is due to its status as the last word listed in several dictionaries." Including OED.

We should've let *Zydeco* play us on off.

But *hop* is an interesting word, in any number of connections. *Hops* in basketball means jumping ability. *Hopped up* is an old reference to opium. *Between hops* is a baseball term of potentially broad application. (You don't want your sentences to catch people between hops.) And how about the simple bunny-associated verb, which goes back at least to around the year 1000: "To spring a short way upon the ground or any surface with an elastic or bounding movement, or a succession of such movements: said of persons, animals, and things. Formerly a general synonym of *leap*; now implying a short or undignified leap" (OED). Oh, man, can OED define a word? (See **"Is the pope fallible?," alternatives to**.) But enough. Here's hopping we meet now and then, maybe in *Alphabest Juice*.

See *jump*.

Acknowledgments

I want to thank my editor, Sarah Crichton; my production editor, Chris Peterson; and my copy editor, Cynthia Merman, for their meticulous (no comma here) sweet perusal.

A NOTE ABOUT THE AUTHOR

Roy Blount Jr. is the author of twenty-two previous books, covering subjects from the Pittsburgh Steelers to Robert E. Lee to *Duck Soup* to what dogs are thinking. He is a regular panelist on NPR's *Wait, Wait . . . Don't Tell Me!* and a member of the Fellowship of Southern Writers and the American Heritage Dictionary Usage Panel. Born in Indianapolis and raised in Decatur, Georgia, Blount now lives in western Massachusetts with his wife, the painter Joan Griswold.